The Integration
of the Personality

THE
INTEGRATION
OF THE
PERSONALITY

BY

CARL G. JUNG, M.D.

Translated by Stanley Dell

Illustrated

FARRAR & RINEHART, INC.

NEW YORK   TORONTO

Contents

The Integration
of the Personality

CHAPTER ONE

The Meaning of Individuation

The chapters in this volume were originally written as lectures given at the Eranos Meeting at Ascona, Switzerland. A number of scholars from different fields of knowledge meet there annually to discuss certain topics of human interest. My contributions represent the psychological aspect of the problems under discussion, and turn upon a question of peculiar interest—the so-called *process of individuation*.

I will try to explain the term "individuation" as simply as possible. By it I mean the psychological process that makes of a human being an "individual"—a unique, indivisible unit or "whole man." In the past, it has been generally assumed that consciousness—or the sum total of representations, ideas, emotions, perceptions, and other mental contents which the ego acknowledges—is equal to the psychological "whole" of an individual. But nowadays the rapidly increasing knowledge of phenomena that can be explained only on the hypothesis of unconscious mental processes has made us doubt whether the ego and its contents are really identical with the "whole." If unconscious processes exist at all, they must surely belong to the totality of the individual, even though they form no part of the conscious ego. If they were a part of the ego, they would be conscious, because anything directly connected with the ego is conscious; consciousness is by definition the relationship between the ego and the various mental contents. So-called unconscious phenomena are those that have no connection

3

with the ego. For this reason the ego usually denies their existence, and yet they reveal themselves in an individual's behaviour. A careful observer can easily see evidence of them, although the individual himself is blissfully unaware of the fact that he is exhibiting his most secret thoughts, or even something he has never consciously thought.

Only prejudice could lead anyone to suppose that, because he has never entertained a certain thought, it cannot be a content of his psyche. This might be the case if, as I said before, the psychic totality were identical with consciousness. But there is plenty of evidence to show that consciousness is far from covering the whole of the psyche. Many things happen semi-consciously, and an incalculable number of occurrences may even be entirely unconscious. The careful investigation of dual—or multiple—personality, of dissociation in nervous and mental diseases, and of approximately similar phenomena in normal people has yielded a wealth of data. I cannot imagine how one would set about explaining such phenomena without the hypothesis of the unconscious, a concept which acknowledges the fact that things live and function in the psyche just as if they were conscious and while the ego is unaware of their existence. For further information on this point the reader may wish to consult the works of Pierre Janet, Théodore Flournoy, Sigmund Freud, Morton Prince, and others.

At all events, medical psychology has been profoundly impressed with the number and importance of the unconscious processes that give rise to functional symptoms and even organic disturbances. These facts have undermined the view that the ego expresses the psychic totality. It has become obvious that the "whole" must needs include, besides consciousness, the field of unconscious events, and must constitute a sum total embracing both. The ego, once the monarch of this totality, is dethroned. It remains merely the centre of consciousness.

We may well ask whether the unconscious part of the psyche itself has a centre or not. I should hardly dare to assume that there is such a thing in the unconscious as a ruling principle analogous to the ego. Actually, everything points to the contrary. If there were such a centre, we should expect almost regular signs of its existence—for instance, intentional and purposeful opposition. Cases of dual personality would be frequent occurrences, and not rare curiosities.

Unconscious phenomena usually appear chaotic and unsystematic. For instance, dreams—one of the most frequent manifestations of the unconscious—show no apparent order, nor any tendency to systematization such as might be expected from a personal entity endowed with consciousness of itself.

Neither the philosophers nor the more modern explorers of the unconscious have ventured to assume the existence of an unconscious equivalent to the conscious ego. On the contrary, such philosophers as C. G. Carus and Eduard von Hartmann treat the unconscious as a cosmic principle, something like a universal mind without any trace of personality or of ego-consciousness. Modern scientists regard the unconscious as a psychic function below the threshold of consciousness, too feeble and too dim to be perceived. In opposition to the philosophers, they are inclined to derive all subliminal phenomena from consciousness and its contents. Janet speaks of consciousness as occasionally being too feeble to maintain the connection between certain processes and the ego. Freud, on the other hand, rather prefers the idea that there exist conscious factors that repress certain tendencies on account of their painful, or otherwise incompatible, character. There is much to be said in favour of both theories, for there are plenty of cases where a debility of consciousness causes distinct functions or contents to drop below the threshold and become subliminal; or where disagreeable contents are obviously repressed or forgotten; or where debility and repression together account for losses to the personality.

It is obvious that such careful observers as Janet and Freud would not have formed theories in which the unconscious is mainly derived from conscious sources had they discovered a trace of independent personality or autonomous volition. According to both theories, the unconscious is little else than psychic material that happens to lack the quality of consciousness, though it need not do so, and that differs in no other way from conscious contents.

If it were true that the unconscious consists of nothing but contents incidentally deprived of consciousness, then it would be preposterous—or at least unnecessarily meticulous —to worry about the question of whether the ego represents the whole of the psychical individual, or not. A normal ego could, and would, adequately embody the "whole," since its losses through unconsciousness would be trifles, and of significance only in cases of neuroses.

The situation, however, is not so simple. Both theories are based chiefly upon experience with cases of neurosis. Neither of the authors had any psychiatric experience.[1] If they had, they would certainly have been impressed with the fact that the unconscious displays certain contents that are utterly different from those of consciousness; such strange ones, indeed, that nobody can understand them, neither the patient himself nor his doctors. The doctors agree that he is crazy, and he agrees too, if his consciousness be still capable of realizing the uncanny incomprehensibility of the phenomena that invade his mind. He is clearly engulfed by a flood of thoughts and experiences that have never before been in his mind, nor in those of his doctors, nor in any other normal mind. That is why we call him crazy: we cannot understand his ideas. We understand something only when we already possess the necessary prem-

ises. But the premises of the patient's ideas are just as remote from our consciousness as from the patient's mind
before he became crazy.

As a matter of fact, there are certain insane ideas which
cannot be derived from the contents of any conscious mind.
Certainly they are not normal contents incidentally deprived
of consciousness, like something forgotten, repressed, or
habitually neglected. They are quite obviously the products
of an autonomous, independent mental functioning never
before known or experienced. They are thoroughly different
from the products of a neurotic mind, which no responsible
observer would judge to be crazy. The neurotic complex is
always within the reach of consciousness and is, therefore,
capable of reintegration into consciousness. Except in the
case of a neurosis that is an indirect expression of a latent
psychosis, the revelation of the unconscious neurotic contents
will never produce a psychosis, simply because they are hu-
manly understandable. The unconscious material of a psychosis is not understandable.[2]

No matter what the causality (ætiology) of a psychosis,
its very existence implies a condition in which certain mental activities appear spontaneously out of the unconscious.
They cannot be derived from consciousness, for consciousness
offers no premises that can explain or assimilate the utterly
strange and abnormal ideas. Neurotic contents can be integrated with no fatal injury to the ego. Insane ideas, on the
contrary, cannot be assimilated. They remain inaccessible
and more or less overgrow the ego-consciousness. They even
show a marked tendency to draw the ego into their own
"system," thus treating the ego as the latter is supposed to
treat the unconscious.

The existence of such cases is not infrequent, and proves
irrefutably that, under certain conditions, the unconscious
is capable of taking over the rôle of the ego. The result of
this exchange is chaos and destruction because the uncon-

scious is not a second personality with an organised and centralized functioning, but on the contrary an apparently irrational and paradoxical coexistence of mental processes. So, while the psychosis demonstrates the possible existence of an autonomous unconscious mind, one should not be satisfied with the verdict that any form of unconscious autonomy is nothing but insanity.

We have known for a long time that the mentality of the neurotic is basically normal, though marred on the surface by exaggeration and disproportion. In other words, a neurotic is normal apart from certain anomalies. Normal psychology has gleaned a wealth of information from the study and analysis of neuroses, for they exhibit certain normal traits in such exaggeration that one cannot fail to notice them.

In spite of the utter strangeness of mental behaviour in psychoses, we may venture the same assertion as to the study of the insane. Nothing produced by the human mind is completely outside our psychic range. Even the craziest idea must derive from something within the human mind, from some hidden root or premise. Without definitive evidence to the contrary, we cannot suppose certain minds to contain elements that other minds do not contain at all. We cannot assume that the unconscious has the faculty of becoming autonomous only in certain minds predestined later to become insane. It is very much more likely that the autonomy peculiar to the unconscious is a more or less general possibility. Insanity is merely the manifestation of a hidden, yet generally existent, condition.

Of course, the lunatic is an individual completely overcome by the unconscious. The same condition may exist to a less degree in the case of a person whom we cannot characterize as lunatic. We then have to deal with a man who is only partially overcome by his unconscious. He is not entirely "beside himself," but only partially or metaphorically.

Or, the condition may be temporary. Such a case can be a matter of ordinary panic or some other emotional upset. In such a state of violent emotion one says or does things out of proportion, things one regrets afterward when reason is restored. Even the most normal individual is not proof against this danger. Under suitable conditions he will "jump out of his skin" and temporarily imitate the insane, with more or less success. Not much is needed; love, hatred, joy, or sadness is often strong enough to reverse the relation between the ego and the unconscious.

On such occasions, strange ideas may seize upon otherwise sound individuals. Groups and societies, even whole peoples, may have seizures of a similar kind; these are mental epidemics. In such a case only malevolent critics speak of a psychosis, while others speak of an "ism." The ordinary lunatic is generally a harmless, isolated case; since everyone sees that something is wrong with him, he is quickly taken care of. But the unconscious infections of groups of so-called normal people are more subtle and far more dangerous, although they derive from the autonomy of unconscious processes just as much as does insanity.

Ordinary common sense always imagines itself to be anywhere but in the immediate vicinity of the lunatic asylum. Yet common sense consists of the minds of average people, who have no idea that their consciousness may easily be invaded, in parts at least, by a strange and dangerous unconscious activity. It is one of the most ridiculous illusions of civilized man that the "perils of the soul" have entirely disappeared along with primitive superstitions. Even the superstitions have not disappeared from any civilized nation as a whole. They have only changed their names, and often not even that. The clan of uprooted intellectual highbrows usually goes on believing in permanent and universal enlightenment. That technical progress and social improvements do not mean psychological differentiation or a higher level of consciousness is a lesson that we are unwilling to learn. The enormous increase of technical facilities only serves to occupy the mind with all sorts of sensations and impressions that lure the attention and interest from the inner world. The relentless flood of newspapers, radio programs, and movies may widen or fill the external mind, while at the same time, and in the same measure, consciousness of the inner world becomes darkened and may eventually disappear altogether. But "forgetting" is not identical with "getting rid of." On the contrary, the situation has become worse: instead of facing the enemy, we risk being attacked from the rear, where we are unaware and defenceless.

"Normal insanity" begins when the emotions are aroused. In these days we have ample opportunity to observe this process on a grand scale. We can see every form of mental contagion, from the crudest sentimentalism to the most subtle, secret poisoning of reason, and this among the so-called normal people—the average individuals who largely make up a nation or a state. Their amazing defencelessness against suggestions, even against the wildest social and political ideas and ideals, is not exactly a proof of the strength of consciousness and reason. But since there must be strength somewhere, it is presumably in that which overcomes reason —in the *irrational and emotional factors*.

Emotions are instinctive, involuntary reactions that upset the rational order of consciousness by their elementary outbursts. Emotions are not "made," or wilfully produced, in and by consciousness. Instead, they appear suddenly, leaping up from an unconscious region. As long as the unconscious is in a dormant condition, it is just as if there were nothing at all in that hidden region. We are really and most thoroughly unconscious of the existence of the unconscious. We are therefore always surprised afresh to discover that something can jump upon our back or fall upon our head out of mere nothingness, radically altering the pattern of our individual or social lives.

Afterward the historian, or the psychologist, steps in and shows us convincingly that things happened as they did because for such and such reasons it had to be so. But who could have told us this before? The public mind was long ago in possession of the main pieces of evidence for the subsequent trial in the court of historical reason. But nobody was conscious of it at the time. When John Huss and Wycliffe preached, the age of the Reformation had begun—but nobody knew it. It was there *in potentia,* but no one could see it with the eyes or touch it with the hands, and thus it was not in consciousness. But it existed below the threshold of awareness. It was *still* unconscious, like a sun below the horizon, of which a savage might say, "There is no sun." We are like those primitives who believe that every evening the sun dies and vanishes, and that if anything rises next morning, it is a new sun. We are always surprised by the fact that something comes out of what we call "nothing."

That is our attitude toward the unconscious. We call it nothing, and yet it is a whole reality *in potentia:* the sun that rises tomorrow, the thought we are going to think, the deed we are going to do, even the fate we are going to lament—tomorrow. Since we now know that, from the beginning, it has always been the same sun that sets in the evening and rises in the morning, we could, or should, afford to be less surprised at the sempiternal nature of the unconscious. But, whereas we think in terms of years, the unconscious thinks and behaves in terms of thousands of years. When something happens which we call an unheard-of innovation, it is really a very old story. Like little children, we still forget what we were yesterday. We still live in a miraculously new world, in which man imagines himself to be astonishingly new, or "modern."

Such a state of affairs is an unmistakable symptom of

the youth of human consciousness, which is still unaware of its origins.

"Normal" man convinces me, even more than the lunatic, of the powerful autonomy of the unconscious. The psychological theory of the psychoses can take refuge behind real or imaginary organic disturbances of the brain and thus invalidate the importance of the unconscious. But such a device is not applicable to normal humanity. What is actually happening in the world is due not merely to "dim remnants of formerly conscious activities," but to volcanic outbursts from the very bottom of things. Otherwise, nobody could be astonished. Yet the very people who give the least credit to the autonomy of the unconscious are the most surprised.

Our consciousness, being still young and frail, has a tendency to make little of the unconscious. This is understandable enough, for a young boy should not be too deeply impressed by the majesty of his parents if he wants to accomplish something in his own right and way. Our consciousness has developed cumulatively, as well as individually, from the darkness and the twilight of the primordial unconscious. There were psychical processes and functions long before there was an ego-consciousness. Thinking existed long before any human voice said, "I am conscious of thinking."

The primitive "perils of the soul" consist mainly of dangers to consciousness. Fascination, bewitchment, loss of soul, possession, and so on are clearly phenomena of dissociation, regression, and suppression of consciousness by unconscious contents. As we have seen, even civilized man is not yet out of the woods. The unconscious is the *mother* of consciousness. Where there is a mother there should also be a father, but he seems to be unknown. Consciousness, the frail youngster, may deny his father, but he cannot deny his mother. That would be too preposterous, since one can see in every child how hesitatingly and haltingly the ego-consciousness develops from a fragmentary consciousness of the moment, and how it slowly appears out of the complete darkness of mere instinctivity.

The careful analysis of human personality has accumulated a vast amount of evidence affording definite proof of the existence of an autonomous, instinctive activity, beginning in an unconscious layer of the mind and ending in activities that strongly influence conscious behaviour. I omit a discussion of this evidence here, as the reader will find plenty of such material in the following essays.

The conscious mind is based upon, and results from, an unconscious psyche which is prior to consciousness and continues to function together with, or despite, consciousness. Although there are many cases of conscious contents that become unconscious again—through repression, for instance—the unconscious as a whole is far from being a relic of consciousness. (Are the psychic functions of animals remnants of consciousness?) The unconscious is prior to conscious mind, and it is autonomous; it has a law unto itself.

As I pointed out earlier, there is little hope of finding in the unconscious an order similar to that of the ego-consciousness. Superficially studied, at least, the unconscious is not encouraging in this respect. So far as research has gone, it does not look as if we were likely to discover an unconscious ego-personality, something like a Pythagorean "countersun." Yet we cannot overlook the fact that, just as consciousness arises from unconsciousness, the ego-centre also emerges from a dark depth in which it was somehow contained *in potentia*. As a human mother can only produce a child potentially human, whose nature was concealed in her during gestation, so we are almost forced to believe that the unconscious cannot be an altogether chaotic accumulation of instincts and images. Something must hold it together. Its centre cannot be the ego, since the ego was born in the conscious mind and turns its back on the unconscious, seeking to deny it as best it can. Or can it be that the unconscious lost its centre when the ego was born? If this is so, we should expect the ego to be far superior to the unconscious in strength of influence and of purpose. The unconscious would follow meekly in the wake of ego-consciousness. This, however, is only how we wish things to be. I admit that it is possible to base a manly and healthy ideal upon this view; it is good for youthful illusions, but its truth is questionable. The facts unfortunately point quite the other way: consciousness all too easily succumbs to unconscious influences, and these are often enough more to the point or more intelligent than the conscious judgements. It is also true that unconscious motives often overrule conscious decisions in the main issues of life. Even individual fate largely hangs upon the fact that unconscious factors are often predominant.

A close examination of the conscious functions shows how much they depend upon an undisturbed use of *memory*. But memory often suffers from interference by unconscious processes. Moreover, it generally functions in an automatic way. It ordinarily uses the bridges of association, but frequently in such an extraordinary way that we must attentively reconsider the whole process of remembering if we wish to discover how certain memories managed to appear in consciousness. And not rarely the bridges remain altogether undiscoverable. In such cases it is impossible to refute the hypothesis of unconscious spontaneity. Another case is the function of *intuition*, which largely depends upon unconscious operations of a complex nature. Because of this peculiarity, I have defined it as "perception of relations via the unconscious."

Normally, the unconscious collaborates with consciousness in a smooth and unobtrusive way, so that one does not even realize its existence. But if an individual deviates too much from the original instinctive pattern, then he realizes the full impact of the unconscious forces. What is true of the individual holds also for the social group. The collaboration of the unconscious is intelligible and purposive. Even when it is in opposition to consciousness, it acts in a compensatory or complementary way, as if it were trying to re-establish the lost balance. The more serious the mental difficulty, however, the more incomprehensible are the manifestations of the unconscious. This is particularly the case in neuroses and psychoses.

There are *dreams* and *visions* of such an informative kind that the people who have them refuse to believe that they derive from an unconscious psyche. They prefer to suppose that they issue from a sort of *superconsciousness.* Such people usually distinguish between a quasi-physiological, or instinctive, unconscious and a psychic sphere, or layer, "above" consciousness which they style the superconsciousness. As a matter of fact, the psyche called the superior or the universal mind in Hindu philosophy corresponds to what the West calls the unconscious. Certain dreams, visions, and mystical experiences, however, suggest the existence of a consciousness in the unconscious. But, if we assume a consciousness in the unconscious, we are at once faced with the difficulty that consciousness cannot exist unless there is a subject—an ego—to which mental contents are related. Consciousness needs a centre, an ego to whom something is conscious. We know of no other kind of consciousness, nor can we imagine a consciousness without an ego. Consciousness cannot exist when there is no one to say, "I am conscious."

I must admit that there are experiences that give plausibility to the hypothesis of an ego in the unconscious realm. Still, for the reasons already mentioned, I feel rather hesitant to adopt it, the more so as I should not know what or whom to call the ego of that consciousness. Moreover, I am unable to separate an unconscious below from an unconscious above, since I find intelligence and purposiveness below as well as above. It is obvious that the centre of a transcendental consciousness cannot be the human ego, since the ego has neither a hand in producing such experiences nor the necessary intelligence to understand them. It can only be their victim—or the receiver of divine grace.

There is not much merit in speculating about things we cannot know. It is best to refrain from venturesome statements that go beyond the boundaries of science. This is neither malevolent criticism nor scepticism; I simply hold that honesty demands that we remain within the narrow confines of our knowledge. It is not only immodest, it is intellectually immoral to make assertions that go beyond the reach of human cognition. The matters we have just considered are partial manifestations of processes that in their entirety are inaccessible to our cognition. As I said before, they may have, and occasionally they seem to have, qualities that we might refer to a consciousness not identical with our own. But as long as we have no other means of ascertaining the existence of a transcendental consciousness we have to admit our uncertainty.

As far, then, as my observations go, I have not discovered in the unconscious anything like a personality comparable to the conscious ego. But, although a definite alter ego seems not to exist (except in the rare cases of dual personality), there are at least *traces of personalities* in the manifestations of the unconscious. A simple example is the dream, in which a variety of real and imaginary people enact the dream thoughts. In nearly all important cases of dissociation the manifestations of the unconscious assume a distinctive character. The unconscious *personates*. This phenomenon has supported and renewed the belief in spirits. But a careful examination of the behaviour and psychic make-up of such personations reveals their fragmentary character. They seem to represent complexes split off from a greater whole; splinters chipped from the main block.

I have constantly been impressed by the peculiarly organized character of dissociated fragments. They resemble
whole or partial personalities. Often I have asked myself
whether we are not justified in assuming that, if the splinters
have personality, then the block from which they were
separated must have personality to a still higher degree. The
conclusion seems logical, and the case is the same whether
the fragments are big or small. Why, then, should not the
whole have personality too? This personality, of course,
would be a completely concealed and inaccessible entity.
*Personality does not necessarily include consciousness. It can
be dormant or, at most, dreaming.*

Nevertheless, the general aspect of unconscious manifestations is in the main chaotic and irrational, in spite of
many symptoms of intelligence and purposiveness. The unconscious produces dreams, irrational fantasies, peculiar
visions, primitive emotions, grotesque or fabulous ideas, and
the like—exactly what one would expect of a dreaming person stirring in his sleep. The unconscious seems to have a
personality that has never been awake or conscious either of
a continuity in itself or of a life lived. The only question is
whether the hypothesis of such a dormant and deeply concealed personality is tenable. It may be that all of the personality to be found in the unconscious is contained in the
personations mentioned before. If this is the case, all my
guesswork would be futile. On the other hand, there possibly
exist concealed personalities that are far less fragmentary—
which is to say, more complete.

I am convinced that there is evidence for this view,
although unfortunately it belongs to the intricacies and
subtleties of psychological analysis.

It is the accepted theory that sex is determined by a
preponderance of male- or female-producing genes in the
combined chromosomes of sperm and ovum after fertiliza-

tion has taken place. Biologically, therefore, a man contains female-producing elements, a woman male-producing elements, a fact of which each, as a rule, is quite unaware. Certainly there are few men who could or would care to tell us what they would be like if they were females. Yet all men must have more or less latent female components if it is true that the female-forming elements continue to live and perpetuate themselves throughout the body cells of the entire male organism. How these sex-determining elements function in the body is not known, but there can be no doubt that they are at least indirectly responsible for the existence of the male and female sex hormones which in turn govern the secondary sex characters, that is, the traits we associate with "masculineness" or "feminineness" in the individual.

It is easy to observe that women at a more advanced age develop masculine qualities, grow a moustache, acquire a rather acute and sometimes obstinate mind, and often develop a deeper voice. Men of advanced age, on the contrary, become mellow, "lovely" old men—soft, kind to children, sentimental, and rather emotional; their anatomical forms become rounded, they take interest in the family and home life, in genealogy, gossip, and so on. It is by no means rare for the wife to take over business responsibilities in later life, while the husband plays a merely helpful rôle. If you study the photographs of a primitive tribe, and if you compare the old people with the young, you will see what becomes at a more advanced age of lovely young girls and of animalistic, brutal young men. A completely hidden character of the opposite sex comes into the foreground.

The observer who has sharpened his eyes and acquired a good deal of practical experience begins to discover symptoms (often astonishing ones) of the man in the woman, and of the woman in the man. When people are at their best, there is not much chance of seeing anything of their other side. But if you observe a man when he is caught in a mood, you find him to be a different person. Sometimes the change is quite remarkable: a man who is ordinarily altruistic, generous, amiable, and intelligent becomes, when a certain mood seizes upon him, a slightly mean, nastily egotistical, and illogically prejudiced character. A woman of a usually kind and peaceable disposition becomes an argumentative, obstinate, narrow-minded shrew if it should come into her head to use a half-understood idea heard in a conversation six weeks or months ago. (If the man is the woman's husband, they will soon have learned the art of picking out irritating topics that inevitably bring out the "other side!")

Should you study this world-wide experience with due attention, and regard the "other side" as a trait of character, you will produce a picture that shows what I mean by the *anima,* the woman in a man, and the *animus,* the man in a woman. By putting together all the cases in which a man has reacted to the influence of a mood (which is an emotion or affect without sufficient cause), you can build up a definite personality. We avoid doing this, as a rule, because when we are fond of people we hate to put them in an unfavourable light. For the psychologist, however, to do so is a professional task. The analysis is not simple for most of us to make, because we are not used to dividing an intimate friend into two separate characters. We are merely irritated by the contradictions in the one person. We do habitually sketch out the presumable character of a man, whom we have never met, from the contents of the letters he has written us; and in a similar way we can sum up all of a man's traits that become visible under the stress of emotion, which affords the ideal condition for the manifestation of unconscious contents. Under its possession one is "beside one's self," and the unconscious gets a chance to occupy the foreground.

As a matter of fact, an emotion *is* the intrusion of an unconscious personality. The unconscious contents it brings to light have a personal character, and it is merely because we never sum them up that we have not discovered this other character long ago. To the primitive mind, a man who is seized by strong emotion is possessed by a devil or a spirit; and our language still expresses the same idea, at least metaphorically. There is much to be said in favour of this point of view.

The character that summarizes a person's uncontrolled emotional manifestations consists, in the first place, of his inferior qualities or peculiarities. Even people we like and appreciate suffer from certain imperfections of character that have to be taken into the bargain. When people are not at their best, such flaws become clearly visible. I have called the inferior and less commendable part of a person the *shadow*. We have met with this figure in literature; for instance, Faust and his shadow Mephistopheles. There is an excellent description of this figure in E. T. A. Hoffmann's *The Elixirs of the Devil*.

But the shadow is not all that becomes manifest in emotional disturbance; and it is not sufficient to explain why a man has the rather definite feeling that "he is not himself" or that "he is beside himself." There is at such times a peculiar *strangeness* about a man, which we positively dislike to attribute to him in our ordinary thought of him. Therefore, we say, "I did not recognize him any more," "he forgot himself," or "he did not know himself any longer." Such colloquial expressions clearly formulate a peculiar strangeness or alienation. "Aliéné" is the French word for insane, and we freely use the word "mad" for angry. As a matter of fact, emotions are coupled with a greater or smaller loss of consciousness, and with a narrowing down of the mind to a remarkable single-mindedness, not to say imbecility. When the storm has blown over, and the former self has appeared again, we prefer to think that the strange presence has disappeared altogether, we hope that the whole thing has not been true.

Yet nothing of this kind really disappears. It merely returns to the unconscious, where it awaits its next opportunity. For a keen eye, even, it does not disappear completely. Its influence is still there, less obvious, yet more subtle and cunning.

The strangeness is due to the emergence of a different character—one that we hesitate to ascribe to the ego personality. This formulation of the matter sounds as if it pretended to be new or unexpected. But there is actually nothing new about it. Practically everybody knows it. Do we not always expect something different behind our first impressions of people? Do we not say, "Wait, until you know him better"? Or a wife says, "You have not been married to him for twenty years." Are we quite sure of ourselves? Are we absolutely certain about our own character, should we find ourselves in a tight corner?

If people are honest with themselves they must admit a certain fear of something that may overcome them. Even saints, or rather just the saints, have their specific devils, and even if they fight them successfully, it is often a close call. Otherwise saintliness would be cheap.

"Strangeness" is, of course, a relative term. One should probably say "relatively strange," since it usually depends upon circumstances whether we can draw a favourable picture of ourselves or not. Certain people may never have an inkling of another side, either because circumstances prevented their seeing it or because they themselves were too unconscious and too unreflective to realize it.

This rather cursory description of two groups of contents that make up personalities in the unconscious—the anima (or animus) and the shadow—would be inadequate, if I did not emphasize the fact that, in a man's case, the anima has a definitely feminine and the shadow an equally definite masculine character. It may strike the reader that my description of the shadow does not markedly differ from my picture of the anima. This is due to the fact that I have spoken only of the immediate and superficial aspects of these figures. Particularly the description of the anima is most incomplete. In the following essays, the reader will find a fuller demonstration of the anima's nature.

If we compare a number of emotional events, we can easily see that the same character reappears in every one of them. For this reason we can attribute continuity to the unconscious personality, and ascribe to it the emotional intrusions. This point of view is at bottom nothing but an imitation, or repetition, of the way in which primitive man comes to the conclusion that there are such things as witches and ghosts. But he is satisfied with the general assertion that witches and ghosts exist, and does not try to specify their nature. The psychological procedure of which I speak is an attempt to reconstruct an individual character. It is not only of theoretical interest, in certain cases, but of great practical importance. Patients often suffer so much from intrusions of the unconscious that it helps them considerably to know their opponent "personally."

It is not always a laborious process to reconstruct the anima. Sometimes she appears already personified in dreams and other products of unconscious activity. We also find her as a classical figure in prose fiction; for instance, in books by Haggard,[3] Benoit,[4] Sloane,[5] and others. These authors have fully succeeded in reconstructing the collective picture of the anima. They are clearly dealing with one and the same mythological and transcendental figure, yet with individual variations. An element of the supernatural always adheres to the anima. This must be so, since she is an entity living almost entirely in the "other world" of the unconscious.

Although the anima is a reconstruction and a hypothesis, the idea explains for us many tragic or puzzling love affairs and their amazing reversals. As long as a man is unconscious of his anima she is frequently projected upon a real woman, and the man's fantasy equips her with all the fascinating qualities peculiar to the anima. Her moral range is rather wide: she embraces the degraded woman and the *femme inspiratrice*, Faust's Gretchen, and the Virgin. Edouard Schuré [6] has given us an almost schematic description of the anima, but he had to present her as two figures, since he could not fit all the paradoxes into one person. Charles Kingsley's *Hypatia* describes a similar case.

The figure of the animus, the man in the woman, is equally paradoxical. The best literary description I have come across is that by Ronald Frazer.[7] It is a curious fact that no woman of talent has succeeded in producing an adequate picture. It may be that a woman's animus writes her novels for her, and thus escapes portrayal. But Frazer has produced a clever and accurate picture of the animus, running the whole gamut from utter banality to supreme mystery.

Animus and anima are natural "archetypes," primordial figures of the unconscious, and have given rise to the mythological gods and goddesses. It is, therefore, rather a futile undertaking to disinfect Olympus with rational enlightenment. The gods are not there; they are ensconced in the shadows of the unconscious, where we cannot uproot them. Whenever a projection of these archetypes is destroyed by rational criticism, the disembodied image returns to its origin, the archetype. There it awaits a new opportunity to project itself. Rationalism is certainly called for in many pursuits, but as soon as it leaves the scientific laboratory to trespass in the domains of life it always expects the things that never happen. Reason has never ruled life, and presumably it never will. The questions of life and fate are too often—and perhaps for the largest part—decided by the powers of the unconscious.

To the psychological beginner, animus and anima are

certainly nothing but elusive wraiths. It needs a good deal of specific experience to recognize and understand their subtle but powerful activity. But when the student has acquired the necessary powers of psychological criticism, he can derive a fairly accurate picture of their nature. They appear as strange, unconscious entities, which he would like to endow with ego-consciousness. They seem almost capable of it.

But the facts do not support this idea. There is nothing in their behaviour that bespeaks an ego-consciousness, as we know it. On the contrary, they show every sign of being fragmentary personalities. They are masklike, wraithlike, without problems of their own or any self-reflection, with no conflict, no doubt, no suffering; something like the gods, who have no philosophy; like the Brahma-gods of the Buddhist Samyutta-nikāya whose erroneous views need Gautama Buddha's correction. They seem to be functions or instincts which appear in a personal form when aroused from their dormant condition. But contrary to the functions attached to consciousness, they are always strangers in the conscious world. Because they permeate the atmosphere with a feeling of uncanny foreboding, or even with the fear of mental derangement, they are unwelcome intruders.

In studying their psychic constituents—that is, the imaginative material manifested through them—we find any number of archaic and "historical" connections, contents, archetypal images that we call mythological themes. The reader will find many such parallels in the following chapters.[8] This peculiarity allows one to locate the anima and animus: they obviously live or function in the deeper layers of the unconscious mind, in the phylogenetic substructures of the modern mind, the so-called *collective unconscious*.

This localization explains a good deal of their strangeness: they bring into our ephemeral consciousness an unknown psychic life belonging to a remote past. This psychic life is the mind of our ancient ancestors, the way in which they thought and felt, the way in which they conceived of life and the world, of gods and human beings. The existence of these historical layers is presumably the source of the belief in reincarnation and in memories of past lives. As the body is a sort of museum of its phylogenetic history, so is the mind. There is no reason for believing that the psyche, with its peculiar structure, is the only thing in the world that has no history beyond its individual manifestation. Even the conscious mind cannot be denied a history extending over at least five thousand years. It is only individual ego-consciousness that has forever a new beginning and an early end. But the unconscious psyche is not only immensely old, it is also able to grow unceasingly into an equally remote future. It forms, and is part of, the human species just as much as the body, which is also individually ephemeral, yet collectively of immeasurable duration.

The anima and animus live in a world quite different from our own; in a world where the pulse of time beats ever so slowly; where the birth and death of individuals count little, and where ten thousand years ago is yesterday. No wonder that their aspect is strange—so strange that their intrusion into consciousness often blasts into fragments the all-too-feeble brainpans of unfortunate mortals. Anima and animus contain the greater part of the material which appears in insanity, more especially in schizophrenia.

The anima and animus are not the only figures discernible in the unconscious. I could mention others with aspects of their own that can be distinguished from the animus and anima. But as they are just as baffling to the ego-consciousness, I shall not discuss them here.

What I have said about the unconscious may give an approximate idea of what is meant by that term. Coming now to the problem of individuation, we see that we are confronted with a rather extraordinary task: the psyche consists of two incongruous halves that should properly make a "whole" together. One is inclined to think that the ego-consciousness is capable of assimilating and integrating the unconscious; one hopes, at least, that such a solution is possible. But, unfortunately, the unconscious is really unconscious; it is unknown. And how can you assimilate something unknown? Even if one has a pretty complete idea of his anima and of other such figures, he has not yet sounded the depths of the unconscious. One hopes to dominate the unconscious, but the past masters of this art of domination— the yogis—wind up with samadhi, an ecstatic condition that seems to be equivalent to an unconscious state. The fact that they call our unconscious the universal consciousness, does not change things in the least: in their case the unconscious has devoured the ego-consciousness. They do not realize that a "universal" consciousness is a contradiction in terms, since exclusiveness, selection, and discrimination are the root and essence of all that can claim the name of consciousness.

A "universal" consciousness is logically identical with unconsciousness. It is true that an accurate application of the methods of the Pali-canon, or of the Yogasutra, produces a remarkable extension of consciousness. But the contents of consciousness lose in clearness of detail with increasing extension. In the end, consciousness becomes vast but dim, with an infinite multitude of objects merging into an indistinct totality—a state in which the subjective and objective are almost completely identical. This is all very well, but scarcely to be recommended anywhere north of the Tropic of Cancer.

We must attempt a different solution. We believe in ego-consciousness and in what we call reality. The realities of a northern climate are somehow so convincing that we are better off if we do not forget them. It makes sense to deal with reality: "My ego-consciousness is, therefore, inclined to swallow the unconscious, and if that should not be feasible, I will try to repress it." That is how we look at the question. But if we understand anything about the unconscious we know that it cannot be swallowed. We know also that it is dangerous to repress it, for we have learned that the unconscious is life, and that if life is repressed it will live against us, as is the case in neuroses.

Consciousness and the unconscious do not make a whole when either is suppressed or damaged by the other. If they must contend, let it be a fair fight with equal right on both sides. Both are aspects of life. Let consciousness defend its reason and its self-protective ways, and let the chaotic life of the unconscious be given a fair chance to have its own way, as much of it as we can stand. This means at once open conflict and open collaboration. Yet, paradoxically, this is presumably what human life should be. It is the old play of hammer and anvil: the suffering iron between them will in the end be shaped into an unbreakable whole, the individual. This experience is what is called, in the later sections of this book, the process of individuation.

Particularly in one of the following chapters I try to show how the psyche behaves under the strain of the conflict, what it produces in the individual, and how it has been exemplified in the history of the human mind. In this second connection, the reader will perhaps be astonished at the emphasis I lay on alchemy, which is discussed in the fifth chapter. Alchemy is not an old hobby of mine; I began a thorough study of the subject only within the last few years. My reason for making a fairly extensive use of alchemistic parallels is that in my psychological practice I have observed quite a number of actual patients' cases which show unmistakable similarities to alchemistic symbolism. In my next chapter I deal with one of those cases. Because a psychologist must be particularly careful not to suggest his own theories to a patient, I wish to point out that none of the cases mentioned were under my care after I had begun the study of alchemy.

If the process of individuation is an empirical fact, rather than a theory, one must expect the problem to have its history. It must have played a more or less important rôle in former centuries. And that historic background does, indeed, exist. I have known for twenty-five years that Gnosticism contains striking parallels to the symbolism of the process of individuation. But a gap of almost 1,600 years separates us from that peculiar religious philosophy. For a long time I was unable to find the mediæval parallel to this problem. Even Silberer's book [9] did not convince me that alchemy was the missing link.

The reason it took me so long to bridge the gulf between Gnosticism and modern psychology was my profound ignorance of Greek and Latin alchemy and its symbolism. The little I knew of German alchemistic treatises did not do much to enlighten me about their abstruse symbolism. At all events, I was unable to make the connection with what I knew of psychological individuation.

That the parallel dawned upon me at all is due to the visionary dreams contained in the next chapter. I must confess that it cost me quite a struggle to overcome the prejudice, which I shared with many others, against the seeming absurdity of alchemy. There is no hope of an approach to the subject if it is considered from the standpoint of modern chemistry, and it appears hopeless when one first tries to understand it psychologically. But my patience has been richly rewarded. I am now satisfied that alchemy is the requisite mediæval exemplar of this concept of individuation. There is a real continuity in the unremitting attempts of human minds to deal with the problem from the first century of our era on to the middle of the eighteenth. Goethe's Faust is the last magnificent link in "Homer's golden chain," and at the same time the introduction of the problem to a new, psychologically minded age. The fifth chapter gives a psychological explanation of alchemy, and also presents the idea of individuation as a fundamental alchemistic symbol. The problem necessarily involves the question of religion. If the reader is particularly interested in the relation of religion to psychology, I call his attention to my Terry Lectures on "Psychology and Religion." [10]

FOOTNOTES TO CHAPTER ONE

1. The first time Freud applied his point of view to a psychosis was in the famous Schreber case, to which I had called his attention: Sigmund Freud, "Psychoanalytische Bemerkungen über einen autobiographisch beschriebenen Fall von Paranoia," *Jahrbuch für Psychoanal. & Psychopathol. Forschungen,* Bd. III, p. 9.

2. There are many different kinds of psychoses. I refer here chiefly to a certain category of schizophrenia.

3. Rider Haggard, *She.* New York: Longmans, Green and Company, 1918.

4. Pierre Benoit, *L'Atlantide.* Paris: A. Michel, 1920.

5. William Sloane, *To Walk the Night.* New York: Farrar & Rinehart, 1937.

6. Edouard Schuré, *La Prêtresse d'Isis.* Paris: Perrin et Cie, 1907.

7. Ronald Frazer, *The Flying Draper.* New York: P. Smith, 1931.

8. In my *Psychology of the Unconscious* (New York: Moffat, Yard & Company, 1916; Dodd, Mead & Company, 1931) I have described the case of a young woman with a "hero story," that is, an animus-fantasy, which yielded a rich harvest of mythological material. Rider Haggard (*op. cit.*), Pierre Benoit (*op. cit.*), and Goethe, in *Faust,* have emphasized the "historical" character of the anima.

9. Herbert Silberer, *Problems of Mysticism and Its Symbolism.* New York: Moffat, Yard and Company, 1917.

10. Jung, *Psychology and Religion.* New Haven: Yale University Press, 1938.

CHAPTER TWO

A Study in the Process of Individuation

In the twentieth chapter of the *Tao Tê Ching,* Laotse says:

> Give up your learnedness,
> Then you will be free from cares!
> Between "yes" and "yes indeed," what difference is there?
> Between good and bad, what difference is there?
> But what all men honour,
> *That* one may not with impunity set aside.
> O wilderness, have I not yet reached your centre?
> The men of the multitude are radiant
> As at the celebration of great feasts,
> As when in the spring people climb upon the towers.
> I alone am undecided, still without a sign to act by,
> Like a little child that is not yet able to laugh—
> A weary wanderer, who has no home.
> The men of the multitude all live in superabundance;
> I alone am like one abandoned.
> Truly, I have the heart of a fool!
>
> Chaos, O chaos!
> The men of the world are clear, so clear—
> I alone am as if beclouded.
> The men of the world lust so after knowledge—
> I alone am downcast, so downcast;
> Restless, alas, as the sea!
> Driven hither and yon, alas, like one who dwells nowhere!
> The men of the multitude all have something to do—
> I alone am as idle as a ne'er-do-well.
> I alone am not as other people are,
> For I value the lavishing Mother.

I have had to borrow these verses from the East because the European has not yet framed the question they contain. Laotse also gives the answer:

> The form of the full life wholly follows the Tao.
> The Tao, invisible, ungraspable, brings things about!
> It contains images, ungraspable, invisible!
> It contains things, invisible, ungraspable!
> It contains seed, unfathomable and dark!
> This seed is the truth.
> This truth embraces faith.
> From the very beginning until today
> The name of Tao has been indispensable
> For the understanding of the origin of all things.
> And how do I know
> That the origin of all things is of this nature?
> Through the Tao!

This avowal of Laotse's expresses a mood that is characteristic also of the white man when he bethinks himself. But he is full of unrest; he knows only the premises, and not the conclusion that would furnish him an answer; only the surface, and not the depths from which it could spring. We are in reality unable to borrow or absorb anything from outside, from the world, or from history. What is essential to us can only grow out of ourselves. When the white man is true to his instincts, he reacts defensively against any advice that one might give him. What he has already swallowed, he is forced to reject again as if it were a foreign body, for his blood refuses to assimilate anything sprung from foreign soil.

This being so, it is the part of wisdom not to tell the white man anything or give him any advice. The best cannot be told, anyhow, and the second best does not strike home. One must be able to *let things happen*. I have learned from the East what it means by the phrase "Wu wei": namely, not-doing, letting be, which is quite different from doing nothing. Some Occidentals, also, have known what this not-doing means; for instance, Meister Eckhardt, who speaks of "sich lassen," to let oneself be. The region of darkness into which one falls is not empty; it is the "lavishing mother" of Laotse, the "images" and the "seed." When the surface has been cleared, things can grow out of the depths. People always suppose that they have lost their way when they come up against these depths of experience. But if they do not know how to go on, the only answer, the only advice, that makes any sense is "to wait for what the unconscious has to say about the situation." A way is only *the* way when one finds it and follows it oneself.

The question of Laotse's is a hard one for the Occidental to confront. To find its answer is not simple; there is no general prescription for "how one should do it." But I can show by an example how, in a given case, it may be done. And this brings us directly up against the reality of our Western world. With us the beginning is always wholly a matter of the personal life, for there is nothing in the more traditional aspect of our culture that offers a true equivalent to the East. All attempts to do as the East does, or to feel as the East feels; all imitation and lofty ideas; every "but one should"—these are nothing but empty words and fine notions that bring absolutely nothing to pass in the psyche, and nothing living to growth. For us, the integration of the personality waits upon a challenge which, willingly or unwillingly, we offer to ourselves.

It is a problem that appears to haunt a great many of us, for the process of individuation is far from an automatic psychic development. For example, take the case of a patient of mine, a woman, fifty-five years old and unmarried. She is an intellectual person with a good academic education, in no way morbid or neurotic. For nine years she had had a warm interest in psychology. In the tenth year she came to a region

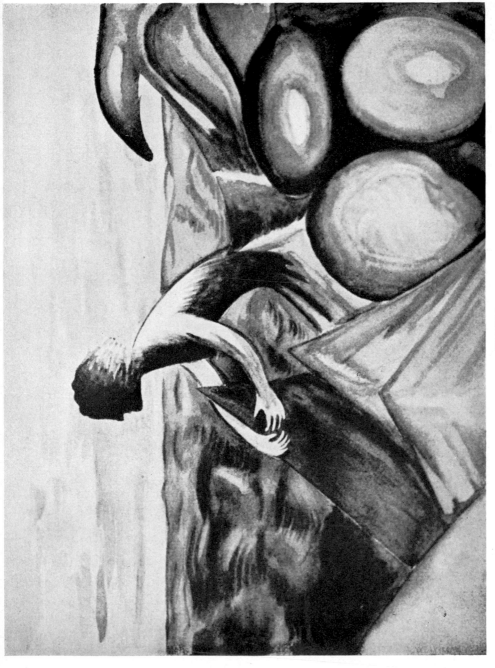

PLATE I

See page 33]

PLATE II

See page 33]

of inner darkness where the road apparently ended, and she no longer knew how to go on. In a last attempt to try something or other she came to me. I was, so to speak, the last piece on her chessboard.

At the same time it occurred to her that she had never been to the country where her mother was born; indeed, she had had a very unsatisfactory relation with her mother. So, on her way to Zurich, she travelled first to her ancestral homeland, and there was seized with an unexpected desire to paint landscapes of the countryside. Up to that time she had had no æsthetic inclinations, nor did she have any aptitude in painting or drawing. Her modest attempts at landscape painting, however, gave her a peculiar sense of new life. When she arrived in Zurich, she continued her attempts. On the day before she came to me for the first time, she again painted a landscape; and while she was doing so a mental image suddenly appeared to her. She saw the lower part of her body thrust into the earth, or rather, among boulders. In the background of her mental picture is the sea. I myself pass by in the form of a sorcerer with his magic wand. She calls to me to help her; I touch the rock in which she is caught with my magic wand; it breaks apart, and her form emerges.

She then had the feeling that she should paint this fantasy, and did so. But as she had no skill, the picture, which she showed me on the following day, was a rather inadequate attempt. In it (Plate I), the boulders look like eggs cut open, with seeds in the centre. There is a hole in the sky, and the wind blows out of it.

She said that the figure represented herself—that she needed to be set free; and her fantasy had anticipated this statement. Analysis, however, soon showed her that I possessed no magic wand—that her release had to be won for herself through honest effort. But what kind of effort? I set her the task of representing her release. In the picture (Plate

II) that she drew for this purpose, the rocks divide themselves and a sphere emerges. This second picture contains no magician.

Why was it necessary for her to represent these feelings and states of mind in terms of actual drawing? Such pictures seem to have, for the patient, a psychological magic. Because pictorial expression fixes certain unconscious contents and draws others around it, he can work magic by this means, but only upon himself. Instead of merely being in a subjective state, he is confronted with objective form that reflects the psychological situation. Before this particular patient had painted her picture she was aware only of her standstill on the subjective side. She was not a human being, for only half of her personality was alive, and the upper half at that— this being all that seemed to her acceptable, genteel, good, and so forth. In other words, only the upper half of her personality was developed. The lower half was unconscious— mere earth, mere stone. The picture that so clearly expressed this state raised the challenge of liberation. She also discovered that she painted with two parts of herself: with the mind and with the eye. The mind always wanted to compose the picture as it *should* be, and the eye as it really was. But the eyes always won the decision against the mind. As she could hardly paint at all, I advised her simply to portray the human figure in the form of a hieroglyph, but to execute everything else as carefully and in as much detail as possible. Like a child, or like primitive man, the unconscious loves to see its contents represented in the brightest colours. They exercise upon it a magical attraction.

My patient said that a struggle always took place between the understanding and the eyes, but that the latter always had the last say. In the case of the picture of her liberation, for instance, the understanding wanted a painting as bright as day, with radiant sunlight melting out of the rocks the hieroglyph that represented herself. But the eyes

balked, and saw instead a gloomy night scene in which lightning, or something else as dangerous, played the rôle of
liberator. This is the picture she painted.

In the second picture the human figure is represented
by a ball, or sphere, with a red centre containing a seed.
A stroke of lightning liberates the figure from the rock. Being dangerous, the lightning is unfavourable; yet she painted
it in gold, and this colour is always the indication of something highly valuable to her. She treated it as though it were
of greater worth than the seed. In order to lessen the danger,
the mind wanted to have the sphere blue and red; but the
eye saw it differently, and the colours were intermingled
with grey. The same disagreement between the conscious
opinion and the unconscious intention came to light in her
interpretation as well. The mind said that the lightning was
intuition, and that she was about to free herself from her
present condition by developing this function. To this the
eye said nothing at all.

This second picture represents the moment when the
human being is being liberated from the state of identity
with the earth. But what is the state of freedom like? Her
next fantasy gave the answer. She saw the sphere, still denot-
ing the human being, floating free in the sky and held in
equilibrium by two opposed and equal forces. The mind said,
"This is a planet in the nascent state." It occurred to her that
several years before, during an operation, she had had an
ether dream—a "big dream." (The Africans make a dis-
tinction between "big dreams" and the "little" ones, which
are merely of a personal nature. The chief and the medicine
man have "big dreams" and these are accepted as revelations
that decide the fate of the tribe.) The patient told of her
ether dream as follows:

"I saw a *grey* world, with a *silver* band around its
equator, rotating in such a way that the band formed zones
of condensation and rarefaction. At the points of condensa-

tion appeared numbers from 1 to 12, and it was clear to me that these were twelve points of junction in world history, and at the same time twelve great personalities." The twelfth was the most important point or the greatest man; it was also the highest point in her own development.

A year after this she had another big dream. Instead of a world-sphere hovering in space, she saw in the sky a golden serpent gazing down upon a crowd of people. She herself was one of the crowd. The serpent chose a young man as a victim, and devoured him. Then it looked for another victim, and this time pointed to the dreamer herself. She was led away to the sacrifice, and awoke.

Because of her recollection of this dream, she now painted another picture (Plate III), in which she placed the golden serpent in the sky. Beneath it hovers the sphere she had drawn in the preceding picture, this being the globe of the ether dream. In the centre is the number 12. The globe has the power to float; it has a field of oscillation about it that causes it to soar. In commenting upon this, the patient says that the field of oscillation is like the wings of the god Mercury, the guide of souls in the underworld; it is not made of silver, but of quicksilver. She tells me that I call it the animus, because she takes the animus in the negative sense as the understanding that gives unsuitable interpretations. The eye must correct this understanding. The eye is an analogue of the sphere. The mercury-animus-understanding is thus outside; it should be within.

The discrepancy between the understanding and the eye is again apparent from this third picture. The sphere is the totality of the whole human being. In the case of the white man, the ego is on top—it is identical with his consciousness. It should, however, be contained within the totality of the psyche. The number 12 is the point of culmination. It occurred to her that she was born in the night of the 28th-29th

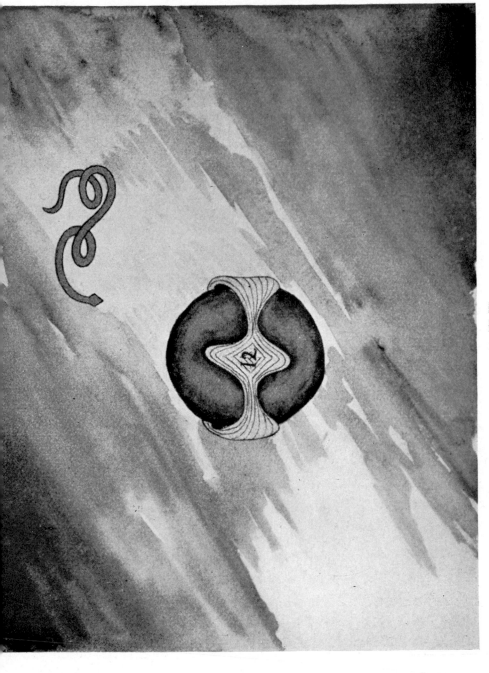

PLATE III

See page 36]

See page 371

PLATE IV

of August—either in the twelfth hour of the 28th or in the first hour of the 29th. Her interpretation of this was: "Either in the eleventh hour or at the break of the new day." The number twelve is thus her birth hour.

Since the band of quicksilver disturbed her, she tried to observe whether it would change in her fantasy. She saw the silver (the mercury) gradually approaching the sphere. Its black lines of force condensed to form the body of a black snake, which began to lace itself around the sphere. This brought upon her a sense of danger and an attack of fear; she felt as if the integrity of the sphere were being threatened. A moral danger presents itself here. The black snake is like a demon. Evil is enfolding her and trying to penetrate within. She therefore attempted a picture of an apotropaic nature. To protect herself against the evil influence, she painted the serpent trying to penetrate the sphere, but repelled by its hardness. This, however, was a suggestion of the mind, and the eye pronounced it an unsatisfactory solution. To her own alarm, then, she was forced to paint another picture (Plate IV).

A black snake with golden mercury wings rears itself above the sphere and thrusts downward into it. Fire breaks out at the point of penetration. The mind wished again to suggest that the sphere repulsed the serpent; but the eye denies this. The sphere is red and blue, with a tripartite arrangement within: there are two green elements and one of gold. The kernel is surrounded by the silver of the mercury. A trinity is thus arrayed against the one, the serpent: the three in one against the devil, who is the fourth.

As Goethe puts it in the second part of *Faust*:

> From the giant shield of Chelone
> Shines an austere figure:
> They are gods whom we bring;
> You must now sing lofty songs.

Small in stature,
Great in power,
The saviours of the shipwrecked,
Gods honoured from of old.

Three we have brought with us,
The fourth would not come.
He said, he was the right one
Who thought for all of them.

The devil is here also the animus, the one who is always right with respect to collective opinion, but who always gives false judgments in individual cases.

This picture, with its objective realization of important contents, led up to a turning point in the patient's psychic life. A climax was reached in her spiritual endeavours. To give her courage, I showed her a painting, executed by a man, in which the serpent rises from below. This gave her a sudden light, and she understood that the whole process was impersonal in its nature. She seized upon the important truth that the ego is not the centre of psychic life; that it revolves around the self, the centre, like a planet around the sun; and that this is consonant with universal laws. The discernment of this truth played a decisive rôle in her later life.

Up to this time the patient had lived in a serious error suggested to her by the animus, the black serpent, the devil. He had made her believe that man is only an ego who has to do everything himself, and is responsible for everything; that this responsible attitude was the highest morality, and that even if one could not always achieve it, one *should* nevertheless always hold to it. But this belief burdens man with a responsibility that he is not able to carry. We are not *only* the ego, as is patent enough from a consideration of the bodily functions, which take their course quite independently of the ego. The truth is, rather, that the ego depends in the most abject fashion upon them. For instance, we may have a neurotic gastric disturbance that we cannot get rid of with the best will in the world, if the "how" of it will not dawn on us from the unconscious.

The serpent demon, however, takes us in with the idea that we are seated upon the driver's seat and can direct our lives. He is the devil inasmuch as he raises an insurrection against the godhead, the whole. Certain theologians even pretend to know what God is, what he can do and cannot do. (For one thing, he has not been allowed to publish anything for the last two thousand years!) As to metaphysical truth, it appears that everything has already been said. For instance, Gogarten declares that God can only be good.

All this is the devilish presumption of the ego. This is why the unconscious wishes to force evil upon us—obviously to show us that we know nothing. No doubt the presumption of the ego is at bottom only a compensation—but to what? To forces that we cannot master. These forces are not "my wishes," "my desires," for they fall upon me against my will. My patient had discovered that psychic happening is only for the smallest part under the control of the ego. For the larger part it is literally a *happening*: happening in and for itself. She is not accountable for it. Discernment of this truth provides her with the formula that enables her to free herself from her identity with the earth. She can then accept the earth. She at last knows that there are overpowering forces from which one cannot escape. We cannot live without being approached by evil.

She had, in her earlier development, lifted herself above the earth and was growing into the sky. But when such is the case, the roots grow down into Hell. It is always true that too much upon one side brings about, in the unconscious, a too-much upon the other. She had come to a standstill because she was pulled upon by "above" and "below." From now on she was no longer torn by opposites, for she could accept the "lower" man as he is. She recognized that evil, the serpent, is a necessary part of the process of growth. The dark part must be brought completely above the horizon, so that life can go on; and the serpent raised to the sky illustrates this truth.

When my patient had made this inner gesture of submission, a change took place in her that showed itself in her next picture, in which red and blue were carefully separated. She had the feeling of tremendous psychic activity, expressed in her painting by a streaming of the quicksilver into the centre. As a result, the latter was covered over as if by a veil. When the veil was dissipated, quite other colours appeared, and these colours progressively regrouped themselves in a further series of pictures.

For my patient, red signified Eros, the emotional principle, and blue the intellectual, or Logos, principle. The two principles were not separated, but intermingled, as is the case with primitive man. She must now learn to distinguish them and to differentiate them. But this can happen only when the totality of her being has become conscious to her.

The next picture (Plate V) is motivated by this differentiation. The painting as a whole is red; it contains four blue spheres, and the serpent is placed below. The centre is green, signifying growth, and is surrounded with gold, which indicates value. Round about are some black contours.

The fact that the serpent has been placed below signifies that it has been accepted as an objective world-principle. The picture expresses a consciousness of the structure of man's being. The latter is represented by the number 4, a number which was sacred to the ancients; the Pythagorean tetractys and the four directions of the weather vane are examples. Four is also the number of the basic psychological functions: sensation, thinking, feeling, intuition. It is only at a relatively advanced stage of consciousness that the four functions are separated and given specific valuation. When this happens, the one is preferred to the other, and one function is de-

PLATE V

See page 40]

veloped to the detriment of the others. But man loses in this way his connection with the whole of himself; he identifies himself with his most valued function, and all the rest falls to the share of the serpent.

A perception of the significance of fourness, of the totality of the psychic structure, means illumination of the "inner region." This recognition is a first step, a necessary station on the road of inner development. My patient was occupied with it for quite a long time, and built upon it until she had attained complete clarity. Another process then set in, which I cannot discuss in this connection.

The point of this case history is that the unconscious led my patient to that insight which people of our time have not yet attained in general, and which they ought to attain if they are to experience the illumination of the "inner region." But there is no "way" to this experience. My patient followed one way, but other people may have to take quite a different course. Even drawing or painting is right only if one can do it from an inner motivation. The pictures ought to make themselves. If *we* make them by means of our conscious mind, then it is magic, and we shall go the way of Goethe's sorcerer's apprentice.

It is obvious that this Western example of the process of individuation is far removed from the perfected beauty of Eastern symbols, like those of Laotse, which likewise give expression to this process, and at which the greatest masters have laboured. We Westerners, in spite of our so-called culture, are still barbarians and children when it comes to the psychic world. We have only just rediscovered the precious stone; we have still to polish it. We cannot yet compete with the intuitive clarity of Eastern vision.

Here, then, is an example of the process of individuation, and one which is remarkable for its brevity and concentration. It owes its special character to the unusual intelligence, education, and maturity of the patient in question. Usually the process runs a much longer course, and is far more involved—particularly in the case of neurotic individuals.

The peculiar symbolic terminology that I have used in describing the patient's fantasies is true to the mental images she actually produced. I admit that all this must sound very strange to a reader who is not accustomed to the peculiar language of intuitive processes. They are not directed by the rational mind, which in other ways is man's most valuable achievement. They are spontaneous, dynamic, and bewilderingly devious; they interfuse rational viewpoints with intuitive visions, and ethical values with emotional outbursts. The psychic activity involved in such a process is utterly undifferentiated; it is like a flow of lava in which all sorts of minerals gush forth in one glowing stream, welling up from the entrails of the earth. There is no use in rationalizing and intellectualizing this activity. Yet it is all-important to maintain the sense of mutual understanding between patient and doctor while the eruption lasts, so that the patient never loses the feeling of intelligent companionship. If he does lose contact with his *directeur de conscience,* he may fall a prey to panic inspired by the overwhelming strangeness of his vision.

As a matter of fact, it is the unexpected manifestations from the unconscious that on occasions do drive people crazy. In real psychoses we find the same mental contents, only in these cases they could not be assimilated by consciousness. Whoever finds himself attacked by such ideas, fantasies, and visions is either seized by an irresistible fear of becoming insane or thinks he is a genius. In either case he is at once isolated from his fellow beings, who are, of course, unable to understand what it is all about. The alienist can discern that something is wrong, and is justified in at least suspecting an unsound mental condition. A knowledge that this is so would hardly contribute to the patient's peace of mind. If prudent and careful people, therefore, have such experiences, they prefer to keep quiet about them, or to repress them before they have fully developed.

The dilemma of supposing oneself either a genius or a crank is, of course, nothing but a mistake. It is neither a stroke of genius—as a rule—nor a fit of insanity; it is simply a matter of formerly unconscious contents rising to the level of consciousness—a not infrequent experience. If a person can only keep a cool head, he is threatened neither by insanity nor by the curse of becoming a misunderstood genius. But to keep a cool head is just the difficulty, when something like hot lava is flowing through a system which otherwise appears to be quite well balanced. That is why people in such a predicament prefer to have somebody with them. Mere reasoning with them, or arguing against the facts, would not help them much; on the contrary, it would only be the repetition of an attempt they had already found to be ineffective. They need to feel a certain understanding and sympathy, perhaps even a certainty that they can share their crazy ideas with someone. This relieves them of the fear of capsizing.

It is this kind of understanding that I always try to bring to bear on the situation, and that explains the peculiar language which I am forced to use in such cases. But when the main shock is over, I always try—with the help of my patient—to see what has happened. When we have got thus far along the road, we give up the intuitive language and the symbolic terminology. We try to reduce the seemingly incomprehensible events to rational sequences and to personal or impersonal origins. By such a procedure we hope to assimilate the experience, and to integrate it into the whole of the human personality. Such experiences should never leave a fatal sense of inferiority; rather, they should enrich both the feelings and the mind, because they contain real life and the greatest values. They contain, as a matter of fact, just those values that were painfully lacking before the outburst occurred, and they add just those pieces to the puzzle of life which make the picture complete. It may still be an imperfect picture in the eyes of man, but we may presume it to be satisfactory in the eyes of the unknown creator of the puzzle.

The difficulty of explaining such a case always lies in the fact that one ought to provide a minute biography of the patient, omitting none of the thousand trifles that make up human existence. Since this is obviously impossible, any description or explanation must remain more or less unsatisfactory to those whose live's have yielded no similar experiences. Some people do not know that others exist who feel their lives to be *progressive*, and these people will find it quite unintelligible when I say that the case of my woman patient begins with the fact that she found herself "stuck." But that is exactly what this woman felt: her life had progressed, and then came to a standstill—whatever that means. There had been a flowing river, and it ended in stagnation. There did not seem to be any possibilities ahead, at least none that she could see. There seemed to be a snag somewhere that was holding her back. Something seemed to call to her from the past, perhaps from afar, from a remote place somewhere in her personal history. She followed the call. And since her mother (very often the representative of the past) was long since dead, she at least made the pilgrimage to her mother's country. There a peculiar thing happened: she began to be fascinated by landscapes, so that she had to paint them. Obviously she found something in the landscape worth retaining. Instead of progressing, she regressed to her mother and to the country from which the mother had issued.

Her first picture in Zurich, before she had seen me, caused a peculiar dissociation. While she was again painting a landscape, she had a fantasy that showed her caught in the earth. This fantasy amounts to a statement about her condition: her regression leads her first to her mother, then to her mother's country, and eventually to the earth, in which the lower part of her body is caught. The mother represents her personal past. Her mother's country must mean something beyond the mother—perhaps the maternal ancestors; and the earth means something else again—presumably the cradle of Man. I have reasons for assuming that such symbols really point to psychical layers—to increasingly unconscious pre-stages of individual consciousness. "Mother" refers to childhood and thus to the origins of individual consciousness; "Mother's Country," to ancestral psychical conditions; "Earth," to a layer of collective unconsciousness peculiar to man in general and presumably also to animals. I would, therefore, call such a regression a "descent into the collective unconscious," that region of the psyche which appears vastly older than the individual's personal life. Such a descent into the collective unconscious appears always to precede a more or less intense activation of the unconscious.

Thus far, there is nothing unique about this particular case: it simply exemplifies a consciousness that has lived in truly modern fashion, quite out of touch with the unconscious. Under such conditions the *earth* becomes fascinating and magical, since it stands for the unknown contents of man's unconscious. The earth, underlying and supporting the visible space above it, is indeed an apt symbol for the collective unconscious as the basis of consciousness. However, we have not exhausted the meaning of this fantasy.

The vision states that man's lower body is caught in the earth. The "lower part" is the basis of consciousness, the unconscious. The earth, therefore, symbolizes fertility—the fertile part of the human psyche. This is perhaps why the rocks in the picture remind us of seeds. When I told my patient to use a hieroglyph to denote the human figure, which defied her inexperienced hand, she instantly chose the globe or circle already suggested by the egglike boulders.

From ancient times the circle or globe has been a symbol of completeness, perfection, and totality. In Plato's *Timæus* the *anima mundi*, or universal soul, is spherical, as are also the hermaphroditic primal beings of the *Symposium*. The same idea predominates in speculative philosophy throughout the Middle Ages.

Now it is, to say the least, a curious fact that a person who was not deeply read in the past should spontaneously produce an idea identical with one of the guiding notions of mediæval philosophy and expressing exactly the same underlying thought. The alchemistic idea of the all-round being, the so-called *rotundum*, represents the *materia prima* and its final product, the philosopher's stone. A text of the first century A.D. speaks of "the stone that contains a pneuma" (spirit) and of the Royal Art as the attempt to set it free (pneuma = nous = mind). This spirit was identified as Mercury or quicksilver. I must repeat that my patient had no knowledge of alchemy and least of all of the significance of its most baffling mystery: the identity of quicksilver and mind. The old alchemistic treatises dwell a great deal also upon the seed buried in the earth, from which it shall rise again in the form of the philosophical gold. The mercurial seed was symbolized by the serpent that formed a circle by biting its own tail. As such it was called *ouroboros*, the tail eater. In all this we can find a remarkable analogy to the main contents of the first picture.

In the second picture occurs the liberation of the seed by the aid of a stroke of lightning. In alchemy it was not lightning, but a *sword*, that divided the egg containing the seed, the *sperma* or *semen mercurii*. The emphasis on the grey colour has its alchemistic parallel in the fact that the *materia prima* was "unseemly." It was therefore called "lead" or *plumbum philosophicum*. The division of the alchemistic egg produced a pair of opposed forces, usually regarded as the male and female principles. The "floating in the sky," also, has its bearing upon the alchemistic "sublimation" and upon the fact that the ultimate product, the philosopher's stone, was thought of as a living, winged, and hermaphroditic being of ethereal and luminous nature.

The dream of the golden serpent contains an anticipation of the patient's own development: she will be assimilated by the mercurial serpent, the totality of her own psyche. This obviously means that she will not overcome the unconscious psyche buried in the earth, but that the latter will devour her, thus producing a different being formed from the conjunction of her conscious and unconscious existence. This new personality is presumably hinted at in the former dream by the number 12, which stands for the "greatest man."

I should mention the fact that my patient had been to some extent influenced by Swedenborgianism, which presents the world in the guise of the *homo maximus*. Being devoured by the serpent could mean being devoured by the *anima mundi*. Swedenborg was not a real alchemist, but he was influenced by the mediæval philosophy of nature and had at one time partially succumbed to a tragic invasion of the unconscious; I refer to the psychotic attack during his stay in London, for which there is unmistakable evidence in his own diary. I will not deny that Swedenborg's peculiar mental condition had an influence on the general conscious attitude of my patient. But anyone with a sufficient knowledge of Swedenborg's chief writings will know that it is very unlikely that he could have infected my patient with alchemistic philosophy or that she could have reproduced it by cryptomnesia.

The actual "conjunction" (again an important alchemis-

tic concept) is represented in the fourth picture. There we
have the union of the sphere, representing totality, with the
black serpent, which she cannot help identifying with the
principle of evil, the devil. The devil is here depicted as a
principle opposed to trinity. This is, of course, a Christian
idea that found its place in mediæval philosophy.[1]

An alchemistic philosopher of the sixteenth century,
Gerardus Dorneus,[2] was deeply concerned with the misdeeds
of the number 4 in a trinitarian world. He was just as much
upset by the fact that totality cannot exclude the black substance of evil. He tried desperately to reason away the possibility in the good world of the Trinity of a painful conflict
caused by the inevitable admixture of the *serpens duplex
cornua quatour erigens*—the dual serpent erecting the four
horns (of the quaternity over against the Trinity). He could
not help naïvely following the general human inclination to
avoid conflict by ignoring the dark side of one's own nature.
Yet in human life there is no totality that is not based upon
the conflict of opposites.

The quaternity in alchemy, incidentally, was usually
expressed by the four colours of the old painters, mentioned
in a fragment of Heraclitus: red, black, yellow, and white;
or in diagrams as the four points of the compass. In modern
times the unconscious usually chooses red, blue (instead of
black), yellow or gold, and green (instead of white). The
quaternity is merely another expression of totality. These
colours embrace the whole of the rainbow. The alchemists
said that the appearance of the *cauda pavonis*, the peacock's
tail, was a sign that the process was coming to a successful
conclusion.

The last picture by my patient contains these colours
in a balanced arrangement, expressing her acceptance of the
quaternity. The hitherto ignored unconscious, the "lower
part of man," had been admitted to her overt psychic life by

on act of submission in which the ego-consciousness yielded supremacy to a superior totality.

Such a submission means the recognition that man has two sides of such equal importance that they cannot become reconciled; their conflict has to be suffered. The cross of the quaternity is unavoidable and indispensable if we are to continue our pilgrimage through life. If we prefer not to liberate the spirit buried in the earth, dormant in the stone, we get stuck in the earth, caught in an unconscious fascination by material conditions.

The whole modern religious problem seems to be contained in this short series of pictures.

The fact that spontaneous imagination makes such telling use of alchemistic symbolism is rather startling to anyone who has a knowledge of mediæval alchemy. The patient's fantasy-pictures are just as if an ancient alchemist were at work—one of that number who have left us illustrated manuscripts, often consisting only of pictures, like the famous *Mutus Liber* of 1677. Those pictures try to express the seemingly inexhaustible mystery of transmutation by means of a symbolism that is only partly traditional. Often enough the expression is highly individual and closely resembles the pictures produced today by people who are presumably working under similar mental conditions.

Perhaps it is well to admit that there were naturally a great many alchemists who thought that they were learning no more than to make gold. But "making gold" was at the same time taken in an allegorical sense by the alchemistic philosophers; they understood by it a spiritual transmutation, or what we would today call a psychological transformation or readjustment. When he is faced with a transformation of this kind, man always unconsciously chooses such symbolism. And the reason for this choice does not lie in the fact that our ancestors of three or four centuries ago thought largely in terms of alchemy. On the contrary, our ancestors thought as we do today because they found themselves in the same psychic predicament, or at least in a predicament comparable to our modern religious problem.

As a matter of fact, history records the same kind of thought from almost two thousand years ago. There are peculiar parallels to alchemistic ideas in certain passages of the Gospel of St. John and in the baptismal rite.[3] The same holds true of Taoist alchemy in China, and of certain philosophical systems in India called "The Quicksilver Systems." It is difficult to prove that these Eastern systems had any influence on the nearly contemporary philosophy of the West, and it is equally difficult to see how a modern person with the usual education in science could arrive at a correct use of alchemistic symbolism. If my woman patient were the only one who had produced such symbols, I should not be citing her case here. But I have seen numbers of similar cases. One could almost call the phenomenon a regular occurrence, though it is little known—and for obvious reasons.

The most sensible way of explaining such parallelism is by resorting to the hypothesis of the collective unconscious —of a universal similitude or identity of the basic structure of the human psyche. It seems likely that the collective unconscious contains a number of patterns, "archetypes," common to the whole of humanity. We must suppose that, under similar conditions, they function in the same way regardless of place and time, and that they produce the same ideas regardless of tradition. I assume, therefore, that my patients would have produced "alchemistic" symbolism even if alchemy had never existed. It is, in a way, true that it has never existed for us, since modern ignorance of alchemistic philosophy is so profound that it amounts to a complete break in historical continuity. Who in our days would ever identify quicksilver with spirit or mind? Though an astrologer might interpret Mercury as mind, yet, even to an astrologer the planet Mercury would have lost its connotation of quicksilver; there is no longer any apparent correspondence between the metal and the planet. It would be just as unlikely to occur to anyone as the equation of Venus with copper, or of Saturn with lead. And the identity of the serpent to quicksilver, so dear to the ancient alchemist, is entirely lost to modern thought.

I have emphasized the fact that my patient was not acquainted with the peculiar symbolism of ancient alchemy. I should add that, when she came to me, I myself had no knowledge of the ideas I have just mentioned. As a matter of fact, it was this very case that led me to the study of alchemy. Therefore, it is impossible that I could have suggested such ideas to my patient, even unconsciously.

As a whole, this case offers a good, though brief, example of a symbolic series typical for certain phases of what I call the process of individuation. Before considering the subject in more detail, it will be wise to take up the concept of the collective unconscious, and to discuss some of the "figures" to be found in it.

FOOTNOTES TO CHAPTER TWO

1. The reader will find ample material about the problem of 3 and 4—the trinity and the quaternity—in later parts of this book. I should like to call his attention again to my Terry Lectures (see Chapter One, note 10) where I have also dealt with this problem.

2. *De Tenebris contra Naturam et Vita brevi*. Theatr. Chem., 1602, Vol. I. Cf. p. 524 *et seq*.

3. I have pointed out these analogies in an essay, "The Visions of Zosimos." Zurich: *Eranos-Jahrbuch,* 1937.

CHAPTER THREE

Archetypes of the Collective Unconscious

The hypothesis of the (collective unconscious) belongs to the class of ideas that people at first find strange, but soon come to possess and use as familiar conceptions. This has been the case with the general notion of the unconscious. When the philosophic idea of the unconscious, in the form presented chiefly by Carus and von Hartmann, had gone down under the overwhelming wave of materialism and empiricism without leaving any traces of moment, it timidly reappeared in the domain of a medical psychology that shared the aims of natural science.

At first the concept of the unconscious was limited, and denoted the state of subliminal or forgotten contents. Even with Freud, who makes the unconscious—at least metaphorically—take the stage as an active subject, it is really nothing but the gathering place of forgotten and suppressed contents, and has significance as a function only thanks to these. With Freud, accordingly, the unconscious is exclusively of a personal nature, although, on another side, he was aware of its archaic and mythological thought-forms.

A more or less superficial layer of the unconscious is undoubtedly personal. I call it the *personal unconscious*. Yet this personal unconscious appears to rest upon a deeper layer that does not derive from personal experience and achievement but is inborn. This deeper layer I call the *collective unconscious*. I have chosen the term "collective" because this part of the unconscious is not individual, but universal; in contrast to the personal psyche, it has contents and modes of behaviour that are more or less the same everywhere and in all individuals. The collective unconscious, so far as we know, is self-identical in all Western men and thus constitutes a psychic foundation, superpersonal in its nature, that is present in every one of us.

Any kind of psychic existence can be recognized only by the presence of contents that can be made sufficiently conscious for recognition. We can, therefore, speak of an unconscious only in so far as we are able to point out its contents. The contents of the personal unconscious constitute the personal and private side of psychic life. They are chiefly the so-called *feeling-toned complexes*. The contents of the collective unconscious, on the other hand, are the so-called *archetypes*.

The term "archetype" derives from St. Augustine. The term is an explanatory paraphrase of the Platonic εἶδος. For our purposes this designation is appropriate and helpful, for it tells us that with the collective unconscious contents we are dealing with ancient or, better yet, with primordial types —that is to say, with images impressed upon the mind since of old. The phrase *"représentations collectives,"* which Lévy-Bruhl uses to denote the symbolic figures of the primitive view of the world, could easily be applied to the unconscious contents as well, since we are actually dealing with the same thing. Primitive tribal lore treats of archetypes that are modified in a particular way. To be sure, these archetypes are no longer contents of the unconscious, but have already changed into conscious formulas that are taught according to tradition, generally in the form of esoteric teaching. This last is a typical mode of expression for the transmission of collective contents originally derived from the unconscious.

Another well-known expression of the archetype is myth and fable. But here also we are dealing with conscious and specifically moulded forms that have been handed on, relatively unchanged, through long periods of time. It is thus only indirectly that the concept of the archetype fits the *représentations collectives,* for it properly designates the psychic content that has as yet been subjected to no conscious treatment and so represents an immediate, psychic actuality. There is a considerable difference between such an archetype and the formula that has become historic or has been elaborated. Especially on the higher levels of esoteric teaching, the archetypes appear in a form that usually reveals in an unmistakable way the elements of judgement and valuation introduced by conscious elaboration. On the other hand, their immediate manifestation, as it confronts us in dreams and visions, is much more natural, less understandable or more naïve than in the myth, for example. In this respect the fairy tale is, no doubt, much truer to nature.

What the word archetype means in the nominal sense is made sufficiently clear when we have pointed out the occurrence of archetypes in myth, esoteric teaching, and fairy tale. But if we try to establish on *psychological* ground just what an archetype is, the matter becomes more complicated. In mythological research, we have contented ourselves until now with solar, lunar, meteorological, vegetal, and other comparisons. But we have almost completely refused to see that myths are first and foremost psychic manifestations that represent the nature of the psyche. The mind of the primitive is little concerned with an objective explanation of obvious things, but has an imperative need or, rather, its unconscious psyche has an irresistible urge to assimilate all experience through the outer senses into inner, psychic happening. The primitive is not content to see the sun rise and set; this external observation must at the same time be a psychic event—that is, the sun in its course must represent the fate of a god or hero who dwells, in the last analysis, nowhere else than in the psyche of man.

All the mythologized occurrences of nature, such as

summer and winter, the phases of the moon, the rainy seasons, and so forth, are anything but allegories of these same objective experiences, nor are they to be understood as "explanations" of sunrise, sunset, and the rest of the natural phenomena. They are, rather, symbolic expressions for the inner and unconscious psychic drama that becomes accessible to human consciousness by way of projection—that is, mirrored in the events of nature. This projection is so thoroughgoing that it has taken several thousand years of culture to separate it in some measure from the outer object.

In the case of astrology, indeed, this age-old intuitive science came actually to be stamped with heresy because men had not succeeded in making the psychological description of personal character independent of the stars. Whoever today still—or again—believes in astrology succumbs almost as a rule to the old, superstitious acceptance of the influence of the stars. And yet anyone who can calculate a horoscope should know that, since the days of the blessed Hipparchus of Alexandria, the vernal equinox has been arbitrarily fixed at zero degrees of the Ram, and that every horoscope is therefore sixty degrees out of reckoning with reference to the influence of the stars, the vernal equinox having gradually advanced, since then, to the last degrees of the Fishes, thanks to the precession of the equinox!

Primitive man impresses us so strongly with his subjectivity that we really should have surmised in the first place that myths are related to psychic happening. Every analogy to nature which he makes is essentially the language and outer dress of an unconscious psychic process. But in the fact that the latter is unconscious we have the explanation why man has thought of everything else except the psyche. People have simply not *known* that the psyche contains all the images that have ever given rise to myths, and that our unconscious is an acting and suffering subject with an inner drama that primitive man rediscovers, by way of analogy, in the processes of nature both great and small.

"In thine own breast dwell the stars of thy fate," says Seni to Wallenstein—a dictum that would do ample justice to all astrology, if we knew even a little something about this secret of the heart. But for this, so far, men have had little understanding. Nor do I dare to assert that the matter stands any better today.

Every tribal teaching is *sacred-dangerous*, and therefore absolute. All esoteric teachings try to grasp the unseen happening of the psyche, and all assert their own final validity. Whatever is true of this primitive lore is even more unconditionally true of the ruling world religions. They contain what was originally the hidden knowledge of revelation and have set forth the secrets of the psyche in glorious images. Their temples and their sacred writings proclaim in image and word the prescript hallowed from of old and accessible to every believing disposition, every receptive outlook, and every last elaboration of thought. Indeed, we are forced to say that the more beautiful, the more grandiose, the more comprehensive is the image that has come into being and been handed on, *so much the farther is it removed from our experience*. Nowadays we can feel our way into it and perceive something of it, but the original experience is lost.

Why, indeed, is psychology the youngest of all the sciences of experience? Why have we not long ago discovered the unconscious and salvaged its treasures of eternal images? Simply because we had a Christian formula for all the things of the psyche—one that is far more beautiful and comprehensive than direct experience. Though for many persons the Christian view of the world has paled in its turn, the symbolic treasure rooms of the East are still full of wonders that can nourish for a long time to come the passion for show and new clothes. And what is more, these images—be they Christian or Buddhistic or anything else—are lovely, mysterious, and full of presentiment. To be sure, the more we are accustomed to them the more has constant usage polished them smooth, so that what remains of them is banal superficiality, clothed in almost senseless paradoxes. The mystery of the virgin birth, or the oneness of the Son with the Father, or the Trinity which is no triad, no longer lends wings to any philosophical fantasy. They have become mere objects of belief.

It is not surprising that the religious need, the believing mind, and the philosophical speculation of the cultured European feel themselves attracted to the symbols of the East—the grandiose conceptions of divinity in India and the abysms of Taoistic philosophy in China—just as once before the heart and mind of the Græco-Roman were gripped by Christian ideas. There are many Europeans who surrendered so completely to the influence of the Christian symbol that they were enmeshed in the neurosis of a Kierkegaard; and others, again, whose relation to God, owing to a progressive impoverishment of symbolism, developed into an unbearably refined I-you relation. It is not surprising that such persons later succumbed to the magic of the fresh strangeness of Eastern symbols. This surrender is no defeat, but rather bears witness to the receptiveness and vitality of the religious sense. We can observe the same thing in the Oriental man of education, who not seldom feels himself drawn in the same way to the Christian symbol, and even develops an enviable understanding of it.

That people succumb to these eternal images is an entirely normal matter. It is for this very purpose that the images came into being. They are intended to attract, to convince, fascinate, and overpower. They are created out of the primal stuff of revelation, and portray the first-hand experience of divinity that every revelation contains. Thus they always lead men to premonition while defending them against experience. For these images do not stand isolated like volcanoes, but, thanks to a labour of the human spirit often centuries long, have been moulded into a comprehensive system of thought ascribing an order to the world, into an ethical regulation of human actions, and into a mighty, far-spread and ancient institution called church or religion.

I can best illustrate my meaning by the example of a Swiss mystic and hermit, the blessed brother Nicholas von der Flüe. His outstanding religious experience was the so-called vision of threefoldness, which preoccupied him to such an extent that he painted it, or had it painted, on the wall of his cell. The vision is represented in a contemporary painting preserved in the parish church at Sachseln. It is a mandala,[1] divided six ways, whose centre is the crowned countenance of God. Now we know that Brother Nicholas made researches into the nature of his vision with the aid of the illustrated booklet of a German mystic, and struggled to get his original experience into tangible form. He occupied himself with it for years. This is what I call the "treatment" of the symbol. Reflection upon the nature of the symbol led necessarily to the conclusion that he must have gazed upon the holy threefoldness itself—that is, upon the *summum bonum*, eternal love. The glorified representation in Sachseln actually corresponds to this idea.

But the original experience was wholly different. For, in the ecstasy of the blessed brother, such a terrible sight was revealed to him that his own countenance was so changed that people were alarmed and grew afraid of him. What he had really seen was a countenance full of dreadful anger, which shook him to the core.

This vision, undoubtedly fearful and highly perturbing, which had burst like a volcano upon his harmless religious outlook without any introduction on the part of dogma and with no exegetical commentary—this vision must have required a long labour of adaptation before it was changed into the thing that confronts us in his later years, namely, a vision of threefoldness. He came to terms with this experience on the basis of dogma, at that time as firm as a rock; and the dogma showed its power of assimilation in this, that, with a saving grace, it transformed something fearfully alive into the lovely clarity of the idea of the Trinity. But the reconciliation might have taken place on quite a different basis provided by the vision itself with its uncanny actuality —much to the disadvantage of the brother himself, who would then have become not a saint, but a heretic, and would perhaps have ended his life at the stake.

This short example illustrates for us the incomparably useful function of the dogmatic symbol: it protects a person from a direct experience of God as long as he does not mischievously expose himself. But if, like Brother Nick, he leaves home and family, lives too long alone and gazes too deeply into the dark mirror, then the awful event of the meeting may befall him. Yet even then the traditional symbol, come to full flower through the centuries, may operate like a healing draught and divert the fatal incursion of the living godhead into the hallowed spaces of the church.

Jacob Boehme, too, must have met with a quite similar experience. He also knows a God of "the fire of wrath," a true *Absconditus*. But he was able to bridge the deeply felt contradiction by means of the Christian formula of Father-Son, and to embody it speculatively in his view of the world, which, though heretical, was yet in all essential points Christian. Otherwise he would have become a dualist. Nevertheless, this contradiction has left obvious traces in his mandala, which is appended to the forty questions concerning the soul and which pictures the nature of divinity, for the mandala is divided into a light and a dark half. The dogmatic image has rendered him, also, excellent service, by sparing him the evil fate of Angelus Silesius, who fled from his own vision into the very lap of the Catholic Church, and had to counterbalance this fault with a severe neurosis.

Dogma advises us not to have an unconscious. Therefore, the Catholic way of life is completely unaware of
psychological problems in this sense. The whole life of the
collective unconscious has been absorbed without remainder,
so to speak, in the dogmatic archetypes, and flows like a
well-controlled stream in the symbolism of ritual and of the
church calendar. This is not a manifestation of the individual
psyche. It never was, because the Christian Church was
preceded by the Græco-Roman mysteries, and these reach
back into the grey mists of neolithic prehistory. Mankind
has never lacked powerful images to lend magic aid against
the uncanny, living depths of the world and of the psyche.
The figures of the unconscious have always been expressed
in protecting and healing images and thus expelled from the
psyche into cosmic space.

The iconoclasm of the Reformation, however, quite
literally made a breach in the bulwarks of the holy pictures
and, ever since, one after another has crumbled away. They
became dubious, for they collided with awakening reason.
Besides, people had long since forgotten what they meant.
Or had they really forgotten? Could it be that men had
never really known what they meant, and that it first occurred to Protestant mankind in recent times that we
actually have no conception of what it means to believe in
the virgin birth or in the complexities of the Trinity? It
almost seems as if these images had just lived, and as if their
living existence had simply been accepted without question
and without reflection, much as everyone decorates Christ-
mas trees and hides Easter eggs without ever knowing what
these customs mean.

The fact is that archetypal images are so significant in
themselves that people never think of asking what they
mean. That the gods die from time to time is due to man's
discovery that they do not mean anything, that they are
good-for-nothings made by human hands, fashioned out of

wood and stone. In reality, man has thus discovered only this: that up till then he had not achieved one thought concerning these images.

The history of the development of Protestantism is one of chronic iconoclasm. One wall after another fell. And the work of destruction was not too difficult, either, when once the authority of the church had been shattered. We all know how, in large things as in small, in general as well as in particular, piece after piece collapsed, and how the alarming impoverishment of symbolism that is now the condition of our life came about. The power of the church has gone with that loss of symbolism, too—a fortress that has been robbed of its bastions and casemates, a house whose walls have been plucked away, that is exposed to all the winds of the world and to all dangers.

Though properly speaking it is a pitiful collapse which offends our sense of history, the disintegration of Protestantism into nearly four hundred denominations is yet an infallible sign of life, and shows that the restlessness is growing. The Protestant with nothing left but the historical figure of Christ, a much-debated idea of God, and a compulsive faith, in which—Heaven knows!—he has very poor success, is actually thrust forth into a state of defencelessness at which men must shudder who live close to nature and to the past. To be sure, the enlightened, most reasonable Protestant consciousness knows, and wishes to know, nothing about this state of affairs, and yet is quietly looking elsewhere for what has been lost to Europe. Men search for the effective images, the modes of viewing things that satisfy the restlessness of heart and mind; and they find the treasures of the East.

There is no objection to this, taken in and for itself. No one compelled the Romans to import Asiatic cults in bulk. If the Christianity that is called hostile to art had really not suited the Germanic peoples, they could easily have rejected it again when the prestige of the Roman legions had waned. The American Negroes, also, will not be kept away from their voodoo worship, and the Pueblo Indians celebrate their buffalo and snake dances quite merrily in the fold of the church. Still, Christianity in Europe has grown into something that its founder might well have wondered at had he lived to see it; and the Christianity of Negroes and Indians might well be the occasion for historical reflections. Then why should not the West assimilate Eastern forms? The Romans also went to Eleusis, to Samothrace and Egypt to be initiated. There even seems to have been a regular tourist trade of this sort in Egypt.

The gods of Hellas and Rome perished from the same disease as did our Christian symbols; men discovered then, as they do today, that they had no thoughts whatever on the subject. On the other hand, the gods of the strangers still had unexhausted mana. Their names were curious and unintelligible, and their deeds portentously dark—a very different matter from the trite scandalmongery of Olympus. The Asiatic symbols were at least not understandable, and so they were not banal like the long-accustomed gods. That people accepted the new as unreflectively as they had rejected the old did not become a problem at that time.

Is it becoming a problem today? Will we be able to clothe ourselves, as though in a new garment, with ready-made symbols grown on foreign soil, saturated with foreign blood, spoken in a foreign language, nourished by a foreign culture, interwoven in a foreign history, and so resemble a beggar who wraps himself in kingly raiment, a king who disguises himself as a beggar? No doubt, this is possible. Or are we not commanded, somewhere, to hold no masquerade, but perhaps even to make our own garment ourselves?

I believe that history is capable of anything. There exists no folly that men have not tried out. And if anything can be made cheap, then those who would like to make it dear are to be counted among the very stupid. At this point I must take a subjective tone and admit that I belong to those who suffer from convictions. Thus, for example, I am convinced that Protestant man has not in vain been despoiled of his own development, and made to go naked. This development has an inner consistency. Everything that presented him with no thought-content has been torn from him. If now he should go and cover his nakedness with the gorgeous dress of the Orient, like the theosophists, he would be untrue to his own history. A man does not work his way down to beggarhood and then pose as an Indian king on the stage. Finally, it is not necessary to go as far as theosophy does. There are more modest substitutes for the loss of Christian symbolism. But none the less it is a substitute, a mere exchange of symbols, in which the question remains dark as to just what original experiences are expressed by the symbol.

It would seem to me far better to confess strong-mindedly to the spiritual poverty of a want of symbols than to feign a possession of which we can in no case be the spiritual heirs. We are, indeed, the rightful heirs of Christian symbolism, but this inheritance we have somehow squandered. We have let the house that our fathers built fall to pieces, and now we try to break into Oriental palaces that our fathers never knew. Why do we not rather say, "We are poor," and for once deal earnestly with our famous belief in God that people are always talking about? But whenever it comes to a pinch, we stop the dear Lord halfway and wish to do it ourselves, not only as though we were afraid, but because we actually have a terrible fear that things would then go wrong. At bottom we share the view of Napoleon: "God is always on the side of the best artillery." And since the dear Lord does not make cannon, we just stick to our own priggery. The fear is anything but unjustified, for when God is nearest the danger is greatest. It is dangerous to confess to spiritual poverty, for whoever is poor has cravings and whoever craves draws his fate upon himself. A Swiss proverb puts it drastically: "Behind every rich man stands a devil, and behind every poor man—two."

As the Christian vow of worldly poverty turned the senses from the good things of the world, so spiritual poverty seeks to renounce the false riches of the spirit. It wishes to retreat not only from the sorry remnants of a great past that call themselves today the Protestant Church, but also from all the allurements of exotic reputation, in order to dwell with itself where, in the cold light of consciousness, the barrenness of the world extends even to the stars.

We have already inherited this poverty from our fathers. I well remember my confirmation lesson at the hands of my own father. The catechism bored me unspeakably. Once I turned the leaves of the little book in order to find something of interest, and my glance fell on the paragraphs about the Trinity. That interested me, and I waited impatiently till the instruction had advanced to that section. But when the longed-for lesson had arrived, my father said, "We will skip this section; I cannot make anything out of it myself." With that my last hope was laid in the grave.

While our intellect has been achieving colossal things, our spiritual dwelling has fallen to pieces. We are thoroughly convinced that even with the latest and largest reflecting telescope, now being built in America, men will discover behind the farthest nebulæ no empyrean where fire and water intermingle; and we know that our sight will wander despairingly through the emptiness of immeasurable extension. Nor are matters improved when mathematical physics reveals to us the world of the infinitesimally small—swarms of electrons into all eternity! In the end we dig up the wisdom of all times and peoples and find that everything most dear and precious has already been said in the most winning and lovely words. Like yearning children we stretch out our hands to it and suppose that, if we could grasp it, we would possess it too. But what we do possess is no longer valid, and our hands grow weary from reaching out, for riches lie everywhere as far as sight extends. All these possessions turn to *water,* and more than one magician's apprentice has finally been drowned in these waters called up by himself—unless he first succumbed to the saving delusion that *this* wisdom was good and *that* was bad. From these adepts come those disturbing invalids who believe they have a prophetic mission; for, through the artificial sundering of true and false wisdom, there arises a cleft in the psyche, and from it a loneliness and craving like that of the alcoholic who always hopes to find companions in his vice.

When our natural inheritance has been dissipated, then —to use the language of Heraclitus—all spirit has descended from its fiery heights; to be sure a different *descensus spiritus sancti*—every symbol is also prophetic. But when spirit becomes heavy it turns to water, and baptism in fire is replaced by baptism in water. The magic formula of the priest still repeats this process in the night of the *Sabbathus sanctus:* *"Descendat in hanc plenitudinem fontis virtus spiritus sancti,"* and the inevitable has happened: the soul has turned to water, as Heraclitus says, and with Luciferian presumption the intellect has usurped the seat whereon the spirit once throned.

The spirit, indeed, may claim the *patris potestas* over the soul, but not so the earth-born intellect, which is man's sword or hammer, and not a creator of spiritual worlds, a father of the soul.

The way of the soul in search of its lost father leads thus to the water, to the dark mirror that reposes at its bottom. Whoever has chosen the state of spiritual poverty, the true heritage of a Protestantism lived out consistently to the end, goes the way of the soul that leads to the water.

And this water is no idle metaphor, but a living symbol created by the psyche itself. I can no doubt best illustrate this by a concrete example, and one will have to suffice:

A Protestant theologian often dreamed the same dream: that he stood at the edge of an abyss with a deep valley below, and in it a dark lake. He knew in the dream that something had always prevented him from approaching the lake. This time he resolved to go to the water. As he approached the shore an uncanny darkness fell, and a gust of wind suddenly rushed over the face of the water. Then fear seized him and he awoke.

This dream illustrates natural symbolism. The dreamer descends into his own depths, and the way leads him to the mysterious water. And now there occurs the miracle of the pool of Bethesda: an angel descends and touches the water, which thus receives healing power. In the dream it is the wind ὅ πνεῖ ὅπου θ' ἔλει, the spirit that bloweth whither it listeth. Man's descent to the water is needed to evoke the miracle of its coming to life. But the breath of the spirit that rushes over the dark water is uncanny; it is an unseen presence, a *tremendum* to which neither human expectations nor arbitrary machinations have given life. It lives of itself, and a shudder strikes the man to whom spirit was always merely what he believes, what he makes himself, what is found in books, or what other people talk about. But when it happens spontaneously, then it is like an apparition, and primitive fear seizes the naïve mind. The elders of the Elgonyi tribe in Kenya have described for me the activity of the god who comes by night, whom they call the "Maker of Fear." "He comes to you," they said, "like a cold gust of wind, and you shudder, or he goes whistling round about in the tall grass"—an African Pan who goes among the reeds in the haunted noon-hour, playing on his pipes and frightening the shepherds.

So it is that, in the dream, this breath of the pneuma has

again frightened a pastor, a shepherd of the flock, who in the time of night-darkness trod the reed-grown water's edge in the deep valley of the psyche. Yes, that erstwhile fiery spirit has come down to nature, to the trees and rocks and the waters of the psyche, like the old man in Nietzsche's *Zarathustra*, who, wearied of humankind, retired to the woods to growl with the bears in honour of the Creator.

We must surely go the way of the waters, which always go downward, if we would salvage the treasure, the precious legacy of the father. In the Gnostic hymn of the soul, the son is sent forth by his parents to seek the precious pearl. It lies at the bottom of a deep spring, guarded by a dragon, in the land of the Egyptians—that lustful and drunken world of physical and mental riches. The son and heir sets out to fetch the jewel, but forgets himself and his duty in the orgies of Egyptian worldliness, until a letter from the father reminds him what his duty is; he then goes forth to the water and dives into the dark depths of the spring, where he finds the pearl on the bottom, and finally offers it to the highest divinity.

This hymn, ascribed to Bardesanes, dates from a time that resembled ours in more than one respect. Mankind looked and waited, and a wise man said to them, "Seek it in the water wherein it sank of yore."

As I wrote these lines, I received a letter from Vancouver from a person unknown to me. The writer is astonished about his dreams, which continually treat of water: "Almost every time I dream it is about water: either I am having a bath, or the water closet is overflowing, or a pipe is bursting, or my home has drifted down to the water's edge, or the lavatory is overflowing, or I see an acquaintance about to sink into water, or I am trying to get out of water, or I am having a bath and the tub is about to overflow," and so on.

Water is the commonest symbol for the unconscious.

The lake in the valley is the unconscious, which in a certain sense lies beneath consciousness, so that it is often referred to as the subconscious, not infrequently with the unpleasant connotation of an inferior consciousness. The water is the valley-ghost, the water dragon of the Tao, whose nature resembles water—a yang embraced in the yin. Psychologically, therefore, water means spirit that has become unconscious. Thus the dream of the theologian is quite right in saying that at the water he will be able to reattain the consciousness of the living spirit.

This statement by the dream now meets with strong resistance from the side of consciousness, which knows of "spirit" only as something to be found on high. Spirit always comes from above. From below comes everything that is sordid and worthless. Spirit means highest freedom, a soaring over depths, a deliverance from the prison of the chthonian element.

But water is earthly and tangible; it is also the fluid of the body ruled by impulse, blood and the flowing of blood, the odour of the beast, and corporeality weighted with emotion. The unconscious is the psyche that reaches from the daylight of a mentally and morally lucid consciousness down into the nerve system that for ages has been known as sympathetic. This does not support perception and muscular activity like the cerebrospinal system, and thus command surrounding space; it has no sense organs, but it maintains the equilibrium of life and—in mysterious ways, by co-excitement—not only imparts knowledge of the innermost nature of other living beings, but also radiates inner activity upon them. In this sense it is an exceedingly collective system, the actual basis of all *participation mystique,* while the cerebro-spinal function culminates in separating out the specificity of the ego, and always, through the medium of space, grasps surfaces and superficialities alone. The latter experiences everything as external, while the former experiences everything as from within.

Now, the unconscious is commonly regarded as a kind of capsulated, personal intimacy—very nearly what the Bible designates as the heart and considers the source of all evil thoughts. In the chambers of the heart reside the wicked voices of the blood, quick anger and the weakness of the senses. But consciousness is chiefly an affair of the main lobes of the brain, that is to say, of the cerebrum, which sees everything separately and in isolation, and therefore sees the unconscious in this way, regarding it out and out as *my* unconscious. So people generally believe that whoever descends into the unconscious lands himself in the oppressive confinement of egocentric subjectivity, and exposes himself in this blind alley to the attack of all the ferocious beasts the cavern of the psychic underworld is supposed to harbour.

The man who looks into the mirror of the waters does, indeed, see his own face first of all. Whoever goes to himself risks a confrontation with himself. The mirror does not flatter, it faithfully shows whatever looks into it; namely, the face we never show to the world because we cover it with the *persona,* the mask of the actor. But the mirror lies behind the mask and shows the true face.

This confrontation is the first test of courage on the inner way, a test sufficient to frighten off most people, for the meeting with ourselves belongs to the more unpleasant things that may be avoided as long as we possess living symbol-figures in which all that is inner and unknown is projected. The figure of the devil, in particular, is a most valuable and acceptable psychic possession, for as long as he goes about outside in the form of a roaring lion, we know where evil lurks; namely, in that incarnate Old Harry where it has been in this or that form since primeval times. With the rise of consciousness since the Middle Ages, to be sure, he has been considerably reduced in stature. But to take his place there are human beings to whom we gratefully resign our shadows. With what pleasure, for instance, we read newspaper reports of crime! A true criminal becomes a popular figure because he unburdens in no small degree the consciences of his fellow men, for now they know once more where evil is to be found.

The meeting with oneself is the meeting with one's own shadow. To mix a metaphor, the shadow is a tight pass, a narrow door, whose painful constriction is spared to no one who climbs down into the deep wellspring. *But one must learn to know oneself in order to know who one is.* For what comes after the door is, surprisingly enough, a boundless expanse full of unprecedented uncertainty, with apparently no inside and no outside, no above and no below, no here and no there, no mine and no thine, no good and no bad. It is the world of water, where everything living floats in suspension; where the kingdom of the sympathetic system, of the soul of everything living, begins; where *I* am inseparably this and that, and this and that are I; where I experience the other person in myself, and the other, as myself, experiences me.

No, the unconscious is anything but a capsulated, personal system; it is the wide world, and objectivity as open as the world. *I* am the object, even the subject of the object, in a complete reversal of my ordinary consciousness, where I am always a subject that has an object. There I find myself in the closest entanglement with the world, so much a part of it that I forget all too easily who I really am. "Lost in oneself" is a good phrase to describe this state. But this self is the world, if only a consciousness could see it. This is why we must know who we are.

The unconscious no sooner touches us than we are it, in that we become unconscious of ourselves. This is the primal danger, instinctively known and an object of fear to primitive man, who himself stands upon the very brink of this pleroma. For his consciousness is still uncertain, and stands on tottering feet. It is still childish—has just emerged from the primal waters. A wave of the unconscious may easily roll over it, and he forgets who he was and does things in which he no longer recognizes himself. Primitives are wary of uncontrolled emotions, because consciousness all too easily succumbs to them and gives place to the state of possession.

So man's striving, in his primitive past, was turned to the fortification of consciousness. His rituals and dogmatic conceptions served this purpose; they were dams and walls erected against the dangers of the unconscious, the "perils of the soul." Primitive culture consists, in the first place, in the laying of ghosts, the lifting of spells, the turning away of the evil omen, propitiation, and so forth.

It is these walls, erected in primeval times, that later became the foundations of the church. It is also these walls that collapse when the symbols become weak with age. Then the waters rise, and inundating catastrophes burst upon mankind. The religious leader of the Taos pueblo said to me once, "The Americans should stop troubling our religion, for when this goes to ruin and we can no longer help the sun to cross the heavens, then the Americans and the whole world will learn something within ten years; for then the sun will not rise any longer." That is to say, night falls, the light of consciousness is extinguished, and the dark sea of unconsciousness bursts in.

Whether primitive or not, mankind always stands upon the verge of those actions *that it performs itself but does not control*. The whole world wants peace, and the whole world prepares for war, to give but one example. Mankind is powerless against mankind, and gods, as they have ever done, show it the ways of fate. Today we call the gods "factors," which comes from *facere*, "to make." The makers stand behind the wings of the world-theatre. It is in great things as in small. In the realm of consciousness we are our own masters; we seem to be the factors themselves. But if we step through the door of the shadow we discover with fright that we are the objects of factors.

This state of the problem is new, since all ages before ours believed in gods in some form or other. Only an unparalleled impoverishment in symbolism could enable us to rediscover the gods as psychic factors, which is to say, as archetypes of the unconscious. No doubt, this discovery is hardly credible as yet. To be convinced, we need to have the experience which was sketched in the dream of the theologian; only then is the self-activity of the spirit experienced across the waters. Since the stars have fallen from heaven, and our highest symbols have paled, a secret life holds sway in the unconscious. It is for this reason that we have a psychology today, and for this reason that we speak of the unconscious.

All this discussion would be superfluous in an age or culture that possessed symbols. For these are spirit from above; and at such a time, also, spirit is above. It would be a foolish and senseless undertaking for such people to wish to experience or investigate an unconscious that contains nothing but the silent, undisturbed sway of nature. But our unconscious conceals natural spirit, which is to say, spirit turned to water; and this spirit disturbs it. Heaven has become empty space to us, a fair memory of things that once were. But our heart glows, and secret unrest gnaws at the roots of our being. In the words of the *Völuspá* we may ask:

> "What does Wotan still mumble over Mimir's head?"
> "*Already the spring boils—*"

Dealing with the unconscious has become a question of life for us. It is a matter of spiritual being or non-being. All those who have met with the experience suggested in the dream just referred to know that the treasure lies in the depths of the water and will try to salvage it. As they must never forget who they are, so they must never imperil their consciousness. They will keep their standpoint upon solid ground and will thus—to preserve the metaphor—become fishers who catch with hook and net what floats in the water. There may be consummate fools who do not understand what fishermen do, but these will not lose sight of the age-old meaning of their action, for the symbol of their craft is many centuries older than the fisher's ring of the Pope, and their myth is still living in the unfaded story of the Holy Grail. But not every man is a fisher. Sometimes this figure is not fully developed; it is arrested at an early, instinctual stage, and then we have the fantasy image of a fish-otter or the like.

Whoever looks into the water sees his own image, to be sure, but behind it living beings soon loom up, fishes, no doubt, harmless dwellers of the deep—harmless, if only the lake were not haunted. They are water-beings of a peculiar sort. Sometimes a nixie gets into the fisher's net, a female, half-human fish. Nixies are entrancing beings:

> Half drew she him
> Half sank he down
> And nevermore was seen.

The nixie is an early stage, still on the level of instinct, of a magical feminine being that I call the anima, the woman in a man of which I have spoken in the first chapter. Yet, since the collective unconscious is *more* than personal, so the anima is not always merely the feminine aspect of the individual man. It has an archetypal aspect—"the eternal feminine"—which embodies an experience of woman far older than that of the individual. This anima is reflected, of course, in mythology and legend. It can be siren or wood nymph, Grace or Erlking's daughter, lamia, or succubus, who infatuate young men and suck the life out of them.

The critic of morals will say that these figures are states of ardent longing and worthless fantasies in projected form. We cannot help granting a certain validity to this assertion. But is it the whole truth? Is the nixie nature really nothing but a product of moral laxity? Were there not such beings long ago, in an age when dawning human consciousness was still wholly bound to nature? Surely there were ghosts in forest and field and stream long before there existed any question of conscience. What is more, these beings were as much dreaded, so that their rather peculiar sexual charms are only relatively characteristic. Consciousness was then far simpler, and the ownership of the soul was ridiculously small. An unlimited amount of what we now consider an integral part of our own psychic being disports itself merrily for the primitive in projections reaching far and wide.

The word "projection" is actually unsuitable, for nothing has been cast out of the psyche; rather, the psyche has attained its present complexity by a series of acts of introjection. Its complexity has increased in proportion as nature has ceased to be animated by spirits. A weird nixie from long ago is today called "an erotic fantasy," and it may complicate our psychic life in a painful way. It comes upon us, to be sure, just as a nixie might; what is more, it is like a feminine incubus, it changes into many shapes like a witch, and in general shows an unbearable independence that does not seem proper to a psychic content. On occasion it causes fascinations that rival the best bewitchment, or states of fear that are not outdone by any manifestation of the devil. It is a vexatious being that crosses our path in many transformations and disguises, plays all kinds of tricks upon us, and causes happy and unhappy delusions, depressions and ecstasies, uncontrolled emotions, and so forth. Even in the state of reasonable introjection the nixie has not laid aside her roguery. The witch has not ceased to mix her vile potions

of love and death, but her magic power has been refined into
intrigue and self-deception, unseen, to be sure, yet none the
less dangerous.

But how do we dare to call this feminine elf the anima?
Anima means soul, and should designate something very
wonderful and immortal. But this was not always so. We
must not forget that this lofty kind of soul is a dogmatic
conception whose purpose is to bind by a spell and to capture
something uncannily active and alive. The German word
"Seele," soul, is closely connected, through the Gothic form
"saiwolo," with the Greek word αἰόλος, which means "moving," "iridescent," something like a butterfly—ψυχή in Greek
—which reels drunkenly from flower to flower and lives on
honey and love. In the Gnostic study of types, the ἄνθρωπος
ψυχικός stands below the πνευματικός, and finally there are
also bad souls who must roast to all eternity in Hell. Even
the quite innocent soul of the unbaptized, newborn babe is
deprived of the contemplation of God, and thus has none of
the substance akin to God. For the primitive, the soul is the
magic breath of life, therefore anima or demonic flame. An
uncanonical saying of the Master's aptly declares, "Who is
near unto me is near unto the fire." In Heraclitus, the soul
at the highest level is fiery and dry; in itself, ψυχή has the
closest kinship with "cool breath"—ψυχός and ψυχρός mean
cool and damp—and thus has affinity to water.

Being that has soul is living being. Soul is the *living*
in man, that which lives of itself and causes life: God
breathed into Adam a living breath so that he should live.
With cunning and playful deception the soul lures into life
the inertia of matter that does not want to live. It creates
belief in incredible things, in order that life should live. It
is full of snares and traps in order that man should fall,
should reach the earth, entangle himself there, and stay
caught, in order that life should live. Were it not for the
motion and the colour-play of the soul, man would suffocate

and rot away in his greatest passion, idleness. A certain kind of reasonableness is its advocate, and a certain kind of morality adds its blessing. To have soul is the wager of life, for the soul is a life-bestowing demon who plays his elfin game beneath and above human existence, for which reason—in the realm of dogma—he is threatened and propitiated with superhuman punishments and blessings that go far beyond the possible deserts of human beings. Heaven and Hell are the fate of the soul and not of civil man, who, in his God-created nakedness and imbecility, would have no idea of what to do with himself in a heavenly Jerusalem.

The anima is not the soul in the dogmatic sense; this is an apotropaic *représentation collective,* but the anima is a natural archetype that satisfactorily subsumes every pronouncement of the unconscious and of the primitive mind that gave form to language and religion. The anima is a "factor" in the proper sense of the word. Man cannot make it; on the contrary, it is always the *a priori* element in moods, reactions, impulses and whatever else is spontaneous in psychic life. It is something that lives on its own account, that makes us live; it is a life behind consciousness that cannot be completely integrated with it, but from which, on the contrary, consciousness arises. For, in the last analysis, psychic life is for the greater part an unconscious life that embraces consciousness on all sides: a thought that is sufficiently obvious when once we have taken into account how much unconscious preparation is needed, for instance, to recognize a sense impression.

Although it seems as if the whole of unconscious, psychic life could be ascribed to the anima, it is yet only one archetype among many. Therefore, it is not characteristic, out and out, for the life of the unconscious. It is only one of its aspects. This is already shown by the very fact that it has feminine gender. This fact in itself would be astonishing, if the feminine were not the most immediate opposite to the masculine. What is not-I or not-masculine is, therefore, most probably feminine; and it is also for this reason that the anima-image is always projected upon women. Either sex is inhabited by the opposite sex to a certain degree, for, biologically speaking, it is only the greater number of masculine genes that tips the scale in favour of the masculine sex. The smaller number of feminine genes forms a feminine character that usually remains unconscious because of its inferiority, yet always begins to function overtly when the specific masculinity has been damaged, as, for instance, by castration or through the exhaustion of old age.

With the archetype of the anima we enter the realm of the gods or of metaphysics, for everything in which the anima appears takes on the quality of the *numen*—that is, becomes unconditional, dangerous, taboo, magical. The anima is the serpent in the paradise of the harmless man with good resolutions and still better intentions. It affords the most convincing foundation for the prejudice against dealing with the unconscious, according to which moral inhibitions will be destroyed and forces let loose that had better been left in the unconscious. For life in itself is not something good; it is more than that, it is also evil. In that the anima wishes life it wishes good *and* bad. In the domain of elfin being, these categories do not exist. Not only the bodily life, but psychic life as well, has the impudence to get along without current morality—often much better so—and even to become healthier and more beautiful without it.

The anima believes in the καλόν κ'ἀγαθόν, the beautiful and the good, this being a primitive conception antedating the discovery of the opposition between æsthetics and morals. It took more than a thousand years of Christian differentiation to make it clear that the good is not beautiful, and the beautiful not necessarily good. The paradoxicalness of this marriage of concepts was no more obvious to the ancients than it was to the primitives.

But the anima is conservative, and clings in a most exasperating fashion to the ways of earlier mankind. Therefore, it likes to appear in historic dress, with a predilection for Greece and Egypt. On this subject we should compare the classic anima-stories of Rider Haggard and Pierre Benoit. That dream of the Renaissance, the *Ipnerotomachia* of Polifilo, like Goethe's *Faust*, reached far back into the classical world to find the precise word for the situation. The former found Queen Venus suitable; the latter, Trojan Helen. We will not increase the number of irreproachable crown witnesses, for these offer us matter and unintentional, authentic symbolism enough to enrich our meditation. If you wish to know what it is like when the anima appears in the modern society of America today, I can warmly recommend to you Erskine's *Helen of Troy*. She is not shallow, for the breath of eternity lies over all that is living.

Anima is life beyond all categories and can, therefore, dispense with blame as well as praise. The Queen of Heaven or the simple little girl who was tumbled into life—have we ever deeply considered how meagre was the lot that the legend of Mary translated to the divine stars?

Life without sense and measure, that is not satisfied with its own fullness, is an object of fear and aversion to civil man—and one cannot disagree with him, for it is also the mother of all nonsense and of all tragedy. This is why, since the beginning of time, earth-born man, with his healing animal instinct, is engaged in combat with his soul and its demonism.

If the coming to terms with the shadow is the companion-piece to the individual's development, then that with the anima is the masterpiece. For the relation with the anima is again a test of courage and—more than that—a test by fire of all a man's spiritual and moral forces. We must never forget, in the case of the anima, that it is a question of psychic facts which have never before been in man's psychological possession; that hitherto were always to be found outside his consciousness in every possible form of projection. For the child, the anima lurks in the supremacy of the mother, which sometimes leaves a sentimental attachment through the whole of life and seriously impairs the masculine development. To the primitive and to the man of the classic age, the anima appears as a goddess or demonic woman; while for mediæval man, mother church has a place beside the Queen of Heaven and the witch.

The desymbolized world of the Protestant has produced first an unhealthy sentimentality and then a sharpening of the moral conflict logically leading, because of its unbearableness, to Nietzsche's "beyond good and evil." In the centres of civilization, this condition shows itself also in the increasing insecurity of marriage. For instance, in Zurich, we have come to the American form of divorce court, the cases in which prove that the anima seeks to be projected upon the opposite sex, whereby magically complicated relations arise.

Largely because of its pathological results, this situation has led to the recent growth of the psychology of complexes, which, in its Freudian form, professes the opinion that sexuality is the basis of all disturbances—a view that only accentuates the already existing conflict. *Le peuple porte le sceau d'un hiver, qu'on n'explique pas,* "The people bears the stamp of a winter which one cannot explain," as the French translation of a Korean stele inscription says.

In dealing with the shadow or the anima it is not sufficient to know about these concepts and to think them out. Nor can we ever experience the content of these concepts by a feeling or sense-impression of them. Therefore, it does not help in any way to learn a list of the archetypes by heart.

Archetypes are complexes of experience that come upon us fatefully, and their effects begin in our most personal life. The anima no longer confronts us as a sublime goddess, but rather, under certain conditions, as our most personal and bitter misunderstanding. When, for instance, a highly honoured scholar in his seventies deserts his family and marries a twenty-year-old, red-haired actress, then we know that the gods have claimed another victim. It is thus that demonic supremacy shows itself to us. (In the Middle Ages it would still have been an easy matter to do away with the young woman as a witch.)

The picture of the anima that I have drawn in the foregoing paragraphs is not complete. It is chaotic life-urge, to be sure, but something strangely meaningful also clings to it—something like secret knowledge or hidden wisdom, in most curious contrast to its irrational, elfin nature. Here I should like to refer you again to the authors already cited. Rider Haggard calls She "wisdom's daughter." Benoit's queen of Atlantis has an excellent library that even contains a lost book of Plato. Trojan Helen, in her reincarnation, is liberated by the wise Simon Magus from a brothel in Tyre, and accompanies him on his journeys.

I purposely refrained from mentioning at the start this thoroughly characteristic aspect of the anima, because our first meeting with it usually leads us to infer anything except wisdom. This aspect appears only to him who seriously comes to terms with the anima. It is only when this hard task has been faced that he comes more and more to recognize that, behind all the anima's cruel sporting with human fate, there lies something like a secret intention which seems to spring from a superior knowledge of the laws of life. Just the most unexpected, just the alarmingly chaotic, in such psychic experience, reveals the deepest meaning. And the more this meaning is recognized the more does the anima lose its impetuous, impulsive, and compulsive character. Dams against the flood of chaos slowly arise, for the meaningful divides itself from the meaningless. When sense and nonsense are no longer identical, the force of chaos is weakened by the subtraction of sense and non-sense; sense is endowed with the force of meaning, and non-sense with the force of meaninglessness. Thereby a new cosmos arises.

In elfin nature wisdom and buffoonery appear as one and the same; and they *are* one and the same, as long as they are in the anima. Life *is* both nonsensical and signifi-cant. And when we do not laugh about one aspect, and speculate about the other, life is exceedingly banal, and everything is of the smallest proportions; there is then only a tiny sense and a tiny nonsense. In the very first place, nothing signifies anything; for when as yet there were no thinking beings, no one was there to interpret manifesta-tions. It is only for him who does not understand that things must be interpreted. Only the ununderstandable has sig-nificance.

Man has awakened in a world that he does not un-derstand, and this is why he tries to interpret it.

Actually, the anima—and so life itself—is without sig-nificance, yet it has a significant nature, for there is a cosmos in all chaos, secret order in all disorder, unfailing law in all contingency. It takes man's discriminating understanding, which dissolves everything into antinomies of judgement, to recognize this. If a man comes to terms with the anima, its chaos and caprice give him occasion to suspect a secret order, to sense a plan, meaning, and purpose extending beyond its existence—we might almost be tempted into say-ing "to postulate" this, yet that would not correspond to the truth. For we do not actually have at our disposal any power of cool reflection, nor does any science or philosophy help us, and still less the traditional teachings of religion.

We are entangled and confused in aimless experience, and
the power of judgement with all its categories has im-
potently gone to the devil. Human interpretation fails, for
a turbulent life-situation has arisen that cannot be fitted
into any traditional explanations. It is a moment of collapse.
We sink into a final depth, to a spiritual death—as Apuleius
rightly says: *ad instar voluntariæ mortis*. It is a surrender of
our own powers, not arbitrarily willed, but naturally forced
upon us; it is no freely chosen subjection and humiliation
bedecked in moralisms, but a complete and unmistakable
defeat crowned with the panic fear of demoralization.

Only when all supports and crutches are broken, and no
covering from the rear gives any further promise of con-
cealing us in the least, does it become possible to experience
an archetype that up till then had lain concealed in the
anima's significant senselessness. It is the *archetype of meaning,* as the anima is the archetype of life itself.

We always suppose, of course, that meaning is the
younger of the two occurrences, because we assume, with
some justification, that we bestow it of ourselves, and because we also rightly believe that the great world can exist
without being explained. But how do we give meaning?
From what source, in the last analysis, do we derive meaning? The forms of our interpretation are historical categories that reach back into the mists of time—a fact we do
not sufficiently take into account. Interpretations make use
of certain linguistic matrices that are themselves derived
from primordial images. From whatever side we approach
the question, everywhere we are confronted by the history
of language and motivation, and this leads straight back into
the enchanted, primitive world.

Let us take, for example, the word "idea." It goes back
to the εἶδος-concept of Plato, and ideas are primordial
images preserved ἐν οὐρανίῳ τόπῳ, being therefore transcendental, eternal forms perceived by the winged eye of

the seer, the *imagines et lares* of the primitive ghost-seer, images of dream and the revealing vision. Or let us take the concept of energy, which explains physical happening. At an earlier time it was the "phlogiston," the heat-force inherent in matter, like the "primordial warmth" of the Stoics, or the Heraclitean πῦρ ἀειζῶον, which already borders on the primitive notion of an all-prevalent living force, a power of growth and magic healing generally called mana.

I will not go on needlessly giving examples. It is sufficient to know that there is not a single important idea or view that does not possess historical antecedents. They are all founded upon archetypal, primordial forms, whose sensuous nature dates from a time when consciousness did not yet think, but merely perceived. Thought was an object of inner perception, not intellection only, but sensed as a manifestation—seen or heard, so to speak. Thought was essentially revelation, not something invented, but something forced upon us or bringing conviction through its immediate actuality. Thoughts antedate the primitive ego-consciousness, and the latter is the object of thought, rather than its subject, according to the Pauline phrase, *sicut et cognitus sum,* or to the Cartesian *cogito ergo sum.*

But we ourselves have not climbed the last peak of consciousness, and so we also have a pre-existent thinking, of which, to be sure, we are not aware as long as we are supported by traditional symbols—or, expressing ourselves in the language of dreams, as long as the father or the king has not yet died; or again, to speak with Nietzsche, as long as God is not yet dead.

I should like to show by an example how the unconscious opens the way to meaning by revelation. It is the case of a young theological student whom I do not know personally. He was in great straits because of his religious convictions, and during this time dreamed the following dream, which appears again later in this book:

He stood before a handsome old man dressed entirely in *black*. He knew it was the *white* magician. This person had just addressed him at considerable length, and the dreamer could no longer remember what it was about. He had only retained the closing words: "And for this we need the help of the *black* magician." At this moment the door opened, and through it stepped an old man resembling the first, except that he was dressed in *white*. He addressed the white magician, "I need your advice," but cast a questioning side glance upon the dreamer, whereupon the black-robed yet white magician said, "You can speak freely, he is an innocent one."

Then the black magician began to tell his history. He came from a distant land where something extraordinary had happened. For the land was ruled by an old king who felt his death near. He—the king—had sought out a tomb for himself. There were in that land a great number of sepulchres from ancient times, and the king had chosen the finest for himself. According to the legend a virgin had been buried in it. The king caused the tomb to be opened to prepare it for his purpose. Now, as the bones that were in it were exposed to the air, they suddenly took on life and changed into a black horse, which at once fled into the desert and there vanished. He—the black magician—had heard of this story, and at once set forth to pursue the horse. In a journey of many days, always upon the tracks of the horse, he had come to the desert and crossed it to the other side where the grasslands began again. There he had met with the horse grazing, and there also he had come upon the find that made him require the advice of the white magician: for he had found the keys of paradise, and now was at a loss to know what was to be done with them. . . .

At this exciting moment the dreamer unfortunately awoke. . . .

In the light of the earlier remarks in this chapter, you will have little trouble in guessing the meaning of this dream: The old king is the ruling symbol that is about to go to its eternal rest, and in the very place where ancient powers of life already lie buried. His choice falls, rightly enough, upon the grave of the anima, who lies in the death trance of a Sleeping Beauty as long as the king is alive— that is, as long as a valid principle (Prince or *principe*) regulates and expresses life. But when the king draws to his end, she comes to life again and changes into the black horse, which even in the Platonic parable expresses the unruliness of the emotions. Who follows him, comes to the desert, to a wild land remote from men—an image of spiritual and moral isolation. But there lie the keys of paradise.

Now, what is paradise? Clearly, the Garden of Eden with its twofold tree of life and of knowledge, and its four rivers. In the Christian version it is also the heavenly city of the Apocalypse, which, like the Garden of Eden, is conceived as a mandala. But the mandala is a symbol of individuation. It is the black magician who finds the keys to the solution of the difficulties of belief weighing upon the dreamer—the keys that open the way of individuation. So the opposition of desert-paradise means also the other opposition of isolation-individuation, or self-becoming.

This part of the dream is also a noteworthy paraphrase of the Λόγιον Ιησοῦ, edited by Hunt and Grenfell, in which the way to the Kingdom of Heaven is pointed out by the animals, and where we find the admonition: "The Kingdom of Heaven is within you, and whoever shall know himself shall find it." Furthermore, it is also a free rendering of the serpent of paradise who persuaded the first parents to sin and who finally leads to the redemption of mankind through the Son of God. As we know, this causal nexus gave rise to the Ophitic identification of the serpent with the Soter. The black horse and the black magician—and this is a modern achievement of the mind—are evil elements whose relativity in respect to the good is hinted at in the exchange of garments.

The two magicians are, indeed, two aspects of the archetypal *old man* who, beyond good and evil, is the superior master and teacher, a pointer of the ways, the pre-existent meaning concealed in chaotic life, the father of the soul, which, nevertheless, in a miraculous way, is also his virgin-mother.

What an unbearably hard lesson for a young student of theology! Fortunately he was not in the least aware that the father of all prophets spoke to him in dream and brought within his grasp the secret of all mysteries. We may wonder at the inexpediency of such occurrences. Why this prodigality? But I must add that we do not know how this dream affected the student, and I must then emphasize the fact that, to me at least, this dream had an infinite amount to say. It was not allowed to be lost, and just for the reason that the ways of life are very wonderful.

The master in this dream teaches a new reconciliation, namely, that of good and evil, as an answer to the sharpening of the moral conflict in Protestantism. Herewith we approach the ideas of the East, the *nirvandva* of the Upanishads, the escape from the opposites, and these ideas are in a manner brought within our reach. We can see how dangerously meaningful is the relativity of good and evil contained in the opposition, by this aphoristic question from Indian wisdom: "Who takes longer to reach perfection, he who loves God or he who hates God?" And the answer goes: "He who loves God takes seven reincarnations to reach perfection, and he who hates God takes only three, for he who hates God will think of him more than he who loves him."

The escape from the opposites presumes their equivalence, and this contradicts our Christian truth. None the less, the relativity and co-operation of the moral opposites contrived by the unconscious, and illustrated in our dream, is a natural truth that has just as naturally been recognized by the East. Moreover, there are some passages in the New Testament that come suspiciously close to this standpoint; I need only remind you of the parable of the unfaithful steward, not to mention certain uncanonical words of the Master.

Our dream is not by any chance unique in this respect; rather, the tendency to make the opposites relative to each other is an outspoken peculiarity of the unconscious. But it must be added at once that this is true only in the case of a sharpened moral sensitivity; in other cases the unconscious can point just as inexorably to the incurable disunion of the opposites. In this regard the unconscious has no absolute standpoint, but one that is relative to the conscious attitude. So we may, no doubt, assert that only a Protestant theologian needed such a dream. This amounts to an essential restriction of the dream's statement. But even with this limitation of its validity, the dream is significant enough to display the superiority of the unconscious standpoint. And so we find this standpoint personified and presented as the opinion and voice of a wise magician, who in age, experience, knowledge, and ability is by far superior to the dreamer's consciousness.

The magician is the archetype of the old wise man, and the latter is a direct descendant of the medicine man with his function in primitive society. Like the anima, he is an immortal demon, and he penetrates the chaotic darkness of mere life with the light of meaning. He is the enlightener, the teacher and master, a ψυχοπομπός, whose personification even Nietzsche, that breaker of tablets, could not forgo; for he called up his reincarnated form in Zarathustra, the lofty spirit of an almost Homeric age, as the carrier and announcer of his own Dionysian inspiration and rapture. God was dead for him, indeed, but the demon of wisdom had become his bodily double, so to speak. He himself says:

> Then one was changed to two
> And Zarathustra passed me by.

Zarathustra is more for Nietzsche than a poetic figure; he is an involuntary confession. Nietzsche also had lost himself in the darkness of a life that turned its back upon God and Christianity, and that is why the revealer and enlightener came to him as the speaking fountainhead of his soul. Here is the source of the hieratic language of *Zarathustra,* for that is the style of this archetype. It has the effect of solemnity and sublimity. Its manner is the *species æternitatis.*

Even modern man, in experiencing this archetype, comes to know the primordial form of thinking as an autonomous activity whose object he is. It is a so-called occult or religious experience, thanks to which the Logos, for instance, attained divinity. Hermes Trismegistus, or the Thoth of Hermetic literature, the mystic Orpheus, Poimandres and his relation, the Poimen of *The Shepherd of Hermas,* are other formulations of the same experience. If the name "Lucifer" were not prejudicial, it would without doubt be suitable for this archetype. But I have been content to call it the *archetype of the old wise man* or *of meaning.*

The three archetypes so far mentioned—the shadow, the anima, and the old wise man—are of the kind immediately experienced in personified form. In the preceding pages, I have tried to present the general psychological conditions from which this experience arises. But what I conveyed were only abstract rationalizations. Actually, we could —or better, we should—give a description of the process as it appears in immediate experience. For, in the course of the process, these archetypes come upon the scene as active personalities.

The process itself involves another class of archetypes, which we may roughly call the *archetypes of transformation*. These are not personalities, but rather typical situations, places, ways, animals, plants, and so forth that symbolize the kind of change, whatever it is. Like the personalities, these archetypes are genuine and true symbols that cannot be taken as σημεῖα or as allegories, and exhaustively interpreted. They are, rather, genuine symbols just in so far as they are ambiguous, full of intimations, and, in the last analysis, inexhaustible. The basic principles, the ἀρχαί of the unconscious, are indescribably vague because of their wealth of reference, their "pleromatic" character—and this despite their being unmistakably specific. Our intellectual judgement, of course, keeps trying to establish their singleness of meaning, and so misses the essential point; for what we should above all establish, as alone corresponding to their nature, is their manifold meaning, their almost unbounded fullness of reference.

If one wishes to form a picture of the symbolic process, the series of alchemistic images discussed in Chapter V are good examples; yet we must note that these symbols, though of obscure origin, are for the most part traditional. An excellent Eastern example is the Tantric system of the chakras, or the mystical nerve system of Chinese yoga. It also seems as if the image series of the tarot cards were descendants of the archetypes of transformation; a very enlightening lecture of Professor Bernoulli's has confirmed this view.

The symbolic process is an *experience in the image and of the image*. The continuation of the process usually shows an enantiodromal arrangement like that in the text of the *I-ging*, and so presents a rhythm of destruction and con-

struction, of error and truth, of loss and gain, of depth and
height. As a rule, the stations of the way also have the characteristics of the ἄθλον, of the heavy labour. For instance, the
ἄθλα of Heracles could very well correspond to a symbolic
process. The beginning of the process is almost always indicated by a blind alley or other unbearable situation. Putting it generally, the goal is illumination, whereby the initial
situation is surmounted and a higher level is reached.

As regards the element of time, the process may be com-
pressed into a single dream or into a short moment of experience, or be extended over months or years, according
to the initial situation, the person involved in the process,
and the goal to be reached. Of course, the wealth in symbols also fluctuates strongly. Almost all the symbols are capable of a positive as well as a negative meaning, and we
meet as often with the one as the other, for the way through
transformation is ambushed by all possible dangers. Though
everything is experienced in image form, symbolically, it is
by no means a question of playhouse dangers, but of very
real risks upon which the fate of a whole life may depend.
The chief danger is that of succumbing to the uncannily
fascinating influence of living archetypes. If we do, we may
come to a standstill either in a symbolic situation or in an
identification with an archetypal personality.

The symbolic process is possible only when one allows
the ego-consciousness to enter the image, whatever it is;
that is, when no obstruction is offered to the happening in
the unconscious. But this is tantamount to a temporary re-
nunciation of the state of being the subject. One might,
therefore, call the necessary condition for the process a *psychosis brought about by free choice*. For a psychosis is a
largely involuntary yielding before an irruption from the
unconscious that has attained a higher potential than consciousness, and so overflows the inhibiting barrier—called
the threshold of consciousness—that is otherwise always

maintained intact. This analogy is again no empty metaphor, but represents a constant danger in the process—threatening, indeed, yet fortunately remaining for the most part at some distance.

Now, by becoming to such an extent an object of unconscious happening, consciousness is drawn into the realm of images and is brought, or sometimes even compelled, to live them by performing them. In this way conscious and unconscious are interfused, and a decided change of consciousness is brought about. That is why I call this a process of transformation. At the same time, the abyss opened up by the aberration of consciousness is filled in, so that the natural order is re-established.

But because consciousness, at least temporarily, becomes the object of the unconscious, there arises the possibility that it will also be drawn completely into the archetype; and this may occur quite at the beginning, when, as a rule, the meeting with the shadow takes place. If the shadow succeeds in assimilating the ego, a reversal of the whole personality comes about. Outwardly, this becomes perceptible through a change for the worse in character. When this is the case, there also unfailingly arises a kind of possession through the anima, and spirit—the archetype of meaning —becomes a destructive wrongdoer.

The fact is that the single archetypes are not isolated from each other in the unconscious, but are in a state of contamination, of the most complete, mutual interpenetration and interfusion. Under so-called normal conditions, the shadow is largely identical with the anima, and so on. When, therefore, the ego is assimilated to the shadow, a certain state of possession through the unconscious automatically occurs. As the shadow, according to its definition, is the historically older human being, the ego becomes more infantile and primitive as a result of the assimilation; the man becomes boyish, the woman becomes a flapper, and both give

themselves airs that belong to the past. The puerile man
bedecks himself with the wreaths of bygone days; he identifies himself, like the Negroes of Central Australia in their
religious ceremonies, with the heroes of eld, thus compen-
sating his powerlessness in the present. He lives in the past
and its ideals. In this way he does something right in the
wrong place, as is always the case in important errors. For
the shadow is a formidable thing. The harder and more
disappointing are the conditions of life, and the more de-
spondent consciousness becomes, so much the more grows
the shadow, till the darkness at last is overpowering.

When, in France at the beginning of the eleventh century, famines and plagues swept across the land, the dis-
illusioned people, feeling themselves God-forsaken, invented
the cult of Satan and the Black Mass with its heathenish
practices. In this the attempt to escape to the metaphysical
and spiritual was right, but the regression to the past and
to the dark, opposite principle was wrong. The palæolithic
Australians do things in a better style: as a result of hard
conditions of life they are often in need, and so might easily
be turned to the negative side. In order to counteract this
danger, they identify themselves, *within the bounds of ritual,* with their ancestors of the so-called alcheringa period,
these being direct descendants of the totem animal, as the
Homeric heroes were of the gods. In this way they grant
life to the shadow, and yet prevent it from taking the upper
hand in their daily life. And they do well, for the animals
they hunt would not be in the least impressed if they came
strutting in the guise of Homeric heroes. Thus they know
how to protect themselves in the right way from the megalomania that comes from distress.

Many primitives have a fine feeling for this, so that
they sometimes forbid the women, under pain of death, to
look on at the men's ceremonies, as if they suspected they
would laugh at the puerile goings-on. When the danger of

the shadow must be exorcised, rather let the darkness of mystery cover the ceremony that brings salvation, that its secrets may not seem a childish farce in the daylight of reality. Taking it in its deepest sense, the shadow is the invisible saurian tail that man still drags behind him. Carefully amputated, it becomes the serpent of healing of the mystery. Only monkeys parade with it.

When one has succeeded in some such way in preserving one's humanity, in spite of the danger of the shadow, then the discovery of the soul becomes possible, and with it the new danger of identification with the soul. I will not now take up this possibility in detail. Let the example of the shadow suffice, for I have used it to show what happens, in small things as in great, when an achetype assimilates consciousness.

The symbols of transformation portray the process, as well as its dangers, in typical images. The traditional images of the way of initiation are extraordinarily multifarious, at least to a superficial view; on the other hand, the individual course of initiation shows images that are comparable in spite of individual variations. To the beginning of the process belong chiefly animal symbols, such as the serpent, bird, horse, wolf, bull, lion, and so forth. The serpent is a chapter in itself, for it has outspoken kinship in myth with the dragon, the black amphibian or reptile (in the diminutive, also the houseless wood snail and worm), the crocodile, the crab (in the diminutive, insects of every kind). The frog, on the other hand, stands upon a higher level and counts, because of its anatomy, as an anticipation of man on the level of cold-blooded animality. Here belong likewise the cellar and cave, watery depths and the sea, as also fire, weapons, and instruments. The birds and mammals are various forms of the sanguine instincts, whereas the serpent, the saurians, and monsters personify primordial, cold-blooded animal nature, and, as adversaries of warm-blooded, emotional nature with its panic excitement, are anticipations of everything divinely pre-eminent. Cave and sea refer to the unconscious state with its darkness and secrecy. Insects, as a rule, are allusions to the states of the sympathetic nerve system, which is always excited by contents that cannot be consciously realized. Fire is emotional excitement or sudden bursts of impulse, and if a pot is set upon the fire, then one knows that transformation is under way. So the kitchen, also, is a place of creative change. Quite at the beginning, sometimes, stands the cosmic catastrophe. Weapons and instruments represent the will.

To the intermediate symbols belong the frog, the hermaphrodite, the crossing, the dangerous passage, the transitus, this last being the bearing of an animal, corpse, tree, or cross; also hanging, soaring, or swimming. Here, too, the tree has its place, or transformation into a tree, and represents rootedness, repose, growth, and a spreading forth in the upper regions of air and light, as also the union of sky and earth.

The hero and the *puer æternus* may appear as themes throughout the whole process.

To the end of the process belong all the symbols of the self in its various aspects. While the Christian cross is a symbol of the beginning, the *cross with equal arms* appears later (as it did in early Christianity), then geometric symbols, the circle, the square, the fourfold opposed to the threefold in all possible forms, the flower, especially the rose, the wheel, star, egg, sun, likewise the child (as higher form of the *puer æternus*). Negative forms appear as the spider, the net, and the prison.

I am only too well aware of the inadequacy of this rapid survey of the symbols of the inner drama. Each of the above-mentioned symbols should really be presented in a thoroughly documented way. The reader must be content with the somewhat more thorough account of the shadow, the anima, and the wise old man. As for the process of transformation, the development of the three archetypes just mentioned may give an approximate conception of it—a conception, if the truth be told, that in no way approaches the richness of actuality.

Nor could I present the opening scene in the form that is characteristic of a woman's psyche. This differs from man's. But traditional symbolism is chiefly a product of the masculine psyche and is, therefore, not a suitable object of imitation for woman. *Exempla sunt otiosa!*

Altogether, I regard it as a dubious venture to bring too many of these dark things into the light; yet sometimes a wanderer in the black night is thankful for the fitful, yellow glare of a lonely lantern, or for the pale streak of earliest dawn.

FOOTNOTE TO CHAPTER THREE

1. "Mandala," a Sanskrit word, means circle or magic circle. Its symbolism embraces all concentrically arranged figures, all circular or square circumferences having a centre, and all radial or spherical arrangements.

CHAPTER FOUR

Dream Symbols

of the Process of Individuation

Facilis descensus Averni;
Noctes atque dies patet atri janua Ditis.
Sed revocare gradum superasque evadere ad auras,
Hoc opus, hic labor est.

(Æneid, lib. VI.)

The Material

We are now ready to consider the experience of an actual person with the process we have termed individuation. This experience was exemplified in certain symbolic dreams and visual impressions. Symbols of the process of individuation are images, usually of archetypal nature, that appear in dreams and portray the centralizing process, or the production of a new centre of the personality. The general nature of this process is discussed in my essay: *The Relation of the Ego to the Unconscious.*[1] For certain reasons indicated there, I call this centre also the "self," a term that is meant to include the totality of the psyche in so far as this manifests itself in an individual. The self is not only the centre, but also the circumference that encloses consciousness and the unconscious; it is the centre of this totality, as the ego is the centre of consciousness.

The symbols that are dealt with in this chapter do not cover all the manifold steps and transformations of the process of individuation, but are of the order of images exclusively and directly related to the making conscious of the new centre. These images belong to a definite category that I call *mandala symbolism*. In *The Secret of the Golden Flower* [2] I have, in collaboration with Wilhelm, described this symbolism in some detail. In the study under consideration I should like to present an individual series of such symbols in chronological order. The material for this chapter consists of more than one thousand dreams and visual impressions of a scientifically educated, youngish man. But the dreamer's education in history, philology, archæology, and ethnology is not the question here. The bearing of his dreams upon the subject matter of these fields was almost wholly unknown to him.

For the purpose of my present study I have treated this patient's first four hundred dreams after his case came to treatment. They are distributed over a period of nearly ten months. In order to exclude every influencing factor, one of my women pupils, a doctor who was then a beginner, undertook the observation of the process under my direction, and pursued it for five months. Then, for three months, the dreamer continued his observations alone. Except for a short conference at the outset, before the beginning of the observation, I did not see the dreamer at all during the first eight months. So it happened that three hundred and fifty-five of the four hundred dreams occurred without any personal contact with me. Only the last forty-five dreams took place under my observation. No interpretations worth mentioning were undertaken, as the dreamer, thanks to his excellent scientific training and talent, needed no help of any kind. The conditions were, therefore, positively ideal for unprejudiced observation and recording.

First of all, then, I shall present extracts of the *initial* dreams, twenty-two in all, in order to show how the mandala symbolism, of which we have already spoken, and which here appears at an early stage of the process, is embedded in the remaining dream material. Later on I shall select the dreams, in chronological order, that deal particularly with the mandala.

With few exceptions, the dreams as presented here are abbreviated, sometimes by extracting the part that carried the main thought, sometimes by reducing the whole text to essentials. This simplifying operation has not only shortened lengthy excursions, but also removed personal allusions and complications. Such an excision had to be made for reasons of discretion. In spite of this somewhat questionable meddling, I have avoided every arbitrary perversion of meaning according to the best dictates of my knowledge and conscience. I had to exercise the same consideration in interpreting the dreams, for which reason certain passages in them will appear to have been overlooked. Had I not made this sacrifice of absolute completeness, I should not have been in a position to publish this series, which in my opinion is hardly to be surpassed in intelligence, clarity, and consistency. Therefore, I take an especial pleasure in expressing to the "author," at this point, my sincere gratitude for the service he has rendered science.

The Method

A great deal of popular misunderstanding about the interpretation of dreams seems to be current. It is important to understand what a serious approach to this problem entails. In my writings and lectures I have always insisted that we must renounce preconceived opinions in the analysis and interpretation of objective-psychic (so-called "unconscious") contents.[3] We are not yet in possession of a general theory of dreams that would allow us, unchastised, to adopt a deductive procedure, any more than we enjoy a general theory of consciousness that would permit deductive conclusions. The manifestations of the subjective psyche, that is to say, of consciousness, are calculable only to the smallest extent, and there is no theoretic demonstration whatsoever that could convincingly establish the necessity of an apparent causal connection. Quite on the contrary, we have to reckon with an arbitrariness and "fortuitousness" of about one hundred per cent in the complex reactions and actions of consciousness. Likewise, there is no empirical, and still less any theoretic, ground for the assumption that the same is not true of the expressions of the unconscious. The latter are as manifold, as unpredictable, and as arbitrary as the former, and must, accordingly, be subjected to as many ways of approach.

In the case of conscious utterances we are in the advantageous position of being addressed and of having presented to us a content intended to be recognizable; in the case of "unconscious" manifestations, on the other hand, there exists no language that we would consider directed and adapted, but only a psychic phenomenon having apparently but the loosest connection with conscious contents. If the conscious utterance should be ununderstandable, we can always ask for the meaning. But the objective-psychic utterance is strange even to the consciousness in which it expresses itself. In dealing with it we are, therefore, constrained to apply the method demanded by the reading of a fragmentary text or one containing unknown words: *we examine the context.* The comparison of a series of textual passages in which the unknown word occurs shows us what the latter *could* mean. The psychological context of dream contents consists of that web of associations in which the expression of the dream is embedded in a natural manner. In theory we can never know this expression beforehand; actually it is sometimes possible, granting a large experience and much practice; yet a careful analysis will never rely too much on rules of the craft, for the danger of deception and suggestion is too great. Especially in the analysis of isolated dreams, it is worthless to foreknow and presuppose on the ground of practical expectations and general probability. Therefore, it is unconditionally the rule that we first assume that every dream and every part of each dream is unknown.

Only after a careful survey of the context do we make an attempt at interpretation. This is done by inserting in the text of the dream the meaning found by establishing the context; and we can then see whether this makes a flexible explanation possible or, rather, whether it gives rise to a satisfying meaning. But under no circumstance may we anticipate that this meaning will correspond to any subjective expectation, for often the dream says something astonishingly different from what we should have expected. If the discovered meaning of the dream answers to expectation, this is actually a reason to be wary, for the standpoint of the unconscious is as a rule complementary or compensatory to consciousness and hence unexpectedly "different."

I do not in any way deny the possibility of "parallel" dreams, that is, of those whose meaning falls in with the attitude of consciousness, or reinforces it. But, in my experience at least, these are fairly rare.

Now, the method which I follow in this study seems to go directly counter to this basic attitude toward the dream. It seems as if the dreams have been interpreted without the least regard for the context. As a matter of fact, I have nowhere in this chapter established their context, for the series of dreams did not take place under my observation at all. I treat the dreams to a certain extent as if I had had them myself and were for that reason able on my own part to supply the context.

Applied to the *isolated* dreams of someone practically a stranger to me personally, this procedure would be a gross technical blunder. But here we are dealing not with isolated dreams, but with several interconnected *series* in the course of which the meaning gradually develops to a certain extent of itself. *For the series is the context, and the dreamer himself supplies it.* It is as if there lay before us not a single text, but a large number which throw light from all sides upon the unfamiliar terms, so that the reading of all the texts is sufficient in itself to clear up the difficulties of meaning of each single one. Moreover, in the second, larger part of this study we are dealing with a definite archetype that has long been known to us from other sources, and this substantially facilitates the interpretation. Certainly, the interpretation of each single passage is essentially *conjecture;* but the course of the entire series gives us all the necessary supports by which immediately to correct possible errors in preceding parts.

It goes without saying that when the dreamer was under the observation of my pupil he was allowed to know nothing of these interpretations, and was therefore in no way prejudiced by my opinions. Moreover, I hold the view, based on considerable experience, that the possibility and danger of prejudice are exaggerated. The objective psyche, as experience shows us, is independent in the highest degree. If it were not, it could not exercise the function which is peculiar to it, the compensation of consciousness. Consciousness may allow itself to be trained like a parrot, but not the unconscious. That is why St. Augustine thanked God for not making him responsible for his dreams. The unconscious is a psychic element that can only in appearance, and much to the disadvantage of consciousness, be put in training. It is and remains out of reach of all subjective caprice, a realm of nature that cannot be improved upon or perverted. It is part of nature's secret, which we can listen to but cannot handle.

Dreams: First Series

1. (Dream) He dreams he is in company and, on taking his leave, puts on a strange hat instead of his own.

What is the significance of this dream? To begin with, the hat, as the covering of the head, has in general the meaning of something comprising the head. As in the act of subsuming we "bring all ideas under one hat," so the hat, like a universal concept, covers the whole personality and shares its meaning. *Coronation* lends to the ruler the divine nature of the sun, the *mortarboard* bestows the dignity of a scholar, *a strange hat* imparts a strange nature. Meyrink employs this theme in *The Golem,* where the hero puts on the hat of Athanasius Pernath and, as a result, is translated into a strange experience. It is clear enough in *The Golem* that it is the unconscious that entangles the hero in fantastic experiences. (Let me call attention right here in a hypothetical way to the significance of the Golem parallel: *it is the hat of an Athanasius,* of an immortal, of a timeless being, by which we are to understand a universally authentic, perpetually existent human being in contradistinction to the individual who happens but once and is, so to speak, accidental.) The hat, which embraces the head, is round like the sun-disk of the crown and therefore contains the first allusion to the mandala. The ninth mandala dream, discussed on page 132, will confirm the attribute of imperishable duration, and the thirty-fifth, given later on page 179, the mandala nature of the hat. As a general result of the exchange of hats, then, we may perhaps expect in this case a development similar to that in *The Golem,* namely, an emergence of the unconscious. The unconscious with its figures already stands like a shadow behind him and presses into consciousness.

2. (Dream) He rides in the railway and, by standing squarely before the window, deprives his fellow passengers of the view. He must stand aside for them.

With this dream it is beginning to be plain that the process is set in motion. The dreamer discovers that he obstructs the light *for those who stand behind him*, namely, the unconscious components of his personality. We have no eyes behind us; as a consequence, "behind" is the region of the unseen, of the unconscious. If the dreamer opens the way to the window, that is, to consciousness, then the unconscious content becomes conscious.

3. (Hypnogogic, visual impression) The subject "daydreams" that he is on the seacoast. The sea breaks into the land, overflowing everything. Then he is seated on a lonely island.

The sea, as earlier chapters have suggested, is the symbol of the collective unconscious because it hides unsuspected depths under a reflecting surface. Those who stand behind him, the shadowy and demonic συνοπαθοί, the "companions who travel along," have broken like a flood into the *terra firma* of consciousness. Such irruptions are uncanny because they are irrational and inexplicable to the individual concerned. They signify a momentous alteration of the personality in that they immediately constitute a painful, personal secret that estranges the human being from his environment and isolates him from it. It is something that "you can tell to no one," except under fear of being accused of mental abnormality, and with some justification, for something quite similar befalls the insane. It is still a long way from an intuitively sensed irruption to pathological overthrow; but a layman does not know this.

The result of psychic isolation through a secret is, as a

rule, the *vivifying* of the psychic atmosphere as a *surrogate* for the lost contact with the individual's fellow beings. It is the occasion for an activation of the unconscious, and out of it there arises something similar to the illusions and hallucinations of lonely desert travellers, seafarers, and saints. The mechanism of this manifestation can, no doubt, be explained in terms of energy. (The normal relations to the objects of the environment are maintained by a certain expenditure of energy. If the relation to the object is cut off, there arises a "retention" of energy, which, for its part, gives rise to an equivalent surrogate.) For example, just as the idea of persecution issues from a relationship infected with mistrust, so, as a substitute for the normal animation of the world around us, there arises an illusory reality in which uncanny, ghostly shadows move in place of people. Thus it comes about that lonely, desert places are always inhabited for primitive man by "devils" and similar spectres.

4. (Dream) He is surrounded by many indistinct, feminine figures. A voice within him says: "I must first get away from the father."

Here has occurred an animation of the psychic atmosphere by what, in the style of the Middle Ages, would have been called *succubi*. We are reminded of the visions of the Egyptian Anthony, which Flaubert has so learnedly portrayed. The hallucinatory element becomes noticeable in the fact that the *thoughts grow audible*. The "first get away" seems to demand a concluding sentence, which should begin with "in order then." Presumably it runs something like: "in order then to be able to follow the unconscious, that is, the allurements of the women." The father, the embodiment of the traditional spirit as it shows itself in religion and in the general outlook of most individuals, stands in his way. He holds the dreamer a prisoner to consciousness and its values. The traditional masculine world with its intellectualism and rationalism becomes noticeably an obstacle.

From this we must conclude that the unconscious, which approaches him, stands decidedly in opposition to the tendencies of consciousness, and that, in spite of this opposition, the dreamer has already a considerable inclination to the side of the unconscious. In consequence, the latter should not be subordinated to the rational judgement of consciousness, but should rather be an experience of its own unique kind. Naturally, this course is not easily accepted by the intellect, for it demands, if not a complete, then at least a partial sacrifice of the conscious intellect. What is more, the problem thus raised is hard for modern man to grasp, because he can see in the unconscious, at first approach, only an unessential and unreal appendage of consciousness, and not a peculiar sphere of experience of an autonomous kind.

In the course of the young man's later dreams this conflict will often recur, until at last the right formula for the correlation of conscious-unconscious is found, and the correct, intermediate position assigned to the personality. Moreover, such a conflict cannot be solved by understanding it, but only by *living* it. Every stage of the process must be lived through. There is no interpretation or other sleight of hand capable of getting the individual around this difficulty by deception. The coalescence of conscious and unconscious can succeed only a step at a time.

The resistance of consciousness to the unconscious, as well as the underestimation of the latter, is a historic necessity of human psychic development, for otherwise consciousness could never have differentiated itself from the unconscious at all. The consciousness of modern man, however, has withdrawn somewhat too far from the reality of the unconscious. We have even forgotten that the psyche does not correspond to our conscious intention, but is for the most part autonomous and unconscious. For this reason, the approach of the unconscious arouses a panic fear in civilized man, not least of all because of the threatening analogy to insanity. There is nothing questionable to the intellect in describing the unconscious as a passive object; on the contrary, such an activity would correspond to rational expectations. But to let the unconscious happen and to experience it as a reality—this exceeds the courage as well as the powers of the average Occidental. He prefers simply not to understand this problem. It is also better so for the weak in spirit, since this thing is not without its danger.

The experiencing of the unconscious is a personal secret communicable only to the very few, and that with difficulty. It isolates the individual to whom it happens. But isolation effects a compensatory animation of the psychic atmosphere, and this is uncanny. The figures that appear are feminine, whereby the feminine nature of the unconscious is pointed out. They are fairies or beguiling sirens and lamias who infatuate the lonely wanderer and lead him astray.[4]

5. (Visual impression) A snake draws a circle about the dreamer. He stands like a tree, grown fast to the earth.

The drawing of a spellbinding circle is the ancient magic means that everyone resorts to who has a singular and secret purpose. He protects himself with it against the perils of the soul that threaten from without and befall everyone who is isolated by a secret. On the other hand, men from of old have resorted to this means in order to demark a place as holy and inviolable; they would draw around it the *sulcus primigenius,* or original furrow, as, for instance, at the founding of cities.[5] That the dreamer stands rooted in the middle is a compensation for his almost insuperable urge to run away from the unconscious. After this vision he has a pleasant feeling of relief; rightly so, for he has succeeded in forming a protected enclosure, a region of taboo in which it becomes possible for him to experience the unconscious.

His isolation, otherwise uncanny, is thereby elevated to an aim, endowed with purposeful meaning, and thus robbed of its fearfulness.

6. (Visual impression, directly following upon 5) The veiled figure of a woman is seated upon a stair.

The theme of the unknown woman, to which we have given, in an earlier chapter, the technical name of anima, here appears for the first time in this case and represents a personification of the animated psychic atmosphere like the many, indistinct feminine figures in the fourth dream. From now on, the figure of the unknown woman reappears in very many of the subject's dreams.

Personification always means autonomous activity of the unconscious. If the figure of a person presents itself, this means that the unconscious has begun to stir. The activity of such figures often bears the stamp of foreknowledge; that is, an activity to be exercised later on by the dreamer himself is anticipated. In this case the *stair* is indicated, which points to a going up or down.

As the process unrolling in such dreams has a historical analogy in the rites of initiation, it may not be superfluous to point out that the planet stair of seven steps plays an important rôle in many of them, as we know, for instance, from Apuleius. The initiations of the late Græco-Roman syncretism, which are already strongly permeated with alchemy, occupy themselves particularly with the "ascent," that is, *sublimation*. The ascent is also often represented by the *ladder*—whence the Egyptian burial gift of a small ladder for the ka of the dead man. The idea of an ascent through the seven planetary spheres means the return of the soul to the solar godhead from which it took its rise (as we learn, for instance, from Firmicus Maternus). Thus the mystery of Isis, which Apuleius has described for us in *The Golden Ass*, likewise culminates in what the alchemy of the early Middle Ages—transmitted by the Arabs directly from Alexandrian culture [6]—calls *solificatio:* the initiate is crowned as Helios, the sun.

7. (Visual impression) The veiled woman uncovers her face. It shines like the sun.

The *solificatio* is accomplished in the anima. This process corresponds, no doubt, to the ancient *illuminatio.* Now this conception, which might be called mystic, is in strong contradiction to the rationalistic attitude of consciousness, which recognizes only intellectual enlightenment as the highest form of understanding and insight. This attitude, of course, does not reckon with the fact that scientific knowledge is satisfying only to the modern forefront of the personality, but not to the collective psyche, which reaches back into grey antiquity and which always demands a particular ritual when it is to be linked with present-day consciousness. Clearly, then, a *lightening of the unconscious* is in preparation, having far more the quality of the *illuminatio* than of rational elucidation. The *solificatio* stands at an infinite distance from consciousness and seems to it almost chimerical.

8. (Visual impression) A rainbow is to be used as a bridge. Yet one must go, not over it, but through underneath. Whoever goes over it falls to his death.

Only gods succeed in walking on the rainbow bridge; mortals fall to their death, for the rainbow is only a beautiful semblance that stretches across the heavens, and not a road for corporeal human beings: they must go through underneath. But under bridges flows water, which follows its own gradient. This hint will be confirmed in what follows.

9. (Dream) A green land where many sheep are at pasture. It is the "land of sheep."

This curious passage, inscrutable at first glance, may derive from childhood impressions, particularly of a religious sort. In this connection they are not far to seek. For instance: "He maketh me to lie down in green pastures," in connection with the early Christian allegory of the sheep and the shepherd. The next piece points in this direction.

10. (Visual impression) In the land of sheep stands the unknown woman and points the way.

The anima, who has already anticipated the *solificatio,* here appears as the psychopomp showing the way. The way begins in the land of childhood, namely, in that time when the rational, present-day consciousness had not yet separated itself from the historic psyche, the collective unconscious. The separation is unavoidable, to be sure, but leads to such a divorce from that twilight psyche of old that a loss of instinct takes place. The result is an impoverishment of instinct and disorientation in the generally human situations. But it also follows from the separation that the "land of childhood" remains definitely infantile, and thus becomes an enduring source of childish inclinations and impulses.

These intrusions are naturally most unwelcome to consciousness, so it consistently represses them. But the consistency of the repression only serves to bring about a still greater separation from the source, and intensifies the impoverishment of instinct to such an extent that it amounts to barrenness of soul. As a result, either consciousness is completely inundated with childishness or it must constantly defend itself—to no avail—against the latter with cynical agedness or with embittered resignation.

It is necessary to understand that, in spite of its undeniable successes, the reasonable attitude of present-day consciousness has become in many human respects childishly unadapted and therefore hostile to life. Life has grown dry and restricted, and therefore demands the discovery of the source. But the source cannot be found unless consciousness resigns itself to a return to the land of childhood in order to receive there, as before, the guidance from the unconscious. Not only he who remains a child overlong is childish, but also he who separates himself from childhood and supposes that everything he does not see no longer exists. But whoever returns to the land of childhood succumbs to the fear of becoming childlike, not realizing that everything original to the psyche has a double face. The one looks forward, the other back. It is ambiguous and hence symbolic, like all living reality.

In consciousness we stand upon a summit and childishly suppose that the way beyond leads to still greater heights above the summit. That is the chimerical rainbow bridge. But in order to reach the next peak we must first go down into that land where the roads just begin to part from each other.

11. (Dream)   A voice says, "But you are still a child."

This dream forces the recognition that even a differentiated consciousness has in no way made a clean sweep of childish things, and that a return to the world of childhood has become necessary.

2. (Dream)   A dangerous wandering with father and mother up and down over many ladders.

The childish consciousness is always attached to father and mother and never alone. A return to childhood is always a return to father and mother, to the whole burden of the psychic non-ego embodied in the parents, with its long, momentous history. Regression means disintegration into the historical, hereditary determinants from whose embrace we can free ourselves only with the greatest effort. The psychic history of the past is, indeed, the spirit of weight, which needs *steps* and *ladders* because it cannot, like the bodiless and weightless intellect, fly when it wants to. Disintegration into the multiplicity of historical determinants is like losing the way, like a disorientation in which even what is right resembles a disturbing error.

No one can free himself from his childhood without first generously occupying himself with it, as we have long since found out from the Freudian researches. Nor is this freedom accomplished through mere intellectual knowledge; it can be effected only by a re-remembering, which is also a *re-experiencing*. Much childhood material remains undisposed of in the psyche because of the rapid flow of the years and the overwhelming rush of the newly discovered world. We have not *freed* ourselves from it, but only removed ourselves from it. So if, in later years, we return to our childhood memories, we find there still living fragments of our own personalities, which lock us in their embraces and permeate us again with the feeling of our earlier days. Those fragments are still in the childhood state and for that reason strong and immediate. Only when they are joined again to the adult consciousness can they lose their infantile aspect and be corrected. This "personal unconscious" must always first be disposed of—that is to say, made conscious; otherwise, the entrance to the collective unconscious cannot be opened. The journey with father and mother, which leads up and down over many ladders, corresponds to this making conscious of infantile, still unintegrated contents.

13. (Dream) The father calls anxiously, "That is the seventh!"

In the wandering over the many ladders an occurrence has obviously taken place that is spoken of as "the seventh." In the language of initiation, the seventh corresponds to the highest stage, and would be the longed for and coveted. But to the traditional mind the *solificatio* is a strange, mystic, and hence nearly insane conception; people thought of such nonsense only in former ages, in the dark times of misty superstition, while the clear, purified mind of our enlightened age has long since outgrown such hazy notions, and to such a degree that only the madhouse now harbours illuminates of that kind. No wonder that the father is fearfully anxious, like the hen that has hatched duck's eggs and is driven to despair by the aquatic leanings of her progeny. If this interpretation is correct—that the seventh means the highest stage before the enlightenment—then, in principle, the process of the integration of the personal unconscious would actually have been terminated. After that, the disclosure of the collective unconscious would begin, and that would sufficiently explain the anxiety of the father as the embodiment of the traditional mind.

In any case, the return to the early twilight of the unconscious does not mean that one should now wholly renounce that valuable achievement of the fathers: the intellectual differentiation of consciousness. It is rather a question of the human being's taking the place of the intellect.

14. (Dream) The dreamer is in America and is looking for an employee with a pointed beard. It is said that everyone has such an employee.

America, to this subject, is the land of practical, straight lines and is not under suspicion of European excess. In

America people would regard the intellect in a practical way, as an employee. This sounds, to be sure, like lese-majesty, and could be a serious matter. So it is consoling to know that everyone (as is the case in America) does the same. He of the pointed beard is the well-known Mephisto, whom Faust also employed, and whom he did not allow to triumph finally over him, in spite of the fact that he, Faust, had dared to descend into the gloomy chaos of the historic psyche and had taken upon himself the mutable and not unquestionable life that arises from the fullness of chaos. The deposition of the intellect and, at the same time, the separation from the father, are thus accomplished.

15. (Dream) The mother pours water from one bowl into another. (Only in connection with dream 28 does the dreamer remember that this was the bowl of his sister.) This act is accomplished with great solemnity, as it is of the utmost importance to the surrounding world. Then the dreamer is cast out by the father.

We meet here again with the theme of the exchange, introduced with the hat in the first dream. One thing is put in the place of another. The "father" is disposed of; now the action of the "mother" begins.

As the father represents the collective consciousness, the traditional mind, so the mother stands for the collective unconscious, the source of the *water of life*. (Compare the motherly significance of the πυγή,[7] the *fons signatus*[8] as an attribute of Mary.) The unconscious transposes the location of the life forces, and thus a change of standpoint is indicated. The dreamer's later act of remembrance enables us to recognize who it is that now becomes the source of life: it is the "sister." The mother is placed above the son, while the sister is placed by his side.

Thus the deposition of the intellect sets us free from

the supremacy of the unconscious, and therewith from in-
fantilism. To be sure, the sister is still a remainder of the
past, but we know definitely from later dreams that she was
the bearer of the anima image. We may, therefore, assume
that the transference of the water of life to the sister means
at bottom the *replacement of the mother by the anima.*

This is really a process of normal life, but one that
usually takes place in a wholly unconscious way. The anima
is an archetype that is always present. The mother is the
first carrier of this image, and it is this that makes her fascinating and meaningful to the son. By way of the sister and
other figures, the image is then transferred to the loved
woman.

As a result of the replacement just mentioned, the
anima becomes a life-bestowing factor, a psychic reality
that stands in unbearable opposition to the world of the
father. Who would be able, without endangering his mental
health, to declare the guidance of the unconscious binding
in his conduct of life, assuming that anyone exists who can
imagine anything definite under this head? But whoever
can imagine this in any way will, by that very fact, conceive what a tremendous insult such a change of view spells
for the traditional spirit, and especially for the spirit that
has clothed itself with an earthly body in the church. It was
this subtle change of psychic standpoint that made the alchemists resort to intentional mystification, and that stood
godfather to all possible heresies. So, it is logical that the
father thereupon casts him out, which means nothing else
than *excommunication.* (The dreamer, be it noted, is a
Catholic.)

Whoever recognizes the psyche in its reality, and accepts it at least as a co-determining, ethical factor, insults
the traditional spirit, which has for many centuries regi-
mented psychic behaviour from without through institutions as well as through reason. Not that unreasoning in-

stinct of itself rebels against strongly consolidated order, for it is itself, through its conformity to inner laws, the most strongly consolidated structure and—what is more—the creative source of all bounded order. But just because this source is creative, all order issuing from it, even in its "most godly" form, is succession and transition. Yet, all appearances to the contrary, every establishment of order and every dissolution of the established is at bottom beyond the reach of human caprice. The secret is this: only that possesses life which is able to annul itself again.

It is well that these things are hard to understand and thus enjoy a beneficent secrecy, for weak minds are only too easily distracted by them and thrown into confusion. Effective protection against all this is offered by dogma, whether of an ecclesiastical, philosophic, or scientific nature, and excommunication is a necessary and useful consequence, from the social standpoint. But no evil is so great that it does not also have something of good in it. Thus, the excommunicate enjoys the *inner freedom of the living spirit,* which counterbalances the safety offered by dogma.

The water that the mother, the unconscious, pours into the bowl of the anima is an apt symbol for the living quality of psychic being. The ancient alchemists never wearied of thinking up expressive synonyms for it. They called it the *aqua nostra,* also the *mercurius vivus,* the *argentum vivum,* the *vivum ardens,* the *aqua vitæ,* the *succus lunariæ,* and so on, by which they meant to characterize a living being not devoid of substance, in contrast to the incorporeality necessarily attributed to the abstract spirit. The expression: *succus lunariæ* points clearly enough to the nocturnal nature of the source, and both *aqua nostra* and *mercurius vivus* (quicksilver) to its earthliness. The *acetum fontis* is a powerful *aqua fortis* that, on the one hand, dissolves all things that have come into being, while on the other it leads to the most enduring of all structures, namely, to the mysterious *lapis*.

These analogies from mediæval alchemy must inevitably seem rather far-fetched. But at this point I may already refer to dreams 13 and 14 in the following, second section of this chapter, where this symbolism is taken up again. The parallels that I cite are chiefly derived from the Latin literature of the twelfth to fourteenth centuries, one of the most interesting texts being the *Rosarium*, by an anonymous author. Like other texts of the period, it reflects much older sources, even the Greek, through the mediation of Arabic writing. To this author, as to all the "philosophic" alchemists, the transmutation of gold was by no means taken literally; they treated it, rather, as a symbol of transformation embracing psychic change. This is why their writings have a direct bearing upon the process of individuation, and why this obscure field yields such important parallels to the activity of the unconscious—as I shall try to show in the later chapter on alchemy.

The importance of the action "to the surrounding world," which the dreamer himself noticed, points to the collective dimensions of this dream, as also to the fact that a decision is offered that strongly influences the attitude of the dreamer.

That old proverb, *extra ecclesiam nulla salus*—outside the church there is no welfare—rests on the knowledge that an institution is an assured, passable way, with a definite aim that is visible or expressible, whereas outside of it no ways and no aims are to be discovered. We must not underestimate the fact that to be thus lost in chaos means a bitter shock, even when we know that it is the indispensable prerequisite of every renewal of the spirit.

16. (Dream) An ace of clubs lies before him. Beside it appears a seven.

The ace, as a one, is the lowest and, as ace, the highest card. The ace of clubs, with its cross form, points to the basic Christian symbol; it will recur in another guise in the twenty-third dream of the second series. In Swiss-German the club is also called "Chrüz" (cross). At the same time, its trifoliate character contains an allusion to the threefold nature of the one God. Lowest and highest is the beginning and the end, the alpha and omega.

After, and not before, the ace of clubs appears the seven. Thus the sentence perhaps runs: The Christian conception of God, and after that the seven (stages). The seven changes symbolize the transformation. This begins with the symbol of the cross and of the Trinity, and, according to the earlier, archaizing allusion in dream 7, would culminate in the *solificatio*. But this solution is not indicated here. Now, we are acquainted from the Middle Ages with a transition that differs from that regression to the classic Helios which Julian the Apostate attempted without success. This is the transition to the *rose* expressed in the formula *per crucem ad rosam*—through the cross to the rose—and condensed to the rose cross (Rosicrucian) of the late Middle Ages. Here the tokens of the solar nature descend from the heavenly Sol into the *flower*, earth's answer to the solar countenance. (The solar quality has survived in the symbol of the "golden flower" of Chinese and mediæval alchemy.) A last sentimental reminiscence of the "rose" might well be the "blue flower" of the Romantics, which in true romantic fashion looks back to the Middle Ages of ruined cloisters, yet with the modesty of a violet proclaims something new in its lovely earthiness.

But the golden lustre of the sun had also to accept the descent, and found its analogy in the glitter of earthly gold, which as *aurum nostrum* was set apart, at least for subtler minds, from the gross materiality of the metal. For these it was undoubtedly of symbolic nature, and was therefore dis-

tinguished by such attributes as *potabile* or *philosophicum.*
The *Rosarium,* indeed, declares that *"our* gold is not the
gold of the general crowd." It is perhaps just its too obvious
analogy to the sun that denied it the attainment of the
highest philosophical dignity, which fell instead to the *lapis
philosophorum.* For higher in rank than that which is
changed stood that which effects change, and to do this is
one of the magic powers of the wonderful stone. The *Rosarium* also says, *quia lapis noster scilicet argentum vivum
occidentale, quod prætulit se auro et vicit illud, est illud
quod occidit et vivere facit*—"because it is our stone,
the living silver of the West, which has preferred itself to
the gold and conquered it, that slays and makes alive." The
following textual passage from a treatise ascribed to Hermes
is particularly enlightening as to the "philosophical" significance of the *lapis: Intelligite, filii sapientum, quod hic lapis
preciosissimus clamet; . . . et lumen meum omne lumen
superat ac mea bona omnibus bonis sunt sublimiora . . .
Ego gigno lumen, tenebræ autem naturæ meæ sunt . . . :* [9]
"Understand, sons of the wise, what this most worthy stone
might exclaim . . . and my light conquers every light, and
my goods are more sublime than all other goods . . . I beget the light, but the darkness also is of my nature. . . ."

17. (Dream) A long wandering. He finds a blue
flower along the way.

To wander is to tread aimless paths; therefore, it is also
to search for and undergo transformation. And now a blue
flower blossoms aimlessly beside his path, an accidental child
of nature reminding him in a friendly way of romantic
lyricism, having budded in a youthful season when the picture of the world drawn by science had not as yet painfully
divorced itself from the actual experience of the world, or
when the parting just began, and the backward glance al-

ready looked upon things of the past. It is, in fact, like a friendly greeting, a numen of the unconscious. It points out to him who is bereft of the certainty of his way and of his membership in the things that mean the welfare of man, the historic spot where he meets friends and brothers in spirit and finds the seed that wishes to unfold in him also. But the dreamer as yet suspects nothing of the ancient solar gold that connects the innocent flower by a backward step with the repulsive elements of alchemy and with the heathen frivolity of the *solificatio*.

18. (Dream) A man offers him gold coins in the palm of his hand. But the indignant dreamer throws them on the ground and immediately afterward deeply regrets his action. Then, in an enclosure, a variety performance takes place.

Here the blue flower has already begun to draw historical consequences in its train. The "gold" is offered and is indignantly rejected. To be sure, the misinterpretation of the *aurum philosophicum* is understandable. But scarcely has it occurred, when there comes a pang of remorse that the valuable secret was rejected and that a wrong answer was thus given to the question of the Sphinx. The same thing happened to the hero of *The Golem*, when the ghost offered him a handful of grain and he refused it. The gross materiality of the yellow metal with its odious connotation of the standard of value, as well as the unattractiveness of the grain, makes the rejection comprehensible; it is so hard to find the *lapis*, because it is *exilis*—unattractive; because *in via ejectus invenitur*, because it is the cheapest of things and is found everywhere, *in planitie, in montibus et aquis*. It shares this "ordinary" aspect with Spitteler's jewel in *Prometheus and Epimetheus*, for which reason, also, it is unrecognized by all the worldly-wise. But the *lapis in via ejectus* might also become the *angularis;* the stone that was rejected might become the cornerstone. The sense of this possibility awakens the strongest remorse in the dreamer.

That the gold is minted—in other words, shaped, stamped, and appraised—is a banality of the external aspect. Applied to the things of the psyche, this is what Nietzsche declines in *Zarathustra*, namely, the giving of names to the virtues. By the acts of shaping and naming, psychic being is disintegrated into minted and appraised units. But this is possible for the single reason that it is from its origins a plurality, a heaping together of unintegrated, hereditary units. Natural man is no *self*, but a particle of a mass, and even a mass, an aggregate, to such a degree that he is not even sure of his "I." For this reason the mysteries of transformation have been needed since primeval times to make him into "something" and to tear him away from the animal, collective psyche, which is a mere multiplicity.

But if the unattractive multiplicity of the "given" human being is cast aside, then his integration, his *birth into selfhood*, is precluded. And that is spiritual *death*. The requisite for real life is not that life should happen in and for itself, but that it should also be *known*. Only a unified personality can experience life; an occurrence split up into partial aspects, though it likewise call itself a human being, cannot do so. The dangerous *multiplicity* already alluded to in dream 4 is compensated by dream 5, where the serpent protectively draws the spellbinding circle and thus demarks the region of taboo, the temenos, which in ancient times signified a piece of land or a grove consecrated to the god. So, in a similar situation, there arises here the symbol of the temenos, in which the "many" now meet together in a unified action—an enjoyable gathering in its superficial aspect, but one that will shortly lose its pleasant character. The goat-song becomes tragedy. The satyr-play, according to all analogy, was a mystery rite whose presumable purpose was to link the human being regressively to the ranks of his natural ancestors and so to the source of life—much as people supposed that the recounting of obscene stories, the αἰσχρολογία of the Athenian ladies in the ceremonies of the Eleusinian mysteries, was good for the fruitfulness of the earth.[10] (Compare also Herodotus' account of the exhibitions in connection with the festivals of Isis in Bubastis.)

The allusion to the compensatory significance of the temenos, however, remains for the present vague to the dreamer. We can understand that he is far more occupied with the danger of spiritual death, which is evoked by the rejection of the historical relationships.

19. (Visual impression) A death's-head. He wishes to kick it aside, but cannot. Gradually the skull changes into a red ball, then into a woman's head, which emits light.

The skull monologues of Faust and Hamlet remind one of the shocking senselessness of human existence, provided that "the pale cast of thought" is spread over it. It was opinions and judgements transmitted from the past that induced the dreamer to dash aside the unappreciated or unattractive offering. But when he tries to shield himself from the uncanny vision, the dead man's skull turns into the red ball, which we may doubtless regard as an allusion to the rising sun, for it changes at once into the shining woman's head, reminding us directly of vision 7. Clearly, an enantiodromia, a play of opposites, has here taken place; after the rejection, the unconscious comes out only the more strongly, first of all with the ancient symbol of unity and of the divinity of the self, the sun, and then passing over to the theme of the unknown woman, who personifies the unconscious. This theme, of course, comprises not only the archetype of the anima, but also the relationship to real woman who is, on the one hand, human personality and, on the other, a vessel of psychic being; a theme introduced in the fifteenth dream by the "bowl of the sister."

In the Neo-Platonic philosophy the soul has an outspoken relation with the form of the sphere. The soul substance is spread above the heaven of fire around the concentric spheres of the four elements.[11]

20. (Visual impression) A globe. The unknown woman stands upon it praying to the sun.

This impression is an expansion of 7. The rejection obviously signified a destruction of the whole development up to dream 18. That is why the initial symbols reappear at this point although now in amplified form. Such enantiodromias are characteristic for unconscious sequences in general. Without the intervention of consciousness the unconscious would persist in its ineffective wave motion, like the treasure of which it is said that it burgeons upward for nine years, nine months and nine nights, and that, if it is not found in the last night, it sinks down again to begin the game anew.

The *globe* perhaps issues from the idea of the red ball. Whereas this was the sun, the globe is more probably a picture of the earth, upon which the anima stands and prays to the sun. The anima and the sun are thus distinguished from each other, and the fact is pointed out that the sun denotes a principle differing from the anima. The latter is a personification of the unconscious. But the sun is a symbol of the wellspring of life and of the final wholeness of man (as hinted in the *solificatio*). Now, the sun is a classic symbol that even yet stands very close to us. We likewise know that the Christians of the first centuries had some difficulty in distinguishing the ἥλιος ἀνατολῆς from Christ.[12] The anima of the dreamer seems still to be a sun worshipper; that is, she is essentially Græco-Roman, and this for the reason that a rationalistically oriented consciousness had occupied itself with her little or not at all, and in consequence had not allowed her to modernize (or better, to Christianize) herself. It almost seems as if the anima had been caused to regress to antiquity by the differentiation of the intellect that grew out of the Christian Middle Ages through scholastic training. The Renaissance provides us with evidence enough on this point; the clearest of all is the *Ipnerotomachia* of Polifilo, who found his anima—Lady Polia—in the house of Queen Venus, unencumbered by any vestige of Christianity, but graced with all the *virtutes* of the classic age. (Polifilo's century was justified in holding his book for a mystery text.) With this anima, then, we plunge into the classic world. So I would not regard it as an error if anyone should explain the above-described enantiodromia *ex effectu* as an evasion of the dubious and unseemly regression to the classic world. Textually, the basic teachings of alchemistic philosophy go directly back to the late Græco-Roman syncretism, as Rusca, for instance, has sufficiently established in the case of the *Turba*. Allusion to alchemy, accordingly, is sufficient in itself to lead one to suspect the classic and to fear a regression to early heathen stages.

It is perhaps not superfluous to point out here, with all due emphasis, that the dreamer had no *conscious* suspicion of all these things. Yet through the unconscious he has plunged into these connections known to us through their expression in history, and therefore behaves in his dreams as if he were a connoisseur of these curious processes of cultural history. But, as an unconscious personality, he is actually an *exponent* of the unconscious development of symbols, just as was the alchemist of the Middle Ages or the Neo-Platonist of antiquity. One might indeed say, with reservations, that it is possible to write history from his unconscious contents just as well as from the texts that are objectively present.

21. (Visual impression) He is surrounded by nymphs. A voice says, "But we were always there. Only you did not notice us."

Here the regression goes even further back to an antiquity that is out of question. At the same time the situation of dream 4 is taken up again along with the rejection situation of 18, which had led to the enantiodromia of 19. To be sure, the picture is once again enlarged, for there is subjoined to it a recognition, hallucinatory in its nature, that the state of affairs in question has always existed and was merely unnoticed up till now. With the establishment of this fact, the unconscious psyche is joined to consciousness as a coexistent entity. The phenomenon of the "voice" has always for the dreamer the final and indisputable character of the αὐτὸς ἔφα. Whenever the voice appears, then a state is reached that can no longer be seriously held in doubt. The fact that contact with distant times—that is, with deep layers of the psyche—has taken place, is accepted by the unconscious personality of the dreamer and communicates itself also to consciousness as a feeling of relative security. Therefore, the *introitus* can continue a step further.

22. (Visual impression) He is in a primeval forest. An elephant is somewhat threatening; then a large ape man or bear or cave man with a club, who threatens to attack the dreamer. Suddenly he of the "pointed beard" is there and fixes the assailant with his gaze in such a way that the latter is held off by its spell. But the dreamer is in great fear. The voice says, "Everything must be ruled by the light."

The multiplicity of the nymphs has broken down into still more primitive components; that is, the animation of the psychic atmosphere has reached a considerably higher pitch, from which one must conclude that the isolation of the individual from his contemporaries has proportionally increased. The augmented isolation can easily be referred to dream 21, where the union with the unconscious was actually established and accepted. This fact, regarded by consciousness as highly irrational, constitutes a secret that must be anxiously shielded, for naturally we cannot come to an understanding with any so-called reasonable person as to its justification. If we should impart the secret, we would thereupon be branded a complete idiot. As a result, the draining off of the libido into the surrounding world is considerably hampered, and there results a plus of energy on the unconscious side, whence the abnormal increase of the autonomy of the unconscious figures, culminating in aggression and actual fear. The variety show of unconscious figures, which was formerly enjoyable, now begins to grow uncomfortable. One can still easily accept classic nymphs with the help of æsthetic embellishments, for one in no way suspects, behind these gracious figures, the Dionysiac secret of antiquity, the satyr-play and its tragic implication—the bloody dismemberment of the god become a beast. Was not a Nietzsche called for to expose in its whole weakness the grammar-school view of antiquity held by every European? And what did Dionysus mean to him! One must surely take seriously what Nietzsche himself says about it, and even more so what happened to him. He doubtless knew, in the prodromal stage of his fatal disease, that the gloomy fate of Zarreus was appointed for him. Dionysus signifies the depths of the passionate dissolution of all human particularity in the animal divinity of the aboriginal soul—a blessed and terrible experience that a humanity strongly hedged within its culture believes it has escaped, till it succeeds once again in giving rein to a new orgy of blood about which all well-minded persons wonder, and for which they blame high finance, the armament industry, the Jews and the Freemasons.

At the last moment, the friend with the pointed beard

appears upon the stage as a *deus ex machina* to help the dreamer, and averts by a spell the threatened destruction by the momentous ape man. Who knows how much Faust's calm curiosity before the apparitions of the classical Walpurgis Night was indebted to the helpful presence of Mephisto with his contemporary, matter-of-fact standpoint. We could wish for many a person that he would bethink himself in good time of scientific or philosophic reflection, of the much-abused intellect. Whoever abuses it comes under suspicion of never having had the experience that could show him what the intellect is good for, and why humanity has forged this weapon at the cost of unprecedented effort. Not to notice this requires an extraordinary remoteness from life. No doubt, the intellect is the devil, but he is "the whimsical son of chaos" to whom we would soonest grant the capacity to deal effectively with his mother. The Dionysiac experience gives the devil, who seeks employment, enough to do, for the coming to terms with the unconscious, which now follows, far outweighs the labours of Hercules. It seems to me to present a world of problems that the intellect cannot settle even in centuries, for which reason it has taken frequent vacations to recreate itself with easier tasks. This is why the psyche is forgotten so frequently and for so long, and why the intellect so often makes use of the apotropaic sorcerer's wand and calls the psyche "occult" and "mystic," hoping that even intelligent persons will take this accusation seriously.

The voice finally declares, "Everything must be ruled by the light," by which is doubtless meant the light of the discerning consciousness, the real and honestly acquired *illuminatio*. The dark depths of the unconscious are no longer to be denied out of ignorance or out of sophistry inspired by plain fear, poorly dissembled; nor are they to be explained away by pseudo-scientific rationalizations; but it must now be admitted that there are things in our psyche about which we know too little or nothing at all, possessing at least the same degree of reality as all those things of the physical world that we also do not finally understand and that nevertheless affect our bodies in the most persevering way. No research ever led to knowledge by asserting of its object that it was irrelevant.

With the active intervention of the intellect a new phase in the unconscious process begins, namely, the coming to terms of the conscious mind with the figures of the unknown woman, the anima, the unknown man, the shadow, the old wise man or "mana personality," and the symbols of the self. The second part of this chapter will occupy itself with these.

The Mandala Symbolism

As mentioned above, I have put together, out of a connected series of four hundred dreams, all those I regard as mandala dreams. I have chosen the term "mandala" because this word denotes the ritualistic or magical circle employed in Lamaism and also in the Tantric yoga as a yantra, or aid to contemplation. The Eastern mandalas used in ceremonial are formations fixed by tradition, and are not only drawn or painted, but are even represented bodily in certain ritualistic celebrations. I refer the reader to Zimmer's exposition in *Kunstform und Yoga im indischen Kultbild*,[13] as well as to Wilhelm and Jung, *The Secret of the Golden Flower*.

It seems to me unquestionable that even in the East these symbols originally came from dreams and visions, and were not invented by some church father of the Mahayana persuasion. Indeed, they are among the oldest religious symbols of humankind, and are perhaps to be found even in the Palæolithic age, as suggested in part by the Rhodesian rock drawings. Moreover, they are distributed over the whole world, a point I will not insist on here. In this section I wish merely to show, in examples taken from actual experience, how the mandalas arise.

The mandalas employed in ceremonial always have great importance, for they contain at the centre a figure of the highest religious significance: either Shiva himself—generally embracing the Shakti—or Buddha, Amitabha, Avalokiteshvara or one of the great teachers of Mahayana. Or it is simply the Dorje, the symbol of the union of all the divine powers, whether of a creative or a destructive nature. The text of *The Golden Flower*, which derives from the Taoistic syncretism, specifies in addition certain "alchemistic" properties of the centre, resembling the qualities of the *lapis* as well as of the *elixir vitæ*, and thus lends it the attribute of a φάρμακον ἀθανασίας or τῆς ζωῆς.[14]

It is to our purpose to recognize this high valuation, for it accords with the significance that attaches to the individual mandala symbols, and these exemplify the same "metaphysical" qualities, if I may so use the term to characterize the peculiar utterance of the dream. Indeed, they represent—unless I am wholly deceived—a psychic centre of the personality that is not identical with the "I."

For some twenty years I have observed these processes and formations in dealing with fairly extensive materials drawn from experience. During fourteen years I have neither written nor lectured about it, in order not to prejudice my observations. But when in 1929 Richard Wilhelm laid before me the text to *The Golden Flower*, I decided to publish the results of my observations at least in a fragmentary way. One cannot be careful enough in these matters, for all too many persons snatch at such "magical" themes and apply them externally like a salve, being misled, on the one hand, by a compulsion to imitate and, on the other, by a morbid desire to possess themselves of outlandish feathers and deck themselves in this exotic plumage.

People will resort to any external means, even the most

absurd, in order to escape from their own psyches. They practise Indian yoga of every denomination, observe rules of diet, learn theosophy by heart, pray according to mystic texts culled from the literature of the whole world—all this, because they are dissatisfied with themselves and lack every glimmer of faith that anything useful could come out of their own psyches. In this way the psyche has little by little become that Nazareth from which nothing good can come; and for this reason people seek it in the four corners of the world, the farther off and the more out of the way the better.

I do not mean in any way to disturb such people in their pet occupations. But if someone who wishes to be taken seriously is equally deluded and believes that I apply the methods and teachings of yoga—perhaps even have mandalas drawn—in order to lead my patients to the "right point," then I must protest and accuse these people of having read my writings with positively criminal inattention. They must have deeply ingrained in them the very questionable teaching that all evil thoughts arise from the heart, and that the human soul is the vessel of all wickedness. If this teaching were true, then God must have made an eternally sorry job of creation, and it would really be high time to turn aside with Marcion the Gnostic and give the incompetent demiurge the sack. To be sure, there is no greater ethical convenience than to relinquish to God the sole responsibility for such an idiotic children's home—as they conceive the world to be—where no one is able to put the spoon into his own mouth.

A human being is worth the effort of being concerned with himself, and he harbours within his own psyche that from which something can arise. It is rewarding to observe patiently what happens, quietly, in the psyche, and the most and the best happens when nothing is instilled from without and above by regimentation. I gladly admit that I have such reverence for what happens in the human psyche that I

would be afraid of disturbing and distorting the still ways
of nature by clumsy efforts of my own. But, in this case, I
renounced even the activity of an observer, and entrusted
this duty to a beginner not encumbered with my knowledge
—all this, in order to avoid disturbance. The results, which I
merely make public, are, therefore, the pure, conscientious,
and exact observations of himself by a man of untroubled
intellect, upon whom no one has foisted anything and who
would not allow anything to be foisted upon him. Those
who are really familiar with psychic material will easily
recognize the authenticity and directness of the results. In
the second series of dreams, which follows, we shall best
begin, for the sake of completeness, with an enumeration of
the mandala symbolism in the initial dreams already discussed:

1. (Visual impression) A serpent that describes a
circle around the dreamer. This was the fifth "dream" in
the first series.
2. (Dream) Blue *flower*. This was the seventeenth
dream of the initial series.
3. (Dream) Man with *gold coins* in his hand. *Enclosure* for a variety show. Both these symbols occurred in the
eighteenth dream.
4. (Visual impression) *Red ball,* dream 19, and
5. *Globe,* dream 20.

Dreams: Second Series

6. (Dream) An unknown woman follows him. He
keeps running in a circle.

The serpent in the first mandala dream was anticipative.
It is often the case that a figure personifying a certain aspect
of the unconscious behaves or suffers in a way that will be

the subject's own experience later on. The serpent indicates a circular movement in which the subject himself is afterward involved. This is to say that something perceived as a circular movement takes place in the unconscious, and this happening then presses into consciousness with the result that the subject is himself gripped by it. The unknown woman or anima represents the unconscious, which continues to vex the dreamer until he falls into the circular movement. This in itself supplies a potential centre that is not identical with the ego. But the latter rotates around the centre.

7. (Dream) The anima accuses him of being too little concerned about her. There is a watch there according to which it is five minutes before . . . ?

The situation is much the same; the unconscious disturbs him like an exacting woman. From this there arises the watch, on which the pointer goes around in a circle. Five minutes before . . . means a certain state of tension for any man who lives by the watch, for when the five minutes are up, then one must do this or that. Perhaps, even, one is in a hurry. (As will become clear later on, the symbol of the circle is always accompanied by a feeling of tension.)

8. (Dream) On a ship. He occupies himself with a new method of taking the bearings of a point. Now it is too far, again too near; the right spot is in the middle. There is a map on which is drawn a circle with the centre.

The task presented here is clearly to determine the centre, the correct spot. This is the centre of a *circle*. It occurred to the dreamer as he was writing down a dream that he had dreamed shortly before of *target shooting;* now he shot too high, and again too low. The right aim lay in the middle. Both dreams seemed to him *highly significant.* (Compare what was said above about the Eastern mandalas.) The *target* is a circle with a centre. The location at sea is determined by the celestial bodies apparently *rotating* around the earth.

9. (Dream)   A pendulum clock that keeps on running without the weights sinking.

It is a kind of clock whose hands turn *without ceasing,* there being obviously no loss due to friction; it is, therefore, a *perpetuum mobile,* an eternal circular movement. Here we come upon a "metaphysical" attribute. As observed, I use this word in the *psychological* sense, and not literally. I mean by this that I take eternity as a quality predicated by the unconscious, and not as a hypostasis, a subsistent principle. The statement in the dream is clearly objectionable to the scientific discrimination of the dreamer, but the mandala is able to lend this statement a peculiar significance. Very important things are just as often rejected because they seem to contradict reason and put it to an unbearable test. The movement without friction shows the clock to be cosmic, even transcendental; in any case, it raises the question of a quality that escapes from the time-space dimensions of the psychic phenomenon expressing itself in the mandala. And this denotes something so different from the empirical ego that the gap is difficult to bridge.

10. (Dream)   The dreamer finds himself in the Peterhof in Zurich with the doctor, the man with the pointed beard, and the doll woman. She is an unknown woman who does not speak and is not spoken to. Question: to which of the three does the woman belong?

The tower of St. Peter's in Zurich has a strikingly large clock face. The Peterhof is an *enclosure,* a temenos in the word's truest sense, a place belonging to the church. The *four* find themselves in this enclosure. The circle of the *clock* is divided into quarters like the *horizon*. The dreamer represents his own "*I*"; he of the pointed beard, the intellect as "employee" (Mephisto) ; and the "doll woman" the anima. The doll is an object for the child, and so an apt expression for the non-ego nature of the anima, being further characterized as object by the fact that she "is not spoken to." This negative aspect (also present in dreams 6 and 7 above) points to the deficient relationship between consciousness and the unconscious, as does likewise the question to whom the "unknown woman" belongs. The "doctor" is also a part of the non-ego, and perhaps covers a passing allusion to myself. The man with the pointed beard, on the other hand, belongs to the ego. This situation reminds us directly of the relation in the *scheme of functions*. If we think of the functions of consciousness as arranged in a circle, then the most differentiated function is generally the carrier of the ego, and is usually coupled with an auxiliary function. The so-called "inferior" function, on the other hand, is unconscious and for that reason projected upon a non-ego. It also has an auxiliary function proper to it. It is thus not impossible that the four persons represent the four functions as components of the total personality, including the unconscious. But this totality is ego plus non-ego. Hence the centre of the circle as an expression of wholeness would correspond not to the "I," but to the *self* as epitome of the total personality. (The centre with the circle is also a sufficiently well-known allegory of the nature of God.) In the philosophy of the Upanishads the self is first of all the *personal atman,* but the latter is also the *superpersonal atman* with cosmic and metaphysical qualities.

In Gnosticism, too, we meet with similar conceptions. I may mention the ideas of the anthropos, of the pleroma, of the monads, and of the spark of light in a treatise of the

Codex Brucianus: [15] "This same is he (Monogenēs) who dwelleth in the Monad, which is in the Sētheus, and which came from the place of which none can say where it is . . . From Him it is the Monad came, in the manner of a *ship,* laden with all good things, and in the manner of a *field,* filled or planted with every kind of tree, and in the manner of a *city,* filled with all races of mankind . . . This is the fashion of the Monad, all these being in it. There are twelve Monads as a crown upon its head . . . And to its veil which surroundeth it in the manner of a defence (πύργος) there are twelve Gates . . . This same is the Mother-City (μητρόπολις) of the Only-begotten (μονογενής)."

I must add for the sake of clarity that Sētheus is a name for God designating the *creator.* Monogenēs is the Son of God. The comparison of the Monad to a field and a city corresponds to the idea of a temenos. The Monad is likewise *crowned.* Compare with this the "hat" in the first dream of the first series and the thirty-fifth dream of the second series (I:1 and II:35). As metropolis, the Monad is *feminine,* like the padma—lotus—the basic form of the Lamaistic mandala. (In China, the Golden Blossom; in the Occident, the Rose and the Golden Flower.) In it dwells the Son of God, the created God. (Buddha, Shiva, etc., in the lotus. Christ in the Rose, in Mary's womb. The seeding place of the Diamond Body in the Golden Flower. This theme recurs in the animal transformation in the square enclosure, of the sixteenth dream of this series.)

In the Johannine Apocalypse we meet with the Lamb in the centre of the Heavenly Jerusalem. (The vision of Ezekiel frequently served as a model.) In our text it is also stated that Sētheus dwelt in the holy of holies of the pleroma, a city with four gates. (Similarly in India: the city of Brahma on the World-Mountain Meru.) There is a Monad in each gate.[16] (Compare the Vajra-mandala appended to *The Secret of the Golden Flower,* where the great Dorje is found in the centre surrounded by twelve smaller ones, like the Single Monad crowned with twelve monads. Moreover, there is a Dorje in each of the four gates.) To the four gates of the city correspond the limbs of the anthropos who has arisen from the Autogenēs (the Monogenēs). The Monad is a spark of light (spinther) and an image of the Father, identical with the Monogenēs. An invocation runs: "Thou art the House and the Dweller in the House." [17] The Monogenēs stands upon a τετράπεζα,[18] a table or stage with four columns, corresponding to the quaternion of the Four Evangelists. (Compare Irenæus, III, XI, and Clemens, *Stromat*. V, VI. Likewise the tetramorph as the saddle-beast of the church.)

The idea of the *lapis* is connected at several points with these conceptions. So, according to the *Rosarium*, Hermes has the *lapis* say: *Me igitur et filio meo conjuncto, nil melius ac venerabilius in mundo fierie potest:* [19] "Therefore there can exist nothing nobler and more venerable in the world than I together with my son." The Monogenēs is also called, in the *Coptic Treatise*, p. 87, "the dark light." The *Rosarium* makes Hermes say: *Ego lapis gigno lumen, tenebræ autem naturæ meæ sunt:* "I, the lapis, beget the light, yet the darkness is of my nature."

The following passage in the *Tractatus Aureus* [20] shows an interesting parallel to the Monogenēs who dwells in the bosom of the Mother-City and who is actually identical with the crowned Monad wrapped in the veil: "The King, the Ruler, saith: I am crowned, and I am adorned with a diadem; I am clothed with the Royal Garment, and I bring joy and gladness of heart; for, *being chained to the arms and breast of my mother, and to her substance,* I cause my substance to keep together; and I compose the invisible from the visible, making the occult matter to appear. And everything which the philosophers have hidden will be generated from us."

To be sure, the text does not say that the "King" coin-

cides with the *lapis,* but the characteristics that he ascribes
to himself are those of the *lapis.* What is more, the *lapis* is the
"Master," as appears from the following passage of the
Rosarium: *Et sic Philosophus non est Magister lapidis, sed
potius minister:* "And so the Philosopher is not the master
of the *lapis,* but rather the servant."

The final production of the *lapis* in the form of the
crowned hermaphrodite is called the *Ænigma Regis.* A German stanza referring to the *Ænigma,* runs:

> Hie ist geboren der Keyser aller ehren,
> Kein hoher mag uber jn geboren werden.
> Mit kunst, oder durch die natur,
> Von keiner lebendigen creatur.
> Die Philosophy heissen jn jhren Suhn,
> Er vermag alles, was sie thun.

> "Here is born the glory of every Kaiser,
> Than he none can be born who is higher,
> By any art or yet through nature
> Out of any living creature.
> The Philosophers call him their son,
> He can do all that they have done."

The last two verses could apply directly to the concluding
sentence of the citation from Hermes, given above.

It seems as if the thought had dawned upon the alchemists that the classic (and Christian) conception of the Son
eternally dwelling in the Father and revealing Himself to
humankind as a gift from God was something that man himself could *engender* from his own nature, with the assistance
of God, to be sure (*Deo concedente*). The heresy of this
thought is reason enough for mystification.

The feminine nature of the inferior function springs
from its contamination with the unconscious. Because the
unconscious has feminine traits, it is personified in the *anima*
—that is to say, for man; the case is reversed for woman.

Let us now assume that in this dream and in those preceding it something is actually meant that rightly arouses in the dreamer a feeling of great significance; and let us further assume that this significance corresponds to the viewpoints presented in the commentary; we would then have reached a high point of intuitive introspection that cannot be surpassed in daring. The eternal pendulum clock is in itself a mouthful hard to digest, at least for a consciousness unready to receive it, and it might easily cripple an over-venturesome flight of thought.

11. (Dream) The dreamer, the doctor, a pilot, and the unknown woman are travelling in a flying machine. Suddenly a *croquet ball* shatters the *mirror*, an indispensable instrument of navigation, and the flying machine falls. Here again the question: To whom does the unknown woman belong?

Doctor, pilot, and unknown woman are characterized as parts of the non-ego: all three of them are strangers. Thus the dreamer remains possessed only of the most differentiated function, which is to say that the unconscious has won considerable ground. The croquet ball is part of the game in which a ball is *driven through a wicket* (under the bow). In the eighth dream of the first series (I:8) it was said that one must not go (flying?) over the rainbow, but must go through *underneath*. Whoever goes over it falls down. It seems the flight had been too lofty, after all. The game of croquet is played on the ground and not in the air. Man should not raise himself with the aid of "mental" intuitions above the "earth" of solid reality and thus escape from it, as so often happens when he has brilliant intuitions. He never attains the level of his own longings, and should, therefore, not identify himself with them. Only gods pass over the rainbow bridge, while mortals walk upon the earth and are subject to its laws.

It must be granted that man's earthiness is a lamentable imperfection in view of the possibilities revealed to him by longing. But this very imperfection belongs to his innate being—to man's reality. He consists not only of his highest longings, his loftiest ideas and efforts, but also of the invidious conditions of his being, such as heredity and that ineffaceable sequence of memories that calls out to him, "This you have done, and this is what you are like!" Man has lost his ancient saurian's tail, to be sure, but in its place a chain has been hung upon his soul that binds him to the earth—a positively Homeric chain of "conditions" that are so momentous that it is best to remain linked to them at the risk of becoming neither a hero nor a saint. (In reality, history gives us a certain authorization not to lend absolute weight to these collective patterns.) Our earth-bound quality does not mean that we cannot grow; on the contrary, it is even the *conditio sine qua non* of growth. No lofty, well-grown tree ever disowned its dark roots. In fact, it grows not only upward, but downward as well.

The question of where we are going is certainly of the greatest importance, but equally important, it seems to me, is the question: "Who goes where?" But this "Who?" always leads to the "Whither?" *Greatness* is needed for the lasting possession of the heights; but many a man can surpass himself. It is difficult to hit upon the correct middle point, as is exemplified in dreams of this series. For this, awareness of the second side of man's personality, of its aims and origin, is indispensable. These two aspects must never be separated out of arrogance or cowardice.

The "mirror" as "indispensable instrument of navigation" refers, no doubt, to the *intellect,* for it can think, and is always persuading man to identify himself with his discernments (reflections). In Schopenhauer the "mirror" is a favourite metaphor for the intellect. The latter is aptly characterized by the expression "instrument of navigation," for it is man's indispensable guide on pathless oceans. But when he has lost the solid ground underfoot, and begins to speculate under the misguidance of an intuition roving in boundlessness, the situation becomes dangerous.

12. (Dream) The dreamer finds himself with father, mother and sister in a very dangerous situation on a trolley-car platform.

The fall thus takes him all the way down to childhood, a condition in which a human being is far from being in possession of his wholeness. The family stands for his wholeness, its components being still projected on the members of the family and represented in them. But this is a dangerous condition for the adult, because it is regressive; it means a splitting up of his personality, which the primitive experiences as a threatening "loss of soul." In the break-up, the parts of the personality, once integrated with effort, are again drawn outward. The individual loses his guilt in exchange for an infantile innocence; and now the wicked father is guilty of this and the unloving mother of that. He is caught in this undeniable, causal connection like a fly in a spider's web and does not notice that he has lost his moral freedom. In whatever respect the parents and grandparents have sinned against the child, this the *adult* accepts as a *condition of his own being*, with which he has to reckon.

The fault of another, which can in no way be changed, interests only a blockhead. A man of intelligence learns only from his own faults. He will put the question to himself: "Who am I, that all this happens to me?" He will look deeply into himself to find the answer to this question of fate.

13. (Dream) A treasure lies in the sea. One must dive through a narrow opening. It is dangerous, but down below

one will find a companion. The dreamer ventures the leap in the dark and finds down there a beautiful garden, symmetrically laid out, with a fountain in the centre.

In the sea of the unconscious lies hidden the thing of price that is hard to attain and is reached only by the man of courage. I will conjecture that the jewel is also the "companion," one who goes through life by our side, a close parallel to the self, which is first of all unfamiliar non-ego, and in which a "you" becomes associated with the lonely "I." This is the theme of the miraculous fellow traveller. I will name three celebrated examples: the disciples on the road to Emmaus, the *Bhagavad-Gita* (Krishna and Arjuna), and the eighteenth sura of the Koran (Moses and Chidher). I will further conjecture that the treasure in the sea, the companion and the garden with the fountain are one and the same thing, namely, the *self*. For the garden is again the temenos, and the fountain is the source of "living water" that we know from the parable, and that the Moses of the Koran also sought and found with Chidher [21] beside it, "one of our servants whom we have clothed with our grace and wisdom." And around Chidher, too, according to the legend, the desert ground blossoms with spring flowers. The image of the temenos with the wellspring developed in Islamic architecture, under early Christian influence, into the court of the mosque and the ritualistic washing place located in the centre (Achmed Ibn Tulun in Cairo). We have the same thing in the Occidental cloister with the well in the garden. This is also the "rose garden of the philosophers," of which we know from the alchemistic treatises and which was later pictured in numerous lovely engravings. "The Dweller in the House" (compare the commentary to dream 10 of this series) is the "companion." The centre and the circle, here represented as fountain and garden, are analogues to the *lapis*, which is many things and even a *living being*. Hermes has it say: *Pro-*

tege me, protegam te. Largire mihi ius meum, ut te adiuvem: "Protect me, and I will protect you. Give me my due, that I may help you." Here, therefore, the *lapis* is nothing less than a good friend and aid who helps the one who helps him, and this points to a compensatory relationship. (I must here call to mind what was said in the commentary to dream 10 of this series, especially the analogy: Monogenēs-*lapis*-self.)

The fall to earth thus leads into the depths of the sea, that is, of the unconscious, and so the dreamer attains the protection of the temenos against the splitting of the personality that accompanies the regression to childishness. The situation somewhat resembles I:4 and 5, where the spellbinding circle had to protect him against the attraction of the many-sided unconscious. (The dangers of temptation come to Polifilo in a quite similar way at the beginning of his nekuia.)

The source of life is, like Chidher, a good companion, yet is not without equivocal elements, some painful examples of which good old Moses had to swallow. Indeed, this source is the symbol of the life force that always renews itself, of the clock that never runs down. An uncanonical word of the Master's says: "Whoever is near unto me, is near unto the fire." As this esoteric Christ is a source of fire—surely with a certain relation to the πῦρ ἀειζῶον of Heraclitus—so also the *aqua nostra,* according to the conception of the alchemistic philosophers, is *ignis*—fire. The source is not only the flowing of life, but also its warmth, its heat even, the secret of passion, which always has synonyms related to fire. The *aqua nostra,* which dissolves everything, is an indispensable ingredient for the production of the *lapis.* But the source comes from *below,* and so the way leads *through underneath.* The fiery source of life is only to be found *below.* This "below" is the natural history of man, his causal connection with the world of instinct. Without this union no *lapis* and no self can come into being.

14. (Dream) He goes with his father into a chemist's shop. Valuable things are to be had there at a low price, especially a particular kind of water. His father tells him of the land from which the water comes. Then, in a train, he crosses the Rubicon.

The traditional "apothecary's" with its glass receptacles and pots, its waters, its *lapis divinus* and *infernalis,* and its magisteries, preserves the last perceptible remnant of the slop kitchen of those alchemists who saw nothing in the *donum spiritus sancti,* the costly gift, but the chimera of the transmutation of gold. The "particular water" is literally —if we may say so—the *aqua nostra, non vulgi.* We can easily understand that it is his father who leads him to the source of life, since his father is the natural procreator of his life. We could say that the father represents the land or the ground from which the source of his life arose. The water of life can be had cheaply, for everyone possesses it— without knowing its value, to be sure. *Spernitur a stultis;* it is despised by the foolish because they suppose that every good thing is always outside and somewhere else, and the idea that the source is in their own psyches appears to them nonsense. Like the *lapis,* it is *pretio quoque vilis,* of little price, and therefore, as in Spitteler's *Prometheus, in viam ejectus* by everyone from the high priest and the academicians down to the very peasant—dashed upon the street, where Ahasuerus stuffs the jewel into his pocket. The treasure has sunk again into the unconscious.

But the dreamer has noticed something and with vigorous resolve crosses the Rubicon. He has understood that the flowing and the fire of life must not be underestimated, but are indispensable to the realization of his completeness.

15. (Dream) Four persons are sailing down a river: the dreamer, the father, a certain friend, and the unknown woman.

Inasmuch as the "friend" is a definite person intimately known to him, he belongs, like the father, to the dreamer's conscious ego world. Thus something of great importance has taken place. In dream II:11 the unconscious was three against one; now the proportions are reversed: the dreamer is three against one (the unknown woman). So the unconscious is depotentiated. The reason for this consists in the fact that, through the diving under, what is below has been linked to what is above. That is to say, the dreamer has resolved not to live merely as a bodiless thought-being, but to accept the body and the world of instinct, the reality of the problems of love and life,[22] and to translate them into act. That was the Rubicon, and it was crossed. For individuation, the realization of selfhood, is not just a mental problem, but the problem of life itself.

16. (Dream) Many people are there. All walk around within a square, moving to the left. The dreamer is not in the centre, but on one side. The idea is to reconstruct the gibbon.

Here the *square* appears for the first time. It may well arise from the circle by means of the four persons arranged in a circle. (This will be substantiated later on.) The problem of *squaring the circle* has occupied mediæval minds like the *lapis,* the *tinctura magna,* and the *aurum philosophicum.* The Eastern mandala, particularly the lamaic as it is fixed in dogma, generally contains the square ground plan of a stupa. That this really signifies a *building* can be seen from the mandalas that are executed bodily. By the figure of the square, these convey the idea of a *house* or *temple* or of an inner, walled-in space, like the town and castle in the commentary to II:10.

According to ritual, stupas must always be circumambulated from the right, for left-handedness is evil. Left, the

Latin *sinister,* means the unconscious side. The movement to the left hand means a motion in the direction of the unconscious, whereas movement to the right is "correct" and aims at consciousness. Since in the Orient these unconscious contents have gradually, through long practice, grown into conscious forms that express the unconscious, they must be taken over by consciousness and retained.

In so far as we can judge of it as a firmly established practice, yoga—even in its most modern forms—proceeds essentially in the same way. It impresses upon consciousness established forms of an *a priori* nature. Its most significant Western parallel is the *Exercitium* of Ignatius Loyola, for in a similar way the latter impresses upon the conscious psyche certain fixed conceptions of salvation. This practice is thoroughly "right" as long as the symbol gives valid expression to the unconscious situation. Eastern as well as Western yoga ceases to be psychologically right only when the unconscious process that anticipates future changes of consciousness has developed so far that it produces gradations that are no longer properly expressed by the traditional symbol, or have ceased to be quite consonant with it. In such a case, and only then, can it be said that the symbol has forfeited its "rightness."

This process surely amounts to a gradual shifting of the unconscious view of the world over the course of centuries, and has nothing whatever to do with intellectualistic criticism of this view. Religious symbols are manifestations of life, plain facts, and not intellectual opinions. The fact that water reaches its greatest density at 4 Celsius is an actuality beyond all criticism. If, for a certain period, the church holds fast to the belief that the sun rotates about the earth and then abandons this view in the nineteenth century, it can appeal to the psychological fact that for untold millions of people the sun did rotate about the earth, and that only in the nineteenth century had any considerable number of persons attained the assurance in the use of the intellectual function that enabled them to grasp the evidence for the planetary nature of the earth. Unfortunately there are no truths without persons to understand them.

The left-handed circumambulation of the square may point to the circumstance that the squaring of the circle is a stage on the way to the unconscious—that it is a yantra, a transitional point instrumental in the attainment of a goal lying behind it and as yet unformulated. It is one of the ways to the centre of the non-ego, and this way was taken by the natural research of the Middle Ages, in the production of the *lapis*. The *Philosophus,* one of the Latin sources of the *Rosarium,* says: *Fac de masculo et fœmina circulum rotundum, et de eo extrahe quadrangulum et ex quadrangulo triangulum: fac circulum rotundum et habebis lapidem Philosophorum:* "Out of male and female make a round circle, extract from it a quadrangle and from the quadrangle a triangle: make of this a round circle and you will have the Philosopher's Stone."

For the modern intellect, of course, such things mean plain nonsense. But this valuation in no way cancels the fact that such chains of ideas do occur and have even played an important part for many centuries. It is the part of psychology to *understand* these things and to leave it to the layman to scold about nonsense and obscurantism. Many of my critics, who pretend to be "scientific," behave exactly like the bishop who excommunicated the cockchafers because of their unseemly proliferation.

As relics of the Buddha are often contained in the innermost sanctuaries of the stupas, so, in the interior of the lamaic square and in the Chinese earth-square is found the holy of holies or the magically potent, that is, the cosmic source of energy—the god Shiva, the Buddha, a Bodhisattva, or a great teacher. In Chinese religion it is Kien, Heaven with its four beams of cosmic force. In the Western, Chris-

tian mandala of the Middle Ages, also, the Godhead is enthroned in the centre, often in the form of the triumphant
Saviour with the four symbolic figures of the Evangelists.
Now, the dream symbol presents the strongest contrast to
these highly metaphysical conceptions, for in the centre the
"gibbon," unquestionably an *ape*, is to be reconstructed. We
here meet again with the ape who first turned up in I:22.
He is there the occasion of a panic and of the helpful intervention of the intellect. He is now to be "reconstructed,"
and this has no other meaning than that the anthropoid—
man as an archaic fact—is to be reconstituted. The leftward
way thus plainly does not lead up to the kingdom of the
gods and of eternal ideas, but downward into natural history,
into the animal instincts as the basis of human existence. We
are confronted, therefore, with a Dionysiac mystery—to use
the classic expression.

The square corresponds to the temenos where a theatrical performance is being given, in this case an ape-play
instead of a satyr-play. The interior of the golden flower is
a seeding place where the diamond body is produced. The
synonym "land of the ancestors" perhaps even points to the
fact that this creation arises from an integration of the
ancestral stages.

The ancestral spirits played an important rôle in the
primitive rites of renewal. The natives of Central Australia
even identify themselves with their mythical ancestors of the
Alcheringan age, a kind of Homeric era. Likewise, in pre-
paring themselves for the ritual dances, the Pueblo Indians of
Taos identify themselves with the sun, whose sons they are.
The regressive identification with the human and animal
ancestors means psychologically an integration of the unconscious, actually a bath of renewal in the source of life
where the individual becomes again a *fish*, that is, unconscious
as in sleep, drunkenness, and death. Hence the sleep of incubation, the Dionysiac consecration and the ritualistic death

in the initiation. Of course, these processes always take place at the hallowed spot.

We can easily translate these conceptions into the infantile language of Freudian theory: the temenos is then the mother's womb, and the rite is a regression to incest. But these are the neurotic misunderstandings of persons who have in part remained infantile and do not know that it is a question of things that have at all times been practised by adults, and that it is impossible to explain their activities as mere regression to childishness. If this were not so, the most significant and the highest achievements of humankind would in the end be nothing but perverted childhood wishes, and the word "childish" would have lost its *raison d'être*.

If it is taken seriously, the symbolism of the rites of renewal points beyond the affairs of childhood to the innate psychic disposition that is the result and deposit of the whole ancestral life reaching back to the animal level: hence ancestral and animal symbolism. It is a question of attempts to annul the separation of consciousness from the unconscious, this being the actual source of life, and to bring about a reunion of the individual with the maternal soil of the inherited, instinctive disposition. If such rites of renewal did not have a decided effect, they would have died out in prehistoric times; or rather, they would never have arisen in the first place. But the case before us shows that, even when consciousness is miles away from the ancient conceptions of the rite of renewal, the unconscious still tries to make them accessible to consciousness in dreams. The autonomy and autarchy of consciousness are, indeed, characteristics without which consciousness itself could never have arisen, but they also spell the danger of isolation and barrenness in that they produce, by splitting off the unconscious, an unbearable *remoteness from the instincts*. And the loss of instinct is the well-known source of endless errors and confusions.

The following dream is given unabridged, as in the original text.

17. (Dream) All the houses have about them something of the stage, of the theatre. Movable scenes and decorations. The name of Bernard Shaw stands out. The play is supposed to take place in the distant future. Over one of the wings is written in English and German:

"This is the universal Catholic Church. It is the church of the Lord. Let all who feel themselves to be instruments of the Lord, enter."

Under this is printed in smaller letters: "The Church has been founded by Jesus and Paul"—as if to celebrate the age of a business firm. I say to my friend, "Come, let's have a look at this." He answers, "I don't understand why a lot of people have to be together when they have religious feelings." Then I answer, "As a Protestant you will never understand that." A woman strongly agrees with me. Now I see a kind of proclamation on the wall of the church. It reads:

"Soldiers!
If you feel that you stand in the power of the Lord, avoid addressing Him directly. The Lord cannot be reached by words. We further urgently recommend that you do not start any discussions among yourselves as to the attributes of the Lord. It is unfruitful, for what is valuable and important cannot be said.
Signed: Pope . . . (name unreadable)"

Now we go in. The interior is like a mosque, particularly like the Hagia Sofia. No benches—imposing effect of space, no images. Framed texts as ornament on the wall (like texts from the Koran, in the Hagia Sofia). One of the texts reads: "Do not flatter your benefactor." The woman who agreed with me before bursts into tears and cries, "Then nothing is left." I answer, "I find it quite all right," but she disappears. First I stand in such a position that there is a pillar before me and I cannot see anything. Then I change my

place and see a crowd of people before me. I do not belong
with them and stand alone. But they are clearly presented to
me and I see their faces. They all say in unison, "We confess
to stand in the power of the Lord. The Kingdom of Heaven
is within us." This is spoken very solemnly, three times.
Then the organ is played; a fugue from Bach with a chorale
is sung. But the original text has been omitted. Sometimes
only a kind of coloratura, then repeatedly the words,
"Everything else is paper" (means: does not have a living
effect upon me). When the chorale has faded away, there
begins—in collegiate fashion, so to say—the genial part of
the meeting. Many jovial and solid people are there. We all
go back and forth, speak together, greet one another, and
wine (*from an episcopal seminary for priests*) and refresh-
ments are handed around. We wish the *church* a happy increase and, as if to give expression to the joy at the aug-
mentation of the society members, a loud-speaker plays a
song hit with the refrain: "Charles is with us also now." A
priest explains to me: "These somewhat trivial pleasures are
officially approved and permitted. We must adapt ourselves
a little to the American methods. That is unavoidable with
large-scale operation as we have it. But we distinguish ourselves fundamentally from the American churches by an
outspoken anti-ascetic tendency." Then I woke. Feeling of
great relief.

I must unfortunately refrain from commenting upon
the dream as a whole, and will restrict myself to our theme.
The temenos becomes a sacramental building, corresponding
to the earlier intimation. The action is thus characterized as
"devotional." The grotesque-comical elements of the Dionysiac mystery appear in the "genial" part of the action,
when wine is handed around and toasts are drunk to the
well-being of the church. The floor-inscription of an
Orphic-Dionysiac sanctuary expresses it perfectly: μόνον μὴ

ὕδωρ: only no water! [23] Here I will refer merely in passing
to the Dionysiac relics in the church, the fish and wine symbolism, for example, the cup of Damascus, the cylindrical
seal with the crucifix and the inscription ΟΡΦΕΟC ΒΑΚΚΙ-
ΚΟC, and so forth.

The "anti-ascetic" tendency clearly draws the distinc-
tion from the Christian Church, which is here called "American." This same characterization occurred in dream 14 of
the first series. America is the ideal home of reasonable ideas
produced by the practical intellect, which would like to put
a right countenance on the world by means of a "brain
trust." This conception corresponds to the modern formula,
intellect-spirit, and completely forgets that "spirit" was
never a human "activity," much less a "function." The left-
handed motion thus proves to be a withdrawal from the
world of modern ideas, and, for the time being, something
like a regression to pre-Christian Dionysus worship to which
"asceticism" in the Christian sense is foreign. The development is not thereby wholly removed from the hallowed
place; it remains within it, which is to say that it does not
lose its sacramental character. It does not simply become
anarchic and chaotic, but rather brings the church into
immediate relation with the sanctuary of Dionysus, as indeed the historic process has done, though in the reverse
direction. It can, therefore, be said that the regressive development faithfully follows the historic way to reach the
pre-Christian level. It is not a backsliding, but what we
might call a systematic descent *ad inferos*, a psychological
nekuia.

I have found something very similar in the dream of a
clergyman who had a somewhat problematic attitude to his
faith: "He comes at night into his church. There the whole
wall of the choir has fallen together. The altar and the ruins
are grown over with *vines* that are full of *grapes,* and
through the opening that has been made shines the *moon.*"

Mithras has a connection with the early church similar to that of Dionysus. The dream of a person who was also occupied with religious problems goes as follows: "Immense Gothic cathedral, almost completely dark; High Mass is being celebrated. Suddenly the whole wall of the transept collapses. Blinding sunlight streams into the interior of the church, and with it a large herd of bulls and cows." This version is clearly more Mithraic.

In our dream, interestingly enough, the church is a syncretistic structure, for the Hagia Sofia is an ancient Christian church that served as a mosque until recently. The aim of the dream is well served when a combination of Christian and Dionysiac religious ideas is attempted in this edifice. The intention is clearly to bring this about in such a way that the one does not exclude the other, that no values are destroyed in the process. This is a very important tendency, for the reconstruction of the "gibbon" is to take place at this spot. Such a sacrilege would easily allow the dangerous surmise that the left-handed movement is a *diabolica fraus* and the gibbon the *devil,* for the devil is regarded as the "ape" of God. The leftwardness would then be a "distortion" of divine truth to the end of putting his Black Majesty in the place of God. But the unconscious has no such blasphemous intentions; it is simply trying to restore to the world of religion the lost Dionysus who is somehow lacking to modern man—think of Nietzsche! The end of the twenty-second dream of the first series, where the ape first appears, runs: "*Everything* must be ruled by the light"— and so also, we may add, must the Lord of Darkness with horns and goat's feet, actually a Dionysiac corybant who has rather unexpectedly attained the honors of a grand duke.

18. (Dream)   A square space. Complicated ceremonies take place in it, having as their purpose the transformation of animals into men. Two serpents that hurry in opposite

directions must be removed at once. Some animals are there, such as foxes and dogs. Again the dreamer goes around in the square, and in each of the four corners must allow himself to be bitten in the calves by these animals. If he runs away, all is lost. Nobler animals now come into existence, bulls and wild goats. Four snakes go into the four corners. Then the assembly goes out. Two sacrificial priests carry a huge reptile. This is touched to the forehead of a still unformed animal hulk, or *life mass*. There now arises from it a human head, whose aspect is resplendent. A voice calls, "These are attempts at being."

The dream goes on to occupy itself with what might almost be called the "explanation" of the happenings in the square enclosure. Animals are to be changed into men; a still unformed "life mass" is to be transformed into a "resplendent" (illumined) human head through magical contact with a reptile. The bestial life mass, no doubt, stands for the totality of the inherited unconscious, which is to be joined to consciousness. This happens through the ceremonial use of a reptile, presumably a snake. The conception of transformation and renewal by means of a serpent is a well-substantiated archetype. It is the serpent of salvation representing the god. It is told of the mysteries of Sabazios that: *Coluber aureus in sinum demittitur consecratus et eximitur rursus ab inferioribus partibus atque imis:* "A consecrated golden serpent was dropped into the bosom, and then removed from the inferior and lowest parts"—Arnobius. For the Ophites, Christ was the serpent. Surely the most significant development of the serpent symbolism in the sense of a renewal of the personality is to be found in the Kundalini yoga. The shepherd's experience with the snake in Nietzsche's *Zarathustra* would accordingly be a fatal omen (and not the only one in his text: see the prophecy at the death of the rope dancer).

But for this transformation to come about there is an indispensable condition: the *circumambulatio,* that is, the exclusive concentration upon the *centre,* the place of creative transformation. In the process we are "bitten" by the animals; we have to expose ourselves to the animal impulses of the unconscious without identifying ourselves with them and without running away, for the flight from the unconscious would defeat the purpose of the procedure. We must hold our ground.

In the case before us, the process set going by self-observation must be experienced in all its sudden reversals and be joined to consciousness by understanding as best one can. Naturally this means an all but unbearable tension arising from the extraordinary incommensurability of conscious life with the unconscious process. The latter can be experienced only in inner feeling, and may at no point touch the visible surface of life. The principle of conscious life is: *nihil est in intellectu, quod non antea fuerit in sensu:* "There is nothing in the mind that was not first in sensation." But the principle of the unconscious is the autonomy of the psyche reflecting in its play of images not the world but *itself,* although it borrows from the world of sense the materials of perception and uses them to make its images clear. In this activity, however, the sense datum is not a *causa efficiens;* rather, it is *autonomously* chosen and borrowed, with the result that the reasonableness of the cosmos is constantly impaired in the most painful way. Yet the world of sense has just as destructive an effect upon the inner, psychic processes when it breaks in upon them as a *causa efficiens.* If, on the one hand, reason is not to be offended and, on the other, the creative play of images is not to be suppressed in an abrupt and violent way, there is need of a synthetic procedure that is foresighted and circumspect enough to accomplish the paradox of uniting what cannot be united. Hence the alchemical parallels in the dreams before us.

Hardly do consciousness and the unconscious touch each other, when their contradictory elements fly asunder. Thus at the very beginning of the dream the snakes that hurry in opposite directions must be removed: the conflict between conscious and unconscious is at once ended by determination, and consciousness is forced to perform the *circumambulatio* and to bear the tension. But the spellbinding circle whose course is thus followed also prevents the unconscious from breaking through into the outer world; such an eruption would equal a psychosis. We can say with the philosopher of the *Rosarium: nonnulli perierunt in opere nostro*: "not a few have perished in our undertaking." The dream shows that the difficult operation—to think in paradoxes—has succeeded; and this is possible only for a superior intellect. The snakes no longer run away, but arrange themselves in the four corners, and the process of change or integration succeeds. The transfiguration and illumination, the conscious recognition of the centre, has been attained, or at least anticipated by the dream. This achievement, if it is more than potential and can be maintained—that is, if consciousness does not again fall out of connection with it—means a renewal of the personality. Since this is a subjective state whose real existence cannot be demonstrated by any external criterion, every further attempt at description and explanation is fruitless, and only he who has had this experience is in a position to grasp and to substantiate its actuality. For example, "happiness" is so strikingly real that there is no one who does not wish for it, and yet there is not one single objective criterion according to which this state can be shown to be unquestionably and necessarily present. The simple truth is that, in the most important things, we must often "sign off" with a subjective judgement.

The arrangement of the snakes in the four corners points to a disposition of the unconscious. It is as if a pre-existent ground plan were given, a kind of Pythagorean τετρακτύς.

I have often observed the number four in this connection. It probably explains the world-wide dissemination and the magical significance of the cross and the circle divided into four parts. In the case before us it seems to be a matter of laying hold upon and regulating the animal instincts, so that the danger of becoming unconscious is exorcized. This may perhaps be the empirical basis of the cross that conquers the powers of darkness.

In this dream the unconscious has doubtless forged strongly ahead and has thrust its contents into dangerous proximity to consciousness. The dreamer seems to be deeply enmeshed in the secret, synthetic ceremony and will not fail to carry a significant remembrance of this dream into his conscious life. Experience shows that a strong conflict thus arises for consciousness, because it is not always inclined or in a position to make the unusual intellectual and moral effort needed to endure a paradox seriously. Nothing is so jealous as a truth.

As a glance at the history of the mediæval mind will show, our whole modern mentality has been preformed by Christianity. The truth of this fact has nothing to do with our current faith or lack of faith in the truths of Christianity. The reconstruction of the ape in the hallowed enclosure, proposed in the dream, is so disturbing that most people run away from it and protect themselves by failing to understand. Some will quite heedlessly pass by the abyss of the Dionysiac secret and seize upon the rational, Darwinistic element to save themselves from mystic exaltation. Only the very few will feel the collision of two worlds and understand what, at bottom, the question is. Yet the dream says plainly that the ape must arise in the place where, according to old tradition, the Godhead dwells. This exchange is almost as bad as a Black Mass.

In Eastern symbolism the square space as earth (Chinese) and as padma (lotus, Indian) has the character of the yoni, feminality. A man's unconscious is feminine and is personified by the anima. She also represents the *inferior function,* so called, and often has a morally dubious character; she frequently stands for evil itself. As a rule, she is the *fourth person*—see the tenth, eleventh, and fifteenth dreams of this series. She is the dreaded, dark, maternal womb, which is of ambivalent nature. The Christian Godhead is One in Three Persons. The fourth person in the heavenly drama is unquestionably the devil. In the harmless, psychological version he is the inferior function. According to moral valuation he is a man's sin; therefore, a function belonging to him and hence masculine. The femininity in the Godhead is kept secret, and to say that the Holy Ghost is Sofia counts as a heresy. The metaphysical drama of Christianity, the "Prologue in Heaven" in *Faust,* has only masculine performers, a point which it shares with many early mystery rites. Femininity must surely be somewhere; so it is presumably to be found in the dark. At any rate, the old Chinese philosophy has placed it there, in the yin.[24]

Although man and woman unite, they nevertheless represent incompatible opposites that may degenerate into deadly enmity when they are activated. This primeval opposition represents symbolically all conceivable oppositions that may occur, as warm-cold, light-dark, south-north, dry-wet, good-bad, etc. In the masculine psyche it also represents the opposition conscious-unconscious. According to the study of the functions in psychology, two of them, the differentiated function and its auxiliary function, are conscious and, therefore, masculine; in dreams they are pictured, for instance, as father and son; the unconscious functions, on the other hand, as mother and daughter. Since the contrast between the two auxiliary functions is nowhere nearly so great as between the differentiated and the inferior function, it is possible for the third function—that is, the unconscious "auxiliary"—to be raised to consciousness and thus become masculine. But it will bring with it something of its contamination with the inferior function, and so form a certain link with the darkness of the unconscious. It was quite in line with this psychological fact when the Holy Ghost was taken as Sofia according to the heretical interpretation, for the Holy Ghost was the mediator of the birth in the flesh, and thus made it possible for the luminous Godhead to become visible in the darkness of the world. It was this connection that aroused the suspicion that the Holy Ghost was feminine, for Mary was the dark earth of the field, *illa terra virgo nondum pluviis rigata:* "that virgin soil not yet watered by the rains," as Augustine called her.

The fourth function is contaminated with the unconscious and, when it is made conscious, draws the whole unconscious in its train. Then we come to a settlement with the unconscious and must attempt to bring about a synthesis of the opposites. But first of all there breaks out the violent conflict that would beset any reasonable man when it became evident that he must swallow the most absurd superstitions. All his faculties would rise in arms, and he would desperately defend himself against what appeared to him to be murderous nonsense. The following dreams can be explained in the light of this situation.

19. (Dream)   Ferocious war between two peoples.

This dream represents the conflict. Naturally, consciousness defends its position and tries to suppress the unconscious. The first result of this is that the fourth function is forced out; but as it is contaminated with the third, this also threatens to disappear. Matters would thus return to the state that preceded the present one, a state in which only two functions are conscious, while the other two fall back into the unconscious.

20. (Dream)   In a cave are two boys. A third falls in, as if through a pipe.

The cave represents the darkness and seclusion of the unconscious. The two boys correspond to the two functions located in the unconscious. In theory, the third would be the auxiliary function, which would point to the fact that consciousness has withdrawn completely into the differentiated function. The match now stands at 1 to 3, and this gives the unconscious a great preponderance. We may, therefore, expect a new advance of the unconscious and a return to its former position. The "boys" point to the *theme of the dwarfs*. Of this, more later.

21. (Dream)   A large transparent ball that contains many small balls. A green plant grows out of the top.

The ball is a whole that embraces all contents; life that has been brought to a stop by useless struggle is thus made possible again. In the Kundalini yoga the "green womb" is a designation for Ishvara (Shiva) emerging from his latent condition.

22. (Dream)   In an American hotel. He rides in the elevator to about the third or fourth floor. There he has to wait with many others. A friend (a definite person) is there and says he (the dreamer) should not have kept the dark, unknown woman below waiting so long, he should have put her in his charge. He now gives him an unsealed note directed to the dark woman. On it is written: "Salvation does not come from not going along or from running away. Nor does it come from letting oneself be carried along without willing. Salvation comes from complete self-surrender, and one's gaze must be directed upon a centre." On the margin of the note was a drawing: a wheel or wreath with eight spokes.

Now an elevator boy comes and says that his (the dreamer's) room is on the eighth floor. He rides in the elevator to about the seventh or eighth floor. There stands an unknown, red-haired man who greets him in a friendly way. Now a change of scenery takes place. Apparently there is a revolution in Switzerland. A military party is carrying out propaganda for "completely throttling left." To the objection that left is feeble anyhow, the answer is made that this is just why left is to be wholly throttled. Now soldiers appear in old-fashioned uniforms and they all resemble the red-haired man. They load their guns with ramrods, stand in a circle, and prepare to shoot at the centre. But they do not shoot, after all, and seem to march away. He awakes in great fear.

While in the previous dream there was indicated a tendency towards the restoration of completeness, in this dream an obstacle is again presented by consciousness, in that it is directed elsewhere. The dream fittingly plays against an American background. The elevator goes upward, and this is proper if anything from the "sub"-conscious is to come "up" into consciousness. It is the unconscious content that here comes up, the mandala characterized by the number 4. That is why the elevator should run to the fourth floor. But since the fourth function is taboo, it runs only approximately to the third or fourth. This happens not only to the dreamer, but to many others besides, and they must wait, like him, until the fourth function can be accepted. A good friend calls his attention to the fact that he should not have caused the dark woman—the anima who represents the taboo function—to wait "below," that is, in the unconscious. It was just for this reason that he had to wait above with the others. In fact, it is not merely an individual, but a collective problem, for the animation of the unconscious that has become noticeable in recent times, as Friedrich Schiller foresaw, has given rise to questions that the nine-

teenth century did not dare to dream of. In *Zarathustra,*
Nietzsche decided to reject the snake and the "ugliest man"
and thus to expose himself to a heroic constraint of consciousness that led consistently to the collapse foretold in the
selfsame book.

The advice on the note is as profound as it is apt, and
there is positively nothing to add to it. After the advice has
been given and somehow accepted by the dreamer, the journey upward can continue. We must assume that the problem
of the fourth function has been accepted, at least in general,
for the dreamer now comes to the seventh or eighth floor, so
that the fourth function is represented no longer by a quarter, but by an eighth, and seems thus reduced by half.

Curiously enough, this hesitation before the last step to
completeness seems also to play a part in the second part of
Faust. It is a question of the scene of the Cabiri: "resplendent
sea women" come across the water. Nereids and tritons sing:

> What we bring in our hands
> Shall give you all joy.
> From the giant shield of Chelone
> Shines an austere figure:
> They are gods whom we bring;
> You must now sing lofty songs.

Sirens:
> Small in stature,
> Great in power,
> The saviours of the shipwrecked,
> Gods honoured from of old.

Nereids
and
Tritons:
> We bring the Cabiri,
> To celebrate a peaceful feast;
> For where they hold hallowed sway
> Neptune's rule will be friendly.

An "austere figure" is brought by "sea women," that is,
by feminine figures that represent to a certain degree the
unconscious as ocean and ocean wave. The "austere" reminds

us of "severe" architectonic or geometrical forms that present a definite idea without Romantic (feeling-toned) accessories. It "shines" from the shell of a tortoise, which is a primitive, cold-blooded animal like the serpent, and symbolizes the primeval instincts of the unconscious. The "figure" is somehow identical with the unseen, creative dwarf gods, the hidden ones that are kept in the dark cista, but who also appear as little figures about a foot high and stand upon the sea, where, as relatives of the unconscious, they protect navigation, the venture in darkness and uncertainty. For this reason, as Dactyls, they are also gods of invention, small and insignificant, it is true—like the stirrings of the unconscious—but also as mighty as it. *El gabir* is the great, mighty one (Arabian *akbar* for kabira = great).

Nereids and Tritons:	Three we have brought with us, The fourth would not come. He said, he was the right one, Who thought for all of them.
Sirens:	One god makes the other An object of derision. Honour all gifts of grace, Fear every harm.

It is significant of Goethe's sentient nature that the fourth is just the thinker. If "feeling is all" must count as a first principle, then thinking must content itself with an unfavourable rôle and be submerged and disappear. Faust, Part I, portrays this development. No doubt, Goethe himself stood model for it. In this case thinking becomes the fourth (taboo) function. Through contamination with the unconscious it takes on the grotesque form of the Cabir, for the Cabiri, being dwarfs, are chthonic gods and generally deformed. ("I look upon the misshapen shapes as ware that's badly earthen.") Thus they stand in grotesque contrast to the heavenly gods and hold them in derision.

Nereids and Tritons:	There are seven of them in truth.
Sirens:	Where have the three remained?
Nereids and Tritons:	We know not how to say,
	Must be sought for in Olympus;
	There lives the eighth as well
	Whom no one thought of yet.
	Inclined to favour us,
	And yet none ready.
	These incomparable ones
	Press always on,
	Yearning hungerers
	For the unattainable.

We learn that there are "in truth" seven or eight of them, but there is again a difficulty with the eighth, as earlier with the fourth. Contradicting the earlier emphasis placed on their origin from the lower, dark regions, it now appears that the Cabiri are actually to be found in Olympus; since they are eternally striving upward from below, they are probably always to be met with both below and above. The "austere figure" is clearly an unconscious content that always presses towards the light. It seeks, and is itself, what I have designated in *The Psychology of the Unconscious* as the "precious object hard to attain." This assumption is at once borne out:

> The heroes of eld
> Are in want of fame,
> However resplendent
> When they attained the Golden Fleece,
> You, the Cabiri.

The "Golden Fleece" is the longed-for goal of the Argonauts' voyage, the adventurous quest that is one of the numerous synonyms for the attaining of the unattainable.

Thales has this wise remark to make about it: "This is

what men long for: It is the rust that gives value to the coin."

Indeed, the unconscious is always the hair in the soup, the anxiously concealed lack of perfection, the painful lie given to all idealistic pronouncements, the remnant of earth that clings to human nature and sadly clouds the crystal clarity that it longs for. According to the alchemistic conception, rust and verdigris are the sickness of metal. And yet this very scurf is the *vera prima materia,* the basis for the preparation of the philosophical gold. The *Rosarium Philosophorum* says: *Aurum nostrum non est aurum vulgi. Quæsivisti autem de viriditate, putans quod æs esset corpus leprosum propter illam viriditatem quam illud, quod est perfectum in ære, est illa sola viriditas, quæ in ipso est, quia illa viriditas vertitur per nostrum magisterium cito in verissimum aurum nostrum:* "Our gold is not the gold of the multitude. But you have asked concerning the verdigris, deeming the metal a leprous body on account of this greenness, rather than holding what is perfected in the metal to be the sole vitality that is in it, because this verdigris is quickly changed by our magistery into our truest gold."

The *viriditas* is sometimes called "azoth" as well, and this, among other things, is one of the numerous synonyms for the *lapis.*

The paradoxical remark of Thales, that only the rust gives its true value to the coin, is a kind of alchemistic paraphrase, and simply means that there is no light without shadow and no psychic completeness without imperfection. To round itself out, life calls, not for *perfection,* but for *completeness.* For this "the barb in the flesh" is needed, the suffering of imperfection without which there is no forward or upward.

Returning now to our dream, we find at the critical place, on the seventh or eighth floor, the man with the red hair. This is a synonym for "the man with the pointed beard," the clever Mephisto who magically transforms the scene because he is concerned about what Faust never saw, the "austere figure," which means the highest jewel, the "incorruptible." He changes himself into the soldiers, the representatives of uniformity, of collective opinion, which last is, of course, entirely against putting up with inexpedient things. It follows the highest authority in holding 3 and 7 as sacred; but 4 and 8 are evil, "ware that's badly earthen," "nothing but" inferiority that has no standing in the severe judgement of the bonzes of every hue. "Left" is to be "wholly throttled"; this means the unconscious side and everything suspicious that comes from the left, from the unconscious. This opinion is, of course, old-fashioned and resorts to old-fashioned means, but muzzle-loaders can still hit the mark. For reasons unknown, or not given in the dream, nothing comes of this destructive attempt against the "centre" upon which (as the advice ran) "one's gaze must be directed." In the drawing on the margin of the note this centre is portrayed as a wheel with eight spokes.

23. (Dream) In the square space. Opposite the dreamer sits the unknown woman, and he should be drawing her portrait. Yet what he draws is not a face, but three-leaved clovers or distorted crosses in four different colors: red, yellow, green, and blue.

In connection with this dream the dreamer spontaneously draws a circle whose quadrants are tinted with the above colours: a *wheel with eight spokes,* containing a blue flower with four petals in the centre. He produced numerous other drawings at short intervals, all of them dealing with the curious structure of the "centre" and arising from the need to discover the configuration that would give adequate expression to the nature of the "centre." Some of the drawings are based upon visual impressions, some upon sentient intuition, and some upon dreams.

The facts show that the conception of the "centre," which the unconscious again and again brought near to consciousness, now begins to gain a foothold in the latter and to exercise a peculiar fascination upon it. The next drawing is again the blue flower, but this time divided into eight; then follow pictures of four mountains around a crater lake. Also one showing a red circle on the ground, a barren tree standing within it, and on the tree a green snake twining itself upward with a leftward motion.

A serious concern with this problem is probably somewhat puzzling to the layman. Some knowledge of yoga and of the mediæval philosophy of the *lapis* would assist him in understanding. The squaring of the circle, as was mentioned in that connection, is one of the methods for producing the *lapis*; another is the use of the *imaginatio*, as the following text from the *Rosarium* clearly proves: *Et nota, quod ianua tua bene et firmiter sit clausa, ut ille, qui est intus, evolare non possit, et Deo concedente, ita pervenies ad effectum. Natura facit suam operationem paulative: ego vero volo quod tu ita facias, imo secundum naturam tua sit imaginatio. Et vide secundum naturam, de qua regenerantur corpora in visceribus terræ. Et hoc imaginare per veram imaginationem et non phantasticam:* "And see to it that your door is well and firmly closed, so that what is within may not fly away, so with God's help you will attain the result. Nature performs her operations by slow degrees; in truth, I would have you do the same: let your imagination be wholly according to nature. And observe according to nature, by which bodies are regenerated in the bowels of the earth. And you must imagine this with a true, and not a fantastic, imagination."

The alchemistic precautionary rule, which occurs so frequently, the enjoining of the *vas bene clausum*, is equivalent to the spellbinding circle. In both cases the inner is to be protected from the intrusion and admixture of the outer, as it is also to be prevented from escaping. The *imaginatio* is here taken as a real and literal *power of making images* according to the classic use of the word, and is contrasted to "fantasy," which designates a mere "conceit" in the sense of unsubstantial thought. In Petronius the meaning is more pointed still: *phantasia non homo* denotes facetiousness. The *imaginatio* is an active evocation of (inner) images *secundum naturam,* an actual achievement of thought or conception. It does not "spin fantasies" out into empty space without plan and without support, which is to say that it does not play with its objects. Rather, it tries to grasp the inner truth of images faithfully copied from nature. This activity is called an *opus,* a work. And we must surely say that the dreamer's manner of handling these objects of inner experience is nothing less than a true *work,* considering the conscientious, exact and careful notation and expansion of the content accruing to consciousness from the unconscious. The resemblance to the *opus* is surely obvious to anyone familiar with alchemy. Moreover, the dreams bear out the analogy, as dream 24 will show.

The dream before us, from which the drawings just mentioned arose, gives not a hint that the left side has been in any way "throttled." On the contrary, the dreamer finds himself again in the temenos confronted by the unknown woman who personifies the fourth function, called "inferior." His drawing has been anticipated by the dream, and the dreamer repeats in the form of an *abstract ideogram* what the dream presents under a personification. This may well afford us a hint that the *meaning* of personification is a symbol for something that can also be represented in quite another form. This "other form" reaches back to dream 16 in the first series, the *ace of clubs,* whose analogy with the *cross* of unequal arms was there pointed out. The analogy is here verified. I tried to sum up the situation then existing in the formula: Christian Trinity modulated, coloured or over-shadowed by the four (colours). Now the colours appear as a concretion of the τετρακτύς. In a citation from the *Tractatus Aureus,* the *Rosarium* makes a similar statement: *Vultur* [25] . . . *clamat voce magna, inquiens: "Ego sum albus niger et rubeus citrinus"* : "The vulture . . . cries in a loud voice, saying: 'I am the white that is black and the red that is yellow.' "

As to the *lapis,* it is pointed out that it unites in itself *omnes colores.* We might, indeed, surmise that the fourfold-ness represented here by the colours is to a certain extent a preliminary stage. This is substantiated by the *Rosarium: lapis noster est ex quatuor elementis;* also the *Aurum Philosophicum: in auro sunt quatuor elementa in æquali proportione aptata.* The fact is that the four colours in the dream also represent the transition from threefoldness to fourfoldness and thus to the quadripartite circle, which most closely accords with the nature of the *lapis* according to the alchemistic conception, because of its roundness (perfect simplicity). This is why a recipe for the preparation of the *lapis,* ascribed to Raymundus, says: *Recipe de simplicissimo et de rotundo corpore, et noli recipere de triangulo vel quadrangulo sed de rotundo: quia rotundum est propinquius simplicitati quam triangulus. Notandum est ergo, quod corpus simplex nullum habens angulum, quia ipsum est primum et posterius in planetis, sicut sol in stellis (Rosarium)*: "Take of a body that is most simple and round, and do not take of a triangular or quadrangular body, but of a round one: because the round is nearer to simplicity than the triangular. For it is to be noted that a simple body has no angle, because it is the first and last among the planets, like the sun among the stars."

24. (Dream) Two persons are speaking about crystals, especially about a diamond.

At this point it is difficult not to think of the idea of the *lapis*. This dream actually exposes the historic undercurrents and intimates that we are really dealing here with the question of the sought-for *lapis,* the "precious thing hard to attain." The dreamer's *opus* amounts to an unconscious repetition of the endeavours of the mediæval *lapis* philosophy. (For further remarks concerning the "diamond" see dreams 37, 39, 44, and 50 in this series.)

25. (Dream) It is a question of constructing a centre and of making the figure symmetrical by reflections at this point.

The word "constructing" points to the synthetic nature of the *opus* and to the laboriousness—if we may use the term—of the building process that taxes the dreamer's energy. The "making symmetrical" is an answer to the conflict in dream 22 of this series. ("Wholly throttle the left.") The one side must fully correspond to the other as a mirror image, and this image arises in the "centre," which thus appears to have the property of reflection; it is a *vitrum,* a crystal or a surface of water. The act of reflecting seems again to point to the underlying conception of the *lapis,* the *aurum philosophicum,* the elixir, the *aqua nostra,* etc.

Since "right" denotes consciousness, its world and principles, so the "reflection" undertakes to turn the picture of the world around to the left, so that a correspondence in the reversed sense arises. We could also say: after reflection, right appears as a reversal of left. Thus left appears to have the same validity as right; the unconscious and its arrangement, which for the most part is beyond our understanding, symmetrically completes consciousness and its contents, although it is not clear what mirrors itself and what is mirror image. To carry out this train of inference, it is possible to regard the "centre" as the point of intersection of *two worlds that correspond but are reversed in the mirror.*

The idea of symmetrization would thus signify a high point in the recognition of the unconscious and its incorporation in a general picture of the world. The unconscious here attains *cosmic character*.

26. (Dream) Nighttime, starry sky. A voice says, "Now it will begin." The dreamer asks, "What will begin?" To which the voice answers, "The circular course can begin." A shooting star now falls in a curious leftward curve. The scene changes: the dreamer is in a questionable place of amusement. The keeper of the house, who appears to be an unscrupulous exploiter, and girls in fallen circumstances are there. There is a quarrel about right and left. Then the dreamer leaves and drives in a taxicab around the perimeter of a *square*. Then again the bar. The keeper of the house says, "What the people said about right and left did not satisfy my feelings. Is there really a right and left part of human society?" The dreamer answers, "The existence of the left does not contradict that of the right. Both are in every man. Left is the mirror image of right. Always, when I feel it as a *mirror image*, I am at one with myself. There is no right and no left part of human society, but there are *symmetrical* and *crooked* persons. The crooked ones are those who can realize only the *one* side in themselves, the left *or* the right. They are still in a childhood state." The keeper of the house says meditatively, "Now that's much better," and goes again about his business.

I have given this dream in detail because it shows in an excellent way how the ideas hinted at in dream 25 were received by the dreamer. The conception of the symmetrical relation is stripped of its cosmic traits and is translated into psychology with the help of social symbols. "Right" and "left" have been used almost as political catchwords.

The cosmic aspect is present at the beginning of the dream. The dreamer noticed that the curious curve described by the shooting star exactly corresponded to a line that he drew when he sketched the picture of the flower divided into eight parts, as described in connection with the twenty-third dream. The curve forms the edge of the flower petals. We might, therefore, say that the shooting star traces the outline of a flower that is spread over the whole starry heaven. It is the *circulation of the light* that begins here. This *cosmic* flower corresponds to the rose in Dante's *Paradiso*.

In that it pictures an "inner" experience that can be understood only as a psychic event, the cosmic nature of the flower is objectionable and at once provokes a reaction from "what is down below." The cosmic aspect is obviously too "high," and is compensated "downward," so that the symmetry is no longer that of two pictures of the world, but only of human society or of the dreamer himself. When the keeper of the house comments upon this psychological insight, "Now that's much better," he is expressing a recognition whose conclusion should run, "But not yet good enough."

The quarrel about right and left that first arises in the public house is a conflict that breaks out in the dreamer himself when he is called upon to recognize the symmetry. He cannot do it, for the reason that the other side seems so dubious that he would rather not inspect its mirror image too closely. The magical circumambulation (the driving around the square) takes place in order that he should remain within and not run away, but rather learn to bear his mirror image. He does this as best he can, yet not in the way the other side wishes. Therefore, the rather cool recognition of his deserts.

27. (Visual impression) A circle; in the middle a green tree. In the circle a raging fight among savages is taking place. They do not see the tree.

The conflict between right and left has obviously not ended. It goes on because the savages are still in a "childhood state" and, being "crooked," know only either right or left.

28. (Visual impression) A circle: within it steps lead up to a basin in which are fountains.

When a condition is not satisfactory, in that an essential aspect of the unconscious content is lacking to it, then the unconscious process reaches back to earlier symbols, as is here the case. The symbolism returns to dream 13 of this series, where we met with the mandala-garden of the philosophers with the fountain of the *aqua nostra*. Circle and basin emphasize the mandala, which in mediæval symbolism is the rose. The "Rose Garden of the Philosophers" is a favourite alchemistic symbol.

29. (Visual impression) A bouquet of roses, then the sign ≢ : but it should be ✳ .

The bouquet of roses is like a fountain that spreads as it rises. The meaning of the first sign—possibly a tree—is unclear, whereas the correction presents the flower divided into eight parts. An emendation is here made to an error that in some way impairs the completeness of the *rosa*. And in order that it may be restored, the problem of the mandala —the correct valuation and interpretation of the centre— must again draw close to consciousness.

30. (Dream) He sits at a round table with the dark, unknown woman.

When a process has reached a culmination as regards either its clarity or the wealth of inferences that can be drawn from it, a regression is always likely to follow. The dreams that lie between those that I have cited clearly show that the challenge of completeness flung at the dreamer frightens him somewhat, for if he takes it up there will follow far-reaching practical results whose personal nature lies outside the scope of our study.

The roundness of the table points again to the circle of completeness, and the anima belongs to it as the representative of the fourth function, especially in her "dark" form, which always makes itself noticeable when something should be concretized—that is, when something should be translated, or threatens to translate itself, into reality. "Dark" is chthonian, that is, earthy and actual. This is also the source of the fear that causes the regression.

31. (Dream)   He sits with a certain man, whose characteristics are repellent, at a round table. On it stands a glass filled with a gelatinous mass.

As against the preceding one, this dream denotes a step forward inasmuch as the "dark" element is accepted as his *own* "darkness," thus giving rise to a proper shadow that personally belongs to the dreamer.

Although I may not enter here upon a full discussion of the psychology of dreams, a few clarifying remarks are called for. The sitting together at one table means relationship, connection, "composition." The round table here means the composition of wholeness. If the anima figure (the personified unconscious) is separated from the ego-consciousness, and therefore unconscious, this fact means that there exists an isolating layer of the personal unconscious located between the ego and the anima.

The existence of a personal unconscious shows that

contents belonging to the person, which actually could be conscious, are unjustifiably unconscious. Therefore, we have a deficient or non-existent consciousness of the shadow. The shadow, as we saw in earlier chapters, corresponds to a negative ego-personality; it embraces all those characteristics whose existence is found to be painful or regrettable. In this case shadow and anima, being unconscious, are contaminated with each other, a state that is represented in dreams as "marriage" or the like. If now the existence of the anima (or of the shadow) is accepted and understood, a separation of the two figures results, as has happened in the case before us. The shadow is recognized as an ego-adjunct, and the anima as not belonging to the ego.

In this way the anima is relieved of the low moral values that were projected on her, and can take up the creative and living function that is properly her own. This is well represented by the glass with the curious contents, which we—and the dreamer also—compare with the undifferentiated "life mass" of dream 18. There is a question of the gradual transformation of primitive, animal elements into human attributes. We may expect something similar here as well, for it seems as if the spiral of inner development had come around to the same angular degree, though on a higher level.

The glass corresponds to the *unum vas* of alchemy, and its content to the living, half-organic mixture from which the body of the *lapis,* endowed with spirit and life, will emerge. Other parallels are the memorable figure in Goethe's *Faust,* Part II, that three times over dissolves into fire: the Boy Charioteer, the Homunculus that is shattered against the throne of Galatea, and Euphorion. (Dissolution of the "centre" in the unconscious.) It is well known that the *lapis* is not only a "stone," for it is expressly stated in the *Rosarium* that it is put together *de re animali, vegetabili et minerali,* that it is *compositus . . . ex corpore, anima et spiritu,* and *crescit ex carne et sanguine. Ideo dicit Philoso-*

phus, portavit eum ventus in ventre suo. Planum est ergo ventus est aer et aer est vita et vita est anima. Lapis est res media inter perfecta et imperfecta corpora et quod natura ipsa incoepit, hoc per artem ad perfectionem ducitur. " 'Therefore,' says the Philosopher, 'the wind carried it in its belly. And it therefore is plain that the wind is air and air is life and life is soul'. The *lapis* is an intermediary between perfected and imperfected bodies, and what nature herself begins, this is carried to perfection by art." And in addition *dicitur lapis invisibilitatis.*

The dream certainly deals with the question of bringing the "centre" to life, reality, or—as we might say—to birth.

32. (Dream)   He receives a letter from the unknown woman. She writes that she has pains in her womb. A drawing is attached to the letter that looks somewhat like this:

In the primeval forest are many monkeys. Then an outlook opens upon extensive glaciers.

The womb is the center, the life-giving vessel. The *Rosarium* says: *Unus est lapis, una medicina, unum vas.* As the Grail is the life-giving vessel itself, so the stone is the *elixir vitæ.*[26] The drawing contains the spiral with the vessel as its centre. The serpentine line clearly leads to the vessel, and we thus have an analogy to the *serpent of healing* of Æsculapius (*medicina*), as also to the Tantric symbol of the Shiva bindu, the creative, latent god unextended in space, who, in the form of the point or of the linga, has the Kundalini snake coiled around him three and a half times.

Moreover, as I could easily show, this is a relatively common *individual* symbol. As the ape and the primeval forest appeared in second series' dream 16 and first series' dream 22, and led up to "the light that should rule everything" in dream 23 of the first series, and to the "glorified" head in dream 18 of the second series, so at the end of this dream an outlook is opened upon white "glaciers" that remind the dreamer of a previous dream—not included in this chapter —in which he sees the Milky Way, and in which a conversation about *immortality* takes place. The glacier symbol is, therefore, the bridge that again leads across to the *cosmic aspect*—to the aspect that was the occasion for the regression. But as is nearly always the case, things do not here repeat themselves in so simple a fashion as it would seem at first glance; rather, they bring with them a new complication that is no less repugnant to the intellectual consciousness than was the cosmic aspect, though it was to be expected on grounds of consistency. This complication is the memory of the conversation concerning immortality. The *pendulum clock,* which is a *perpetuum mobile,* already hinted at this theme in dream 9 of this series. Immortality is a clock that never runs down, a mandala that revolves eternally like the heavens. Thus the cosmic aspect returns with compound interest. That might easily prove too much for the dreamer, as a scientific stomach has limited digestive powers.

Indeed, the unconscious puts forth a confusing abundance of designations for that obscure thing that we call a mandala or the "self." It seems almost as if we were about to go on dreaming the century-old dream of alchemy, like the unconscious itself, and to continue piling new synonyms on the mountain of the old, only to know as much or as little about it in the end as did the ancients. I will not enlarge upon the significance of the *lapis* to our forefathers, or of the mandala to the Lamaists and Tantrists, the Aztecs and Pueblo Indians, or yet of the "golden pill" to the Taoists, or

of the "golden seed" to the men of India. We know the texts
that give us a living picture of all this. But what does it mean
when the unconscious of a cultured European stubbornly
persists in putting forth such abstruse symbolism? The
psychological viewpoint is the only one I am able to apply in
this case. (There may be others that I do not sufficiently
understand.) From this standpoint, everything that can be
brought together under the general concept of the "mandala" seems to me to express the essence of a definite attitude.

The known attitudes of consciousness have describable
aims and purposes. The attitude that consists of a centring
of the attention upon the self is the only one that has no
specifiable aim and no conceivable purpose. It is easy to say
self, but what is meant by it remains clouded in metaphysical darkness. To be sure, I have previously defined the self as
the totality of the conscious and unconscious psyche. But
this whole is boundless, a true *lapis invisibilitatis*. For, in so
far as the unconscious exists, it is not describable; existen-
tially it is a mere postulate, and nothing whatever can be
predicated as to its possible contents (except those of the
conscious sort). Wholeness is only experienced in its parts
and in so far as these are contents of consciousness; as wholeness it necessarily transcends consciousness. The "self," conse-
quently, is a purely delimiting concept, somewhat like Kant's
"thing-in-itself." Yet it is an idea that, in empirical ways, is
constantly elucidating itself, as our dreams show—without
losing anything of its transcendence, however.

Since it is impossible for us to have any information as
to the limits of something that escapes our knowledge, we
are not in a position to set any limits to the self. It would be
arbitrary and, therefore, unscientific to restrict the self to
the bounds of the individual psyche, quite apart from the
essential fact that we are not acquainted with these bounds,
since these also lie in the unconscious. We can, of course, in-

dicate the boundaries of consciousness; but the unconscious is simply the unknown pysche, and is boundless because it is undeterminable.

This being the state of affairs, we should not be in any way surprised if the empirical manifestations of unconscious contents bear the traits of boundlessness and undeterminability in space and time. In all times and places this is the quality of the numen and is, therefore, alarming to a careful consciousness that knows the value of precisely delimited concepts. We are glad that we are neither philosophers nor theologians and do not have to confront such numena within our own academic field. But it is all the worse when it becomes increasingly clear that numena are psychic entities that force themselves upon consciousness, in that, night after night, our dreams philosophize on their own. Even more: if we try to avoid these numena, and angrily reject the alchemistic gold proffered by the unconscious, then it is an empirical fact that we fare badly and may even develop symptoms, in violation of all common sense; while as soon as we return again to the stumbling block and make of it—even in a hypothetical way—a cornerstone, then the symptoms disappear and everything goes "inexplicably" well.

In this dilemma it might seem that we could console ourselves with the idea that the unconscious is a necessary evil with which we have to reckon, and that it is wiser to accompany it on some of its curious wanderings among symbols, even when their meaning is thoroughly questionable. We might deem it consonant with good health to repeat once more "the lesson of earlier humanity," in Nietzsche's phrase.

To such intellectual expedients I can only object that they often do not hold up in the face of actual events. For we actually can observe that in the course of some years the entelechy of the self asserts itself to such a degree that consciousness must rise to a much higher level of achievement than this in order to keep pace with the unconscious.

What, then, we can ascertain about the mandala symbol today is this: that it represents an autonomous psychic fact known through manifestations that are continually being repeated, are everywhere to be met with, and are always identical. It seems to be a kind of nuclear atom about whose inner structure and final meaning we know nothing. We may also regard it as the real—that is, the effective—mirror image of an attitude of consciousness, an attitude that can state neither its aim nor its purpose, and *whose activity, because of this renouncement, is completely projected upon the virtual centre of the mandala. This cannot happen except under compulsion, and the compulsion always attaches to a situation in which the individual does not know how to help himself in any other way.*

As to its being a merely static psychological reflection, this is contradicted not only by the dynamic nature of the symbol, which occasionally announces itself with overwhelming spontaneity in dreams and visions, but also by the autonomous nature of the unconscious itself, which is not only the original form of psychic activity, but is also that psychic state that we traversed in early childhood and that we return to every night. There is no evidence for the assertion of a merely reactive (reflex) activity of the psyche. This is at best a biological working hypothesis of limited validity. When it is raised to a general truth it is nothing but a materialistic myth, for it overlooks the creative power of the psyche, which—whether we like it or not—exists, and in face of which all so-called *causæ* are mere occasions.

33. (Dream)   A fight among savages in which acts of bestial cruelty occur.

As was to be foreseen, the new complication—immortality—has started a raging conflict.

34. (Dream) Conversation with a friend. The dreamer says to him, "I must persevere before the bleeding Christ and carry on the work of redeeming myself."

Like 33, this dream points to a subtle, unusual suffering caused by the incursion of a strange, hardly acceptable spiritual world; hence the analogy to the tragedy of Christ: "My kingdom is not of this world." It also betrays to us the fact that from now on the dreamer is in deadly earnest about working at his task.

35. (Dream) An actor throws his hat at the wall, where it looks like this:

As shown by certain materials not presented here, the actor points to a particular fact in the personal life of the dreamer. Up to now he had maintained a certain fiction about himself that prevented him from taking himself seriously. The fiction is not compatible with the serious attitude he has now attained. He must abandon the actor, for it was this man who rejected the self. The hat refers to the first dream in the initial series, where it is a *strange* hat that he places on his head. The actor throws the hat against the wall, and the hat proves to be a mandala. The "strange" hat was, therefore, the self, which at that time, when he was still playing a fictitious rôle, seemed foreign to him.

36. (Dream) He rides in a taxicab to the Rathaus-platz, but it is called the Marienhof.

I only mention this dream in passing because it shows the feminine nature of the temenos. *Rosa mystica* is one of the attributes of the Virgin in the Laurentian Litany (also *vas*, see dream 32 in this series).

37. (Dream) Curves outlined with light, around a dark centre. Then a wandering in a dark cave. There a fight between good and evil takes place. There is also a prince who knows everything. The prince presents him with a ring containing a diamond and puts it on the fourth finger of his left hand.

The circulation of light that began in dream 27 of this series comes in again more clearly. The light always denotes consciousness, and here it first runs along the periphery. The centre is still dark. It is the dark cave whose entrance is obviously again the cause of conflict. But it is like the prince who stands over all and knows everything, being also the possessor of the precious stone. The gift means nothing less than the dreamer's vow to the self, for the ring finger of the left hand usually wears the marriage ring. To be sure, left is the unconscious, from which one might infer that the situation is still for the most part covered by unconsciousness. The prince seems to be the representative of the *ænigma regis*. Compare the commentary to dream 10 in this second series.

38. (Dream) A circular table, four chairs around it. Table and chairs are empty.

This dream confirms the above surmise. The mandala is not yet "in use."

39. (Visual impression) He falls into the depths. At the bottom is a bear whose eyes shine successively in four colours: red, yellow, green, blue. He really has four eyes that change themselves into four lights. The bear has disap-

peared. The dreamer goes through a long dark passage. Light shimmers at the end. There lies a treasure, and on it the ring with the diamond. Of this the saying goes that it will lead him far to the east.

This waking dream shows that the dreamer is still occupied with the dark centre. The bear stands for the chthonian element by which he might be seized. But then it appears that the bear is a preliminary phase of the four colours (compare II:23) that form a transition to the *lapis*, namely, the diamond, in whose play of colour all the tints of the rainbow are contained. The way to the east, no doubt, points to the unconscious as an antipode. According to the legend, the stone of the Grail comes from the east and must return thither. In alchemistic parlance, the bear corresponds to the *nigredo* of the *materia prima*.

40. (Dream) Under the guidance of the unknown woman he must discover the pole at the greatest risk of life and limb.

The pole is the point around which everything turns.

41. (Visual impression) Yellow balls that run around in a circle, to the left.

This presents the rotation around the centre, reminding us of a preceding dream in this series, number 21.

42. (Dream) An old master shows him a spot on the ground with red light on it.

The *philosophus* shows him the "centre." The redness might connote the dawn.

43. (Dream) In a fog a yellow light like the sun becomes visible, but it is murky. Eight rays go out from the

centre. It is the point that is to be pierced; the light should thrust itself through, but this has not yet quite happened.

The dreamer himself notices the identity of the piercing point with the pole in dream 40. As we surmised, it is a question of the appearance of the sun, which now becomes yellow. But the light is murky—unquestionably an allusion to the deficiency of understanding.

44. (Dream) In a square enclosure in which he must hold still. It is a prison for Lilliputians or children (?). An ill-natured woman guards them. The children start to move and begin to circulate around the periphery of the enclosure. He would like to run away, but may not. A child changes into an animal that bites him in the calf.

The lack of clarity demands a further effort of concentration. For this reason he finds himself still in a childhood state (therefore "crooked," see II:26), and is imprisoned in the temenos under the care of an ill-natured mother-anima. The animal appears as in II:18 and he is bitten; that is, he must expose himself and pay a *price* for it. The circumambulation means, as always, the concentration upon the unconscious centre. He finds this state of tension almost unbearable. But he awakened with the strong and agreeable sense of a solution, "as if he held the *diamond* in his hand." The "children" connote the theme of the dwarfs that perhaps expresses "Cabiric" elements: unconscious formative powers. This we shall return to in dream 56.

45. (Dream) A drill ground. Troops are there, but they are no longer equipping themselves for war. Instead, they form a star with eight beams rotating to the left.

The essential point here, no doubt, is that the conflict seems to be surmounted. The star is not in the sky and is not a diamond, but a configuration on the ground formed by human beings.

46. (Dream) Imprisoned in the square enclosure. Lions and a wicked sorceress appear.

The chthonian prison does not release him because he is not yet ready to translate something into reality, as he should. It is a question of an important personal affair or duty, rather, and one that raises considerable doubt in his mind.

47. (Dream) The wise old man shows him a spot upon the ground that is marked out in a particular way.

This is no doubt the spot upon the earth where the dreamer belongs if he is to realize his own self.

48. (Dream) An acquaintance receives a prize because he has dug up a potter's wheel out of the ground.

The potter's wheel rotates on earth (compare II:45) and produces earthen—earthly—vessels, which, in a metaphorical sense, we can perhaps call human bodies.

49. (Dream) A rotating star-shaped figure. At the cardinal points of the circle are pictures that represent the seasons of the year.

As it was the place that was previously designated, so now it is the *time*. Place and time are the most general and indispensable elements in every determination. The determination of time and place was emphasized at the very beginning. Compare dreams 7, 8, and 9 in this group.

50. (Dream) An unknown man gives him a precious stone. But a gang of Apaches falls upon him. He runs away

(fear-provoking dream) and is able to save himself. The un-known woman says to him later that this will not always be the case. There would be a time when he might not run away, but would have to hold his ground.

When the particular time is added to the particular place, then one is approaching reality at a rapid pace. Hence, the gift of the precious stone, and also the fear in face of the decision, which robs him of his determination.

51. (Dream)   There is great tension. Many people are circulating around a large rectangle in the middle and four small rectangles that are constructed on the sides of the large one. The circulation goes leftward around the large rectangle and rightward around the small ones. In the centre is the star with the eight rays. In each of the centres of the four small rectangles is placed a bowl containing, re-spectively, red, yellow, green, and colourless water. The water rotates to the left. There arises a question that causes anxiety: whether the water is sufficient?

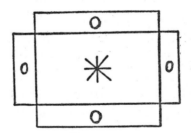

The colours point once again to the preliminary stage. The "anxious" question is whether there is enough *water of life—aqua nostra*, energy, libido—on hand to reach the ker-nel. In the centre the circulation still goes to the left: a movement of consciousness towards the *unconscious*. The centre is not yet sufficiently illuminated. The right-handed circulation around the small rectangles, which represent the four (functions), seems to suggest that the four functions are becoming conscious. The four (functions) are generally distinguished by the four colours of the rainbow. But the *blue is strikingly absent* here, and the square ground plan has been suddenly abandoned. The horizontal has extended itself at the cost of the vertical. We are, therefore, dealing with a mandala that may be called "distorted." It must be observed by way of criticism that there is as yet no antithetical arrangement of the functions; that is to say, the nature of the functions is not as yet so conscious that their peculiar contrariety could be recognized. The preponderance of the horizontal over the vertical denotes the dominance of the ego-consciousness, through which something of height and depth is forfeited.

52. (Dream)   A rectangular dance hall. Everyone goes leftward around the periphery. Suddenly the command is shouted, "To the kernels!" But the dreamer must first go into the next room to crack some nuts. Then the people climb down rope ladders to the water.

Actually, the moment seems to have arrived to press forward to the "kernel," but he must go into the small rectangle ("next room") ; that is, he must first crack a few problem-nuts in one of the four functions. Meanwhile the process goes on downward to the "water." The vertical is thus prolonged and a square again arises from the incorrect rectangle. It is the square that expresses the complete symmetry of conscious and unconscious with everything that the symmetrization of conscious and unconscious means in psychology.

53. (Dream)   He finds himself in an empty, square space that is describing a rotation. A voice calls, "Don't let him out. He won't pay the tax."

This refers to the insufficient realization of himself in the personal affair already mentioned, which in this case is an essential condition of individuation and cannot be avoided. As was to have been expected, after the preparatory emphasis of the vertical in the preceding dream, the square is now reconstituted. The cause of the disturbance lay in appraising the challenge of the unconscious (the vertical) too cheaply, so that a levelling down of the personality (the recumbent rectangle) was brought about.

After this dream the dreamer worked out six mandalas in which he tried to determine the right length of the vertical, the "circulation" and the distribution of colours. At the end of this work came the following dream:

54. (Dream)   I came into a particular, *hallowed house,* the "house of the gathering." In the background are numerous candles that are arranged in a peculiar form with four points running upward. Outside, at the door of the house, stands an old man. People go in. They do not talk, and stand motionless in order to collect themselves inwardly. The man at the door says of the visitants of the house, "As soon as they come out again, they are clean." Now I go into the house myself and am able to concentrate fully. Then a voice speaks: "What you do is dangerous. Religion is not a tax that you can pay to enable you to dispense with the image of the woman, for this image is indispensable. Woe to them who use religion as a substitute for another side of the life of the soul; they are in error and will be accursed. Religion is no substitute, but is to be added to the other activity of the soul as a completion. *Out of the fullness of life shall you bring forth your religion; only then will you be blessed!*" While the last sentence is being spoken in especially loud tones, I hear distant music, simple harmonies upon an organ. Something about it recalls the "fire

magic" theme of Wagner. As I now go out of the house I see a burning mountain and feel: "The fire that is not quenched is a holy fire" (Shaw: *Saint Joan*).

The dreamer notes that this dream was a "strong experience" for him. In truth, the dream has the quality of the numen, and we will therefore not go wrong in assuming that it represents a new summit of insight and understanding. Indeed, the "voice" has as a rule the character of absolute authority and generally presents itself at decisive moments.

The house surely corresponds to the square that is a place of "gathering." The four shining points in the background again denote the four. The remark about the cleansing refers to the transforming function of the taboo enclosure. The production of wholeness, which is prevented by the "flight from the tax," naturally calls for the "image of the woman," since as "anima" it represents the fourth, "inferior" function, feminine because it is contaminated with the unconscious. In what way this "tax" is to be paid depends upon the nature of the inferior function as well as of its auxiliary, and also upon the attitude-type. The achievement can be concrete as well as symbolic in nature. But as to which is the valid form, this decision does not rest with the dictates of consciousness.

The view expressed in the dream that religion may not be a substitute for "another side of the life of the soul" surely spells for many persons a striking innovation. According to this conception, religion is equated with completeness; it even appears to express the integration of the self in the "fullness of life."

The soft chiming in of the fire magic, the Loki theme, is not inappropriate, for what does the "fullness of life" mean? What is the significance of "completeness"? It would seem to me that there are reasons enough here for some anxiety, since a human being as a whole throws a shadow. It was not for nothing that the fourth was separated from the three and banished to the kingdom of everlasting fire. But does not an uncanonical saying of the Master declare, "Who is near unto me, is near unto the fire"? [27]

Such terrible ambiguities are not for grown-up children, and, even of old, people named Heraclitus the "dark one" because he said things that were too plain, and called life itself an "eternally living fire." This is why there are uncanonical sayings for those who can hear plainly; and—last but not least—this is why even the Bible is on the *Index*.

55. (Dream)   A silver dish with four cracked nuts at the cardinal points.

This dream shows how the problems have been disposed of from 52 on. To be sure, they are not completely settled. The goal so far attained is represented by the circle divided into four, whose quadrants are tinted with the four colours. The circulation is leftward. Justice is done to symmetry in this way, but the contrariety of the functions is still unrecognized, in spite of the enlightened dream 54. From this circumstance we must conclude that the "realization" meets with strong inner resistance, partly of a philosophic and ethical nature, having a certain historical justification that is not easily put aside.

56. (Dream)   Four children carry a large, dark ring. They go in a circle. The dark, unknown woman appears and says she will come again, just now it is the festival of the solstice.

The elements of dream 44 are here united again: the children and the dark woman, who was the bad witch before. The solstice indicates the turning point. The children, the dwarf gods, bring the ring.

57. (Visual Impression) The dark ring. In the centre an egg.

58. (Visual impression): Out of the egg comes a black eagle and seizes in his beak the ring that has turned to gold. The dreamer is on a ship and the bird flies before it.

The eagle denotes the heights. Previously it was the depths; people who climb down to the water. He seizes the whole mandala and thus takes the dreamer under his guidance. Carried by a ship, the dreamer sails after the bird. Birds are thoughts and flights of mind. Usually it is fantasies or intuitive ideas that are represented in this way—the winged Mercury, genii, and angels. The ship is the vehicle that carries him over the sea and the depths of the unconscious. As a human construction the ship has the meaning of a system, method or way; compare Hinayana and Mahayana, the small and great vehicle, the two forms of Buddhism. The flight of thought precedes, the methodical elaboration follows after. A man cannot tread upon the rainbow bridge like a god, but must travel across underneath with whatever tools of afterthought he may have at his command. The eagle—synonyms: vulture, raven—is a well-known alchemistic symbol. Even the *lapis*, the *rebis* (made out of two parts, and thus often hermaphroditic, as a coalescence of Sol and Luna) is frequently represented with wings, in this way standing for premonition—intuition. All these symbols in the last analysis depict the state of affairs that we call the self, in its rôle of transcending consciousness. This visual impression is like a snapshot of an unfolding process that leads to the next stage.

59. ("Great vision") There is a vertical and a horizontal circle, having a common centre.

This is the world-clock. It is supported by black birds. The vertical circle is a blue disk with a white edge, divided into $4 \times 8 = 32$ parts. On it revolves a pointer. The horizontal circle consists of four colours. Upon it stand four little men with pendulums, and around it lies the ring that was formerly dark and is now golden (previously carried by the four children).

The "clock" has three rhythms or beats:

The *small* beat: The pointer of the blue, vertical circle advances 1/32.

The *middle* beat: A complete revolution of the pointer. At the same time the horizontal circle advances 1/32.

The *great* beat: 32 middle beats make a revolution of the golden ring.

This curious vision made the deepest and most lasting impression on the dreamer; it was an "impression of the greatest harmony," as he himself puts it. The world-clock is certainly the "austere figure" that is identical with the Cabiri, that is, the four children or four little men with the pendulums. It is a *three-dimensional* mandala; one, therefore, that has attained substantiality and realization. Unfortunately, the discretion required of a doctor forbids my communicating the biographical details. The simple statement must suffice that this realization did actually take place.

Why the vision of this curious figure should give the impression of "greatest harmony" is in one way hard to understand; in another, when we consider the texts that furnish a basis for historical comparison, it is easy to conceive. It is hard to feel our way into the matter because the meaning of the figure is so excessively dark. And when the meaning is incomprehensible, while form and colour have no regard for æsthetic claims, then neither the understanding nor the sense of beauty is satisfied, and we cannot feel in what way the impression of "greatest harmony" could arise. We can only venture the hypothesis that disparate and incongruous elements have combined themselves in the most fortunate way in this figure and have produced an image that realizes to a high degree the "intentions" of the unconscious. We must assume that the picture is the particularly happy expression of an otherwise unknowable psychic fact that could manifest itself up till now only in seemingly disconnected aspects.

The impression is extremely abstract. One of the ideas that underlie it seems to be that two heterogeneous systems intersect by sharing a common centre. If, as heretofore, we start with the assumption that the "centre" and its circumference represent the totality of psychic being, and thus the self, then the figure tells us that in the self two heterogeneous systems intersect, having to each other a functional relation determined by laws and regulated by "three rhythms." The self is by definition the centre and the circumference of the conscious and unconscious system. The regulation of its function by "three rhythms" is something that I cannot support by documentary evidence. I do not know what the rhythms allude to. But I do not doubt for a moment that a valid allusion exists. Since the figure has a cosmic aspect (world-clock!), I must surmise that it is a paraphrase or perhaps even a spontaneous intimation of space-time; in any case, that it is an adumbration of space-time, of a mathematical and, therefore, four-dimensional nature, but only given to perception in a three-dimensional projection. I do not wish to lay too great a weight on this train of argument, as the interpretation of the figure would considerably overtax my present understanding.

As regards the comparative interpretation from history, we are in a more fortunate position—at least as to the general aspects of the subject. First, we have at our disposal the mandala symbolism of three continents; secondly, the special *time symbolism of the mandala* as it developed, particularly in the west, under the influence of astrology. The horoscope itself is a mandala (a clock) with a dark centre and a leftward *circumambulatio* with "houses" and planetary phases. The mandalas of ecclesiastical art, especially the floor mandalas before the high altar and beneath the transept, often employ the circle of zodiacal beasts or the seasons. A related idea is that of the identity of Christ with the calendar of the church, of which he is both the stationary pole and the life. The θεὸς χριστός as υἱὸς τοῦ ἀνθρώπου is a projection of the individual self in the form of a symbolic figure, a plain anticipation of the idea of the self. From this fact arises the Gnostic (Ophitic) blending of Christ with the serpent of the Agathodaimon, and the Horus symbolism as it still showed itself in the Middle Ages in the well-known portrayal: the Christ throned in the mandala with the symbols of the four Evangelists, the three animals and the angel, corresponding to Horus the Father with his four sons, or Osiris with the four sons of Horus.[28] For Horus is also a ἥλιος ἀνατολῆς,[29] and Christ was honoured as such by the early Christians.

We find a peculiar parallel in the works of Guillaume de Digulleville, prior of the Cistercian monastery of Chalis, a Norman poet who, independently of Dante, composed three "Pélerinages" between 1330 and 1335: *Le Pélerinage de la Vie Humaine, de l'Ame et de Jésus Christ.*[30] The last hymn of the *Pélerinage de l'Ame* contains a vision of paradise. This consists of seven large spheres each of which contains seven smaller ones. All the spheres rotate, and this movement is called *siècle—sæculum.* The heavenly *siècles* are the prototypes of the earthly centuries. The angel who guides the poet explains to him: *Quand la sainte Eglise dans ces oraisons ajoute: "in sæcula sæculorum," il ne s'agit point du temps de là-bas, mais de l'éternité.* At the same time, the *siècles* are spherical spaces in which the blessed dwell.

Siècles and *cieux* are identical. In the uppermost sky, which is of pure gold, the king is seated upon his circular throne that shines more brightly than the sun. A crown (*couronne*) of precious stones encompasses him. Beside him upon a circular throne of brown crystal is seated the queen who pleads for the sinners, Mary as the wife of God.

"While gazing at the golden sky, the pilgrim perceived a marvellous circle that seemed to be three feet across. It came out of the golden sky at a certain point and entered it again at another and it followed the whole course of it." This circle is of the colour of the sapphire, *blue*. It is a small circle with a diameter of three feet, that clearly moves like a rolling disk over the large circle. The large circle intersects with the golden circle of the sky.

While Guillaume is absorbed in this sight, there suddenly appear three spirits clothed in purple, with golden crowns and girdles, and they enter the golden heaven. This moment, the angel tells him, is *une fête,* like a church festival on earth. "This circle that you see is the calendar—

> Which in running its whole course
> Shows of the saints their days
> When they must be celebrated.
> Each makes one round of the circle,
> Each star is for a day,
> Each sun for the space
> Of days thirty or zodiacal."

The three figures are saints whose feast day is just being celebrated. The small circle that enters the golden sky is three feet wide, and it is three figures that make their sudden ingress into heaven. They signify the moment of time in eternity, like the circle of the calendar. But just why the "calendar" has a diameter of three feet, and why there are three figures, remains unexplained. We naturally recall the three rhythms of our vision that are set going by the movement of the pointer on the blue circle and that come into the system as inexplicably as the calendar circle into the golden sky.

The guide now continues to inform Guillaume about the meaning of the signs of the zodiac from the point of view of sacred history, and closes with the remark that the feast of the Twelve Fishermen will be celebrated in the Sign of the Fishes; they, therefore, appear before the *Trinity*. Then it suddenly occurs to Guillaume that he has never rightly understood the Trinity, and he asks the angel for an explanation. The angel answers: "Now, there are *three principal colours: green, red and gold.* These three colours are seen to be united in many a work of watered silk and in the feathers of many birds, such as the peacock. The all-powerful king who puts three colours into unison, can he not also bring it about that one substance is three?" The regal colour of gold is ascribed to God the Father, the red to God the Son, because he has spilled his blood, and to the Holy Ghost the green, "the colour that verdures and comforts." Thereupon the angel warns him not to inquire further, and disappears. But Guillaume awakes and finds himself in his bed, and so ends *Le Pélerinage de l'Ame.*

But we must still ask something: "Three there are, where does the fourth remain?" Why is blue missing? It was just this colour that was missing in the "distorted" mandala of our dreamer. Curiously enough, the "calendar" that intersects the golden circle is blue, as likewise the vertical circle in the three-dimensional mandala. We surmise that "blue," standing for the vertical, means height and depth (the blue sky above, the blue sea below), and that the shortening of the vertical lines makes the square into a horizontal rectangle, bringing with it something like an inflation of consciousness; that the vertical, therefore, corresponds to the unconscious. But for man the unconscious has feminine characteristics. Blue is the traditional colour of the Virgin's celestial cloak. In busying himself with the trin-

ity and threefoldness of the *roy,* Guillaume has forgotten
the *reyne.* Faust prays to her in these words:

> "Highest ruler of the world!
> Grant me in the blue
> Outspread tent of the sky
> To gaze upon your secret."

It is inevitable that, for Guillaume, the blue should
be missing from the tetrad of the rainbow colours, because
it is feminine in nature. And like woman herself, the anima
means the height and depth of man. Without the blue vertical circle the golden mandala remains a bodiless, two-di-
mensional thing, a merely abstract picture. Only the interference of time and space in the here and now makes reality.
Completeness becomes real only in the moment, that moment that Faust searched for during a lifetime.

The poet Guillaume did, indeed, suspect the heretical
truth when to the king he joined a royal spouse who is seated
upon an earth-brown crystal. For what is the sky without
Madam Earth? And how can man attain his completion if
the royal spouse does not plead for his black soul? It is she
who understands darkness, for has she not brought her
throne, the earth itself, into the sky with her, albeit as a
delicate metaphor? She adds the missing blue to gold, red,
and green and forms the harmonious whole.

The vision of the "world-clock" is neither the last nor
the highest in the development of the symbols of the objective psyche. But it concludes about the first third of the
material that consists of some 400 dreams and visions. This
series is noteworthy because it describes in an unusually
complete way a psychic fact that I had observed long before
in many individual cases. We owe it not only to the completeness of the objective material, but also to the care and
sharp-sightedness of the dreamer, that we are placed in a
position to follow the synthetic work of the unconscious

step by step. The troubled course of this synthesis would doubtless have been presented much more thoroughly if I had included in the investigation the 340 dreams that occurred in among the 59 notations treated here. Unfortunately, this was not possible, because the dreams reach to some extent into the intimate circumstances of the dreamer's personal life and so could not be made public. Therefore, I had to restrict myself to the impersonal materials.

I trust that I have succeeded in throwing some light upon the development of the symbols of the self, and in mastering to some degree the serious difficulties inherent in materials drawn from experience, like these. At the same time, I am fully aware that the matters adduced in comparison, which are necessary for the explanation and supplementation of the subject, might have been multiplied several times. But so as not to overburden the meaning I have exercised the greatest reserve in this respect. As a result, there is much that is only hinted at, and this is not to be taken as a sign of superficiality. I believe myself to be in a position to offer detailed evidence for my opinions. But in saying this I do not wish to create the impression that I presume to have said anything final on this highly involved subject.

To be sure, it is not the first time that I have treated of a series of spontaneous manifestations of the unconscious. I have done it once before in my book, *Psychology of the Unconscious,* but in that case I dealt rather with a problem of neurosis—puberty—while this is a broader problem involving individuation. Moreover, there is an important difference between the personalities in question. That earlier case, which I never saw at first hand, ended in a psychic catastrophe—psychosis. But the present case represents a normal development such as I have often observed in persons of superior mentality.

But what is particularly noteworthy in this case is

the consistency in the development of the central symbol. We can hardly avoid the impression that the unconscious process moves in a spiral path around a "centre" that it slowly approaches, the "properties" of the "centre," meanwhile, showing themselves always more clearly. We could also put it the other way around and say that the central point, unknowable in itself, acts like a magnet upon the disparate materials and processes of the unconscious and, like a crystal grating, catches them one by one. So we find that, in other cases, the centre is often represented by the *spider in its web,* especially when the conscious attitude is still predominantly one of fear of the unconscious processes. But if the way is opened to the process as happened in this case (objectively and subjectively), then the central symbol forces its way with unrelenting consistency through the apparent chaos of the dramatic entanglements of the personal psyche. In doing so, it constantly renews itself. Thus, in the epitaph of the great Bernoulli, it is said of the spiral: *Eadem mutata resurgo.* Representations of the centre as a spiral are accordingly frequent, as for instance the serpent coiled around the creative point, the egg.

Yes, it seems as if the personal complications and the dramatic, subjective climaxes that make up the quintessence of life and its whole intensity were but hesitation or timid shrinking before the finality of this strange or uncanny process of crystallization, when, indeed, they do not appear to be meticulous objections to it and petty distractions. One often has the impression that the personal psyche chases around this centre like a shy animal, fascinated and frightened at the same time, always running away and yet always approaching.

I hope that I have given no occasion for the false belief that I have any knowledge of the nature of the "centre," for it is simply unknowable—at least for me—and can only be expressed symbolically in phenomenal forms, as is the case—one might add—with every object of experience. Among the properties peculiar to the centre I have always been struck by the phenomenon of fourfoldness. That it is not "simply" a question of "four," as for instance the four cardinal directions or something of that kind, is shown by the fact that there often arises a rivalry of three and four, particularly in the cases of men, whether by chance or not I do not know. Likewise, though not as often, there is a rivalry of four and five, and the rare mandalas with five rays, mainly in the cases of women, are shown to be abnormal by their lack of symmetry. It thus seems as if a clear insistence upon four were the normal thing, or as if there were statistically a greater probability for the four.

Now—and I should not suppress this observation, surely —it is a curious *lusus naturæ* that the chief chemical component of an organic body is carbon, characterized by a valence of four; it is well known, moreover, that the "diamond" is a carbon crystal. Carbon is black—coal, graphite— but the diamond is "clearest water." Such an analogy would be a lamentable intellectual offence if the phenomenon of the four were a matter of mere conscious poetizing and not a spontaneous production of the objective psyche. Even if we supposed that dreams could be influenced to a noteworthy degree by autosuggestion, this being naturally a question of meaning rather than of form, we would still have to prove that the dreamer's consciousness made decided efforts to force the idea of fourfoldness upon the unconscious. But there is absolutely no question of such a possibility in this case, any more than in the many other cases I have observed, not to mention the numerous historical and ethnographic parallels, only a few of which have been mentioned here.

If we survey the situation as a whole, we come to the inevitable conclusion—at least in my opinion—that a psychic element is present that expresses itself through the tetrad. This conclusion demands neither daring speculation nor extravagant fantasy. If I have called the centre the "self," I did so after ripe reflection and a careful assessment of the data of experience as well as of history. A materialistic interpretation might well say that the "centre" was "nothing but" the point at which the psyche becomes unknowable because it there coalesces with the body. A spiritualistic interpretation, on the other hand, could maintain that the "self" was "nothing but" the "spirit" that animates soul and body and that breaks into time and space at this creative point. I explicitly refrain from such physical and metaphysical speculation and content myself with the determination of empirical facts, holding this to be infinitely more important, as regards the advancement of human knowledge, than if I ran after stylish intellectual follies or after supererogations of faith labelled "religious."

As far as my experience informs me, it is a question of significant "nuclear processes" in the objective psyche, of a kind of picturing of the goal that the "purposeful" psychic process apparently sets itself without being led to it by suggestion from without.[31] Externally, of course, there always exists a certain state of psychic insufficiency, something like hunger; but the goal envisioned by this state is some familiar and favourite food, and not a dish that is unknown to consciousness or seems absurd. The goal that the deeper psychic need sets itself, the image that promises to bring "healing" and *completion,* is beyond all measure strange to consciousness and can find entrance into it only with the greatest difficulties. The situation is naturally different with people who live in a time when such images of the goal have dogmatic validity, or in surroundings where this is recognized. In such cases these images are by that very fact presented to consciousness; the unconscious has its mirror image held up to it, in which it recognizes itself and by which it is brought to reunite itself with consciousness. This involves the assumption, of course, that consciousness is really stirred.

As regards the question of the rise of the mandala theme, it would appear to a superficial view that it arises gradually in the course of the dream series. Actually, however, it is unquestionable that it only comes to show itself more clearly and in a more differentiated form; it was always present and, properly speaking, already appeared in the first dream. As the nymphs said, "We were always there, only you did not notice us."

It is, therefore, more probable that we are dealing with a type-form that exists *a priori,* with an archetype that is inherent in the unconscious and therefore has no part in the coming into being and passing away of the individual. We might say that the archetype is an "eternal" presence, and that it is merely a question whether consciousness becomes aware of it or not. I think that we can form a more probable hypothesis, and one that better explains the observed facts, if we assume that the theme's appearing always more clearly and more frequently [32] in the course of the dream series corresponds to a more exact conception of a type existing *a priori,* rather than that the mandala is first produced in the course of the series. This latter assumption is contravened by the fact that such fundamental ideas as that of the hat covering the personality, the encircling snake, and the *perpetuum mobile,* appear at the very beginning.

If the mandala theme is an archetype, it should occur collectively; that is, it should in theory befall every one. Yet in practice it is met with in relatively few cases in a distinct form; but this in no way prevents its playing the part of a concealed pole around which everything turns in the last analysis. Every life is, at bottom, the realization of a whole, that is, of a self, so that the realization can also be called individuation. For all life is bound to individuals who carry and realize it, and apart from them is unimaginable. But every carrier has an individual specification and determination, and the meaning of living existence consists in its realizing itself in these terms. To be sure, the "sense" is often something that could as well be called "nonsense"; yet there is a fair measure of incommensurability between the secret of existence and human understanding. Sense and nonsense are anthropomorphic interpretations serving the purpose of an outlook that we hold to be sufficiently valid.

As the parallels from history show, the mandala symbolism is in no way a matter of unique curiosities, but of what we may well call uniformities. If this were not so, then there would exist no materials for comparison. But it is exactly this possibility of comparison with the mental products of all ages and from all directions of the compass that shows us most plainly what an immense importance was ascribed by the *consensus gentium* to the processes of the objective psyche. This is reason enough not to make light of them in a superficial way. My empirical observations as a doctor only confirm this valuation. Of course, there are persons who hold it unscientific to take anything seriously; they do not wish to have their intellectual playground disturbed by seriousness. But the doctor who disregards human feeling-values commits a bad blunder, and if he tries to set "right" the mysterious and obscure working of nature in order to be scientific, as he calls it, he is substituting his own banal sophistry for the healing processes of nature. He should take to heart the alchemistic wisdom of old:

Naturalissimum et perfectissimum opus est generare tale qua ipsum est.

FOOTNOTES TO CHAPTER FOUR

1. Scholars and students are referred, for Dr. Jung's complete annotation and documentation of this chapter, to the original German version in the *Eranos-Jahrbuch,*

Zurich, Rhein-Verlag, 1935. C. G. Jung, *Two Essays on Analytical Psychology* (II). London: Baillière, Tindall and Cox, 1928.

2. See the bibliography of works by C. G. Jung, page 306.

3. For this concept compare my essay in *Wirlichkeit der Seele* (Zurich: Rascher, 1934, pp. 1 ff.) and T. Wolff, *Einführung in die Grundlagen der komplexen Psychologie* (pp. 34 ff.), in *Die kulturelle Bedeutung der komplexen Psychologie* (Berlin: Julius Springer, 1935).

4. The seductive virgins appear in a similar rôle at the beginning of the nekuia of Polifilo: Nekuia (vekuía from vékus, meaning corpse), title of the eleventh book of the *Odyssey*, is the sacrifice to the dead for conjuring up the departed out of Hades. Nekuia is, therefore, a suitable designation for the "journey to Hades," the descent into the land of the dead, and was used by Dietrich in this sense in his commentary upon the *Codex of Akhmim,* which contains an apocalyptic fragment of the Gospel of Peter. (*Nekyia, Beiträge zur Erklärung der neuentdeckten Petrusapokalypse*, II Aufl. Leipzig: Teubner, 1913). Typical instances are the *Divina Commedia,* the classic *Walpurgisnacht* in *Faust,* the apocryphal descents into Hell of Christ, and so on. The French edition of the *Songe de Poliphile* dates from 1600. Its full title is *Le Tableau des Riches Inventions couvertes du voile des feintes Amoureuses, qui sont représentées dans le Songe de Poliphile Desvoilées des ombres du Songe et subtilement exposées par Beroalde* (Paris: Guillemot). *Poliphilo* is the work of the Dominican Franceso Colonna (1433-1527). See Claudius Popelin, *Le Songe de Poliphile* (Paris: 1833). The *Ipnerotomachia* (Italian title) dates from about 1467 and was printed in 1499 or thereabout.

5. Eduard Fritz Knuchel, *Die Umwandlung in Kult, Magie und Rechtsgebrauch,* Basel: Schweiz. Gesellschaft für Volkskunde, 1919.

6. See Ruska, *Turba Philosophorum,* in *Quellen und Studien zur Geschichte der Naturwissenschaften und der Medizin.* Berlin: Julius Springer, 1931.

7. Wirth, *Aus orientalischen Chroniken,* p. 199, 1894.

8. Laurentian Litany.

9. (*Rosarium*). As to the curious composition of the quotations from Hermes in the *Rosarium* see footnote to Hermes, below.

10. Foucart, *Les Grands Mystères d'Eleusis.* Paris: C. Klincksieck, 1900.

11. See H. L. Fleischer, *Hermes Trismegistus, An die Menschliche Seele* (Leipzig: 1870, p. 6). Also compare the round form of Plato's primeval man, and the σφαῖρος of Empedocles.

12. Compare Augustine's argument that God is not the sun but he who made it, and the testimony of Eusebius who was a witness of "Christian" sun-worship.

13. Heinrich Zimmer, *Kunstform und Yoga im indischen Kultbild.* Berlin: Frankfurter Verlags-Anstalt, 1926.

14. See Reitzenstein, *Die hellenistischen Mysterienreligionen nach ihren Grundgedanken und Wirkungen.* Leipzig: Teubner.

15. Charlotte A. Baynes, *A Coptic Treatise Contained in the Codex Brucianus.* Cambridge: 1933.

16. *Ibid,* p. 58.

17. *Ibid,* p. 94.

18. *Ibid,* p. 70.

19. The quotations from Hermes come from the *Tractatus Aureus.* These quotations by the anonymous author show arbitrary alterations that have far more significance than mere faulty readings. They are actually original interpolations to

which he lends higher authority by using the name of Hermes. I have compared the three printed editions of the *Tractatus Aureus* in the British Museum, of 1566, 1610 and 1692, as well as the English translation by Mrs. Atwood (1850), and have found that they all agree. In the *Tractatus Aureus* the passages from the *Rosarium* read: *Jam Venus ait: Ego genero lumen, nec tenebræ meæ naturæ sunt . . . me igitur et fratri meo conjunctis nihil melius ac venerabilius.*

20. Mrs. Atwood (1850), *A Suggestive Inquiry into Hermetic Philosophy and Alchemy* (Belfast: revised edition, 1920).

21. Vollers, *Chidher* in *Archiv für Religionswissenschaft,* xii, 235.

22. For the most part only darkly hinted at by the alchemists, as, for instance, *de pinguiori carne sume.* The *Tractatus Aureus* runs: "Hear then these words, and understand them; keep them and meditate thereon and seek for nothing more: Man is generated from the principle of Nature, *whose inward substance is fleshy* and not from anything else. Meditate on this letter and reject superfluities."

23. Orphic mosaic from Tramithia: Eisler, *Orpheus the Fisher* (London: 1921). We might easily take this inscription in a humorous sense, and even so we would not offend the spirit of the classic mysteries. One should compare with it the frescoes of the Villa dei Misteri in Pompeii (Amadeo Maiuri, *La Villa dei Misteri,* Rome, 1931) where drunkenness and ecstasy not only approach each other, but are one and the same. But since the initiations have from of old the significance of healing, the advice could also be taken as a warning against the drinking of water, since it is well known that in the southern countries drinking water is the mother of dysentery and *typhus abdominalis.*

24. *Tractatus Aureus,* Chapter ii: "The Masculine truly is the heaven of the feminine, and the Feminine is the earth of the Masculine."

25. In alchemy, the vulture, eagle, and crow are essentially synonymous.

26. The centre of the mandala is sometimes referred to in alchemistic writing as the *vas.* It corresponds to the calix of the Indian lotus, the place of origin and the abode of the gods. It is called the padma, a term that denotes femininity and corresponds to yoni. In alchemy, the *vas* is often taken as the uterus in which the "child" comes into being. In the Laurentian Litany, Mary is three times called the *vas: (vas spirituale, honorabile, insigne devotionis)*; and in mediæval poetry she is referred to as the "ocean flower" that harbours the Christ. Compare dream 36 of this second series.

27. *Ait autem ipse saluator: Qui iuxta me est, iuxta ignem est, qui longe est a me, longe est a regno.* (Origen, in *Jerem. hom.* xx, 3, cited from Preuschen, *Antilegomena,* p. 44. Giessen: 1901).

28. Bas-relief of Philæ, Wallis Budge, *Osiris and the Egyptian Resurrection,* i, 3; the sons of Horus standing in the lotus, in the Hunefer papyrus, Wallis Budge, *Book of the Dead.* Facsimile 1899, Plate 5—Sometimes three with animal heads and one with a human head, as in the Kerasher papyrus, Wallis Budge, *op. cit.* In a manuscript of the seventh century (Gellone) even the Evangelists have their animal heads.

29. So named, in Meliton of Sardes, for instance. (From the *Analecta Sacra,* quoted by Cumont, *Textes et Monuments du culte de Mithras,* i, 355.)

30. Abbé Joseph Delacotte, *Guillaume de Digulleville: Trois Romans-Poèmes du XIVme siècle.* Paris: 1932.

31. The image that presents itself in our subject material as a goal may serve as a picture of the *origin* when regarded from the historical standpoint. I mention, by way of example, the conception of paradise in the Old Testament, and especially the creation

of Adam in the Slavic Book of Enoch. (M. Foerster, *Adams Erschaffung und Namenge-bung, Archiv für Religionswissenschaft*, xi, pp. 478 ff.)

32. If the 400 dreams are divided into 8 groups of 50 each, then the number of mandalas occurring in each group is as follows:

I	6	V	11
II	4	VI	11
III	2	VII	11
IV	9	VIII	17

There is thus a substantial increase in the numerical occurrence of the mandala themes in the course of the whole series.

CHAPTER FIVE

The Idea of Redemption in Alchemy [1]

Slowly, in the course of the eighteenth century, alchemy wasted away through its own obscurity. It tried to explain everything on the principle of: *obscurum per obscurius, ignotum per ignotius* (what is dark by what is darker still, what is unknown by what is still more unknown); and this principle agreed very badly with the spirit of enlightenment and especially with the dawning of chemistry as a science towards the end of the century. These two new forces of the mind, however, only gave to alchemy the finishing stroke. Its inner decay began fully a hundred years before, in the time of Jacob Boehme, when many alchemists deserted their retorts and crucibles to devote themselves exclusively to Hermetic philosophy. It was then that the chemist parted company with the follower of Hermes. Chemistry became a natural science, while Hermetic philosophy lost its contact with the firm ground of empiricism and climbed beyond itself to allegories and speculations that were as bombastic as they were empty of content, and that were kept alive only by memories of a better age. But this better age was the time when the alchemist still wrestled in his mind with the problems of matter—when the exploring consciousness stood face to face with the dark void of the unknown, and was confident of discerning within it forms and laws.

The basic concept of alchemy is the work (*opus*). This consists of a practical part, the actual *operatio*, which we must conceive as an experimentation with metals, particularly quicksilver, but also sulphur and various salts and ashes. In my opinion it is quite hopeless to bring any kind of order out of the boundless chaos of substances and procedures. Only rarely can we form an approximate idea of the manner in which the work was carried on, with what materials and with what results. The reader usually finds himself in the most impenetrable darkness with regard to the names of the substances, which are almost always chosen hit or miss; and it is just the most used substances like mercury, salt, and sulphur whose alchemistic significance belongs to the secrets of the art.

Moreover, it would be a mistake to imagine that the alchemists always understood one another. They themselves complain about the obscurity of the texts, and occasionally betray their inability to understand their own symbols and symbolic figures. So, for example, the very learned Dr. Michael Majer, an encyclopædist of alchemy, accuses Geber, the classical authority, of being the obscurest of all; one would need the help of an Œdipus, he says, to read the riddle of the *Gebrina Sphinx*. Bernhardus Trevisanus, another famous alchemist, even calls Geber an obscurantist and a Proteus who promises the kernel and offers the rind.

The alchemist knows that he writes obscurely. He admits that he veils things intentionally, but nowhere—as far as my knowledge reaches—says that he is unable to write in any other way. He makes a virtue of his necessity by maintaining either that he must be secretive for one reason or another, or that he wishes to make the truth as clear as possible and to tell—not quite above his breath—what the *materia prima* or the *lapis* is.

The heavy darkness that covers the chemical operation comes from the fact that the alchemist actually takes little interest in the purely chemical side, and uses it only to devise a new nomenclature for the psychic transformations that hold a real fascination for him. We could say that every original alchemist builds himself a more or less individual edifice of thought consisting of the dicta of the philosophers and of a combination of analogues to the basic concepts of alchemy—analogues that are often fetched from the four corners of the earth. There even exist treatises written more or less for the purpose of offering the artist building material for analogies.

The method of alchemy, psychologically regarded, is boundless amplification. The *amplificatio* is always in place when a dark experience presents itself—an experience so vaguely adumbrated that it must be reinforced and extended by drawing upon a psychological context, if it is to be made intelligible. This is why, in Analytical Psychology, we resort to amplification in the interpretation of dreams, for a dream is too shadowy an adumbration to be understood until it is enriched through the stuff of association and analogy, and is thus amplified to the level of intelligibility. The *amplificatio* forms the second part of the work, and is taken by the alchemist in the sense of *theoria*.[2] The theory was originally the so-called Hermetic philosophy, but early in the epoch preceding the Reformation it was broadened by the assimilation of ideas taken from Christian dogma. In the earliest Occidental alchemy, Hermetic fragments have for the most part come down from Arabic originals. A direct contact with Hermes Trismegistus was established for the first time in the second half of the fifteenth century, when Marcilio Ficino translated the Greek manuscript of the *Corpus Hermeticum*, which was brought at that time to Italy from Macedonia.

Everything unknown is filled by psychological projection: it is as if the investigator's own psychic depths were mirrored in the darkness. What he sees and thinks he recognizes is, first of all, the facts of his own unconscious. It is a relatively simple matter for us, once psychology has sharpened our insight, to recognize the psychic nature of alchemistic symbols and processes. Professor Bernoulli [3] has contributed an excellent survey of the psychological meaning of the most important manifestations of alchemy. It is well known that Herbert Silberer,[4] also, at an earlier date, succeeded in throwing some light upon the psychological content of alchemy. So as not to repeat unnecessarily what has been said before, I will call to mind only the essential points of the process.

It begins with an unknown *materia prima* in the state of blackness (*nigredo*). Next in time comes the union (*conjunctio*) of contradictory principles, usually designated as ♂ and ♀. There generally follows a disintegration or a death (*putrefactio, mortificatio, calcinatio*); then the washing off (*ablutio*) that produces the whitening (*albedo*). Herewith a certain result has been attained; there has come into being a white stone or a white earth (*terra foliata alba*) representing a kind of extract or sublimate of the formerly united opposites. This, however, is nothing definite as yet, but rather a kind of preliminary stage or basis in which the seed of a following stage either is potentially present, or is sowed or planted.

The next transformation is the reddening (*rubedo*). The white and the red often present themselves as white and red roses, or as stones, sulphur, the eagle, etc. Moreover, the *rubedo* is frequently compared to blood, and—when it is a stone—to the carbuncle. The latter comparison is generally a sign that the climax has been reached. The carbuncle is then the red tincture whose projection upon the base metals changes these into gold or silver; or it is the panacea and the *elixir vitæ*. But the reddening is not always the culmination of the procedure; not, at any rate, when gold is the end in view. In this case the reddening is followed by the yellowing (*citrinitas*), the latter producing the coagulated, solid, or fluid gold (*aurum potabile*). As a variant there is also the vitreous gold (*vitreum aurum*) or the malleable glass (*vitreum malleabile*).

The stone of the philosophers (*lapis philosophorum*), the most prevalent of all alchemistic conceptions, was conceived either as an instrument or as an absolute end in itself. In the first case it may be the red powder or the red tincture; but in the second case it is a thoroughly mystical being having body, soul, and spirit, and depicted as winged or hermaphroditic. ~

Analogous to the unknown *materia prima*, and sometimes even identical with it, is the so-called divine, "eternal" water (*aqua permanens*, ὕδωρ θεῖον), also described as quicksilver (*mercurius, argentum vivum*). It plays its mysterious part throughout the whole process, at the very outset as well as at the very end—this part being essentially instrumental. The same is true of the fire, which is called "our" fire (*ignis noster*), the philosophical or the mercurial fire, and which is thus distinguished from the common one. No less significant is the Hermetic vessel (*vas Hermetis*), typified by the retorts and crucibles, and regarded as the container of the substances to be transformed. Although it is essentially an instrument, it nevertheless has peculiar and fundamental relations both to the *materia prima* and to the stone, and so is not a mere piece of apparatus. The procedure itself had its partial developments—namely, solutions and coagulations, sublimations and separations—and these were repeated in a cyclic manner, the whole cycle being called *circulatio, rotatio,* or *rota* (wheel).

The outline I have roughly traced above presents a more or less superficial view of alchemy as we have commonly come to know it.

From the standpoint of modern chemistry we are unable to form any picture of alchemy whatsoever; and if we turn to the texts with their many hundreds of methods and recipes, as these have come down to us from the Middle

Ages and antiquity, we discover among them relatively few containing a recognizable meaning for the chemist. He will surely find the majority of them senseless, and furthermore no true tincture or artificial gold was ever produced in all the many centuries during which men earnestly slaved in the laboratories.

What then—we may well ask—induced the ancient alchemists steadfastly to go on working—or, as they said, "operating"—and writing further treatises about the "divine" art, when their whole undertaking was so impressively hopeless? We must add, to be sure, that every insight into the nature of chemistry and its limitations was still barred to them, so that they were as much entitled to hope as those who dreamt of flying—and whose late followers achieved it after all. We must not underestimate the satisfaction of the undertaking, of the adventure, of the *quærere* (search) and of the *invenire* (discovery). It could last as long as the alchemist's methods appeared significant to him. Now, there was nothing at that time that could have persuaded him of the senselessness of his chemical operations; and, besides, he could look back upon a long tradition that bore not a few testimonies from those who claimed to have arrived at the wonderful result.[5] Nor was the matter entirely without promise, since here and there, on the side, a few useful inventions did emerge from the labours in the chemical laboratory. As a precursor of chemistry, alchemy had a sufficient reason for existence. Even if alchemy had consisted of an endless series of—let us say—meaningless and fruitless chemical experiments, we should still have no more cause to wonder at the perseverance of the alchemists than at the quixotic attempts of mediæval doctors and pharmacologists.

The decisive point is, however, that we are called upon to deal, not with chemical experimentations as such, but with something resembling psychic processes expressed in pseudo-chemical language. The ancients knew what chemi-

cal processes were; therefore, they must have known that
what they practised was at least no ordinary chemistry. That
they knew of this difference is shown by the title of a treatise
of Democritus ascribed to the first century; it reads τὰ
φυδιχὰ καὶ τὰ μυστιχά (*The Physical and the Philosophical*).
And soon after this there arises a wealth of evidence to
show that, in alchemy, two currents run side by side that to
our way of thinking are heterogeneous. Alchemy's *tam
ethice quam physice* (ethical as well as physical) is not intelligible to our thinking. If the alchemist admittedly uses
the chemical process purely in a symbolical way, then why
does he work in a laboratory with melting pots and retorts? And if, as he ceaselessly asserts, he describes chemical
processes, why does he distort them past recognition by
symbolization?

This riddle has before now caused many an honest and
well-meaning student of alchemy to cudgel his brains. On
the one hand, to be sure, the alchemist declares that he conceals things intentionally in order to prevent wicked or foolish people from taking possession of the gold and thus caus-
ing some calamity. On the other hand, he is likely to inform
us that the sought-for gold is not—as the foolish suppose—
the common one (*aurum vulgi*), but rather the philosophical gold, or even the wonderful stone, the *lapis invisibilitatis* (of invisibility), or the *lapis æthereus* (ethereal), or
finally the unimaginable, hermaphroditic *rebis*, and that absolutely all recipes are to be despised. But on psychological
grounds it is highly improbable that it was consideration
for mankind that drove the alchemist to mystification. For
when something real is discovered it is generally heralded
aloud. The alchemist Basilius Valentinus gives us the best
example of this in his *Triumphal Car of Antimony*.

The fact is that the alchemists had nothing whatever
to divulge, and least of all the secret of manufacturing gold.

Mystification can be pure bluff for the obvious purpose of exploiting the credulous. That alchemy as a whole is to be explained from this angle is contradicted, in my opinion, by the fact that not a few detailed, scholarly, and conscientious treatises were written and printed anonymously, which therefore could not be of unlawful advantage to anyone.

But mystification can also arise from a different source. A real secret does not act secretively—it speaks secretively: it suggests itself by a variety of images pointing to its existence. Now, by this I do not mean a secret personally guarded by someone, that has a content known to the possessor; but a matter or circumstance that is "secret"—known only by intimations—and that is, in its essence, unknown. So, for instance, the real nature of matter was unknown to the alchemist. He knew it only through intimations. Inasmuch as he tried to explore it, he projected the unconscious into the darkness of matter, to illuminate it. In order to explain the mystery of matter, he projected into what was to be explained still another mystery, namely, his own unknown, psychic substratum: *obscurum per obscurius, ignotum per ignotius!*

Strictly taken, projection is never made; it happens; it is met with. In the darkness of some externality I find, without recognizing it as such, a psychic or inner something that is my own. Therefore, in my opinion, it would be a mistake to assign as the source for the formula *tam ethice quam physice* the doctrine of correspondence. I believe, on the contrary, that this doctrine is more probably a rationalization of the experience of projection. The alchemist does not practise his art because he believes on theoretical grounds in correspondence; rather, he has a theory of correspondence because he experiences the presence of the idea in the physical order. I am, therefore, inclined to suppose that the true root of alchemy is less to be sought in transmitted philosophical views than in certain experiences of projection of the individual researchers.

By this I mean that during the carrying out of the chemical experiment the laboratory worker had certain psychic experiences that appeared to him as a particular behaviour of the chemical process. Since it is a question of projections, it was naturally unknown to him that his experience had nothing to do with matter in itself (as we know it today). He experienced his projection as a characteristic of matter; but what he actually experienced was his own unconscious. In this way he retraced the path of man's developing knowledge of nature. As everyone knows, science began with the stars, and mankind discovered in them the dominants of the unconscious, the so-called gods, as well as the curious psychological qualities of the zodiac: a complete doctrine of character, wholly projected. Astrology is a primeval experience, and so is alchemy. Such projections always repeat themselves when man tries to investigate an empty darkness and then unwittingly fills it with living form.

This being so, I have given my attention to the question of whether the alchemists themselves reported such experiences in the course of their practice. I had no reason to hope for a rich find, since it is a question of experiences that are unconscious and therefore unlikely to be reported. As a matter of fact, there are some unmistakable accounts in the literature. It is significant that the later accounts are more detailed and specific than the older ones.

The most recent account derives from a German treatise of 1732, entitled *Abtala Jurain,* etc. It reads (pp. 52 and 54):

The Creation.

"Take a good lot of ordinary rain water, at least ten quarts; preserve it well sealed in glass vessels at least ten days, then it will stink and precipitate fæces. Pour off the clear part and put it in a wooden vessel that is fashioned round like a ball; cut it off in the middle and fill a full third of the vessel and place it in the sun around midday in a secret or remote place.

"When this has happened, then take a drop of the consecrated red wine and let it fall down into the water; then at once thou wilt see a mist and a heavy darkness above on the water such as there was also in the first creation. Then put in two drops, so wilt thou see the light coming forth out of the darkness; hereupon little by little put in every half quarter hour three then four then five then six drops, and then no more, so wilt thou see with thine eyes above on the water bit by bit one thing after the other as God created all things in the six days, and how it all took place, and such secrets as are not to be spoken aloud and I also have not the power to reveal. Fall upon thy knees, before thou undertakest this operation. Let thine eyes judge of it; for thus was the world created. Let everything stand as it is, and it will disappear in half an hour from the time it began.

"By this ye will clearly see the mysteries of God that are at present hidden from you as from a child. Ye will understand what Moses wrote of the creation; ye will see what manner of body Adam and Eve had before and after the fall, what was the serpent and what the tree and what manner of fruits they ate; where and what Paradise is, and in what bodies the righteous will be resurrected, and not in this one that we have received from Adam, but rather in the one we have attained through the Holy Ghost, such a one, namely, as our Saviour brought from Heaven."

The Heavens.

"Ye shall take seven pieces of metal, of each and every metal as they are named after the planets, and shall stamp upon every one of them the character of the planet in the house of that same planet, and each and every piece shall be as large and thick as a rose noble: but of mercury take only the fourth part of an ounce by weight and have nothing marked upon it.

"Then put them in the order in which they stand in the heavens into a crucible and shut all windows in the chamber that it may be quite dark therein; then melt them all together in the midst of the chamber and drop therein seven drops of the blessed stone; so forthwith a flame of fire will come out of the crucible and spread itself over the entire chamber (fear no harm); and the whole chamber will shine more brightly than sun and moon, and ye will behold above your heads the entire firmament, as it is in the starry heavens above, and the planets will hold their true courses, as in the sky; let it cease of itself, in a quarter of an hour everything will find its own place."

We extract another example from a treatise by Theobald van Hoghelande (sixteenth century):

"They say also that different names were given to the stone because of the wonderful manifoldness of the figures that appear in the course of the work—colours that often spring up at the same time. Sometimes also we imagine, as if in clouds or in fire, strange forms of animals, reptiles or trees. I found something similar [the author continues] in a book ascribed to Moses: when the body is dissolved, it is there written, then will appear sometimes two branches, sometimes three or more, sometimes also figures of reptiles; occasionally it also appears as if a man with a head and all his limbs were seated upon a cathedra."

Hoghelande's statements prove, as do the two preceding texts, that, during the practical labour, hallucinatory or visionary perceptions took place that can be nothing else than projections of unconscious contents.

A somewhat different aspect of the relation of the psychic world to the chemical operation is shown by the following citation from the *Theatrum Chemicum* of 1659:

"I demand of thee, look with the eyes of the spirit at the shoot of the grain of wheat in respect to all its circumstances, that thou mayest bring the tree of the philosophers to grow."

This seems to point to the active imagination as that which actually sets the process going (*promovere*).

Trithemius, Abbot of Sponheim (about 1500), the alleged teacher of Paracelsus, says: "Out of other things thou wilt never make the one, unless first the one arises out of thyself." Whatever the alchemist meant by the "one," [6] it is related to the subject of the "artist," whose unity is posited as an indispensable condition for the completion of the work.

There is scarcely any doubt that we are dealing here with the psychological factors in the work, and that these are held to be of fundamental importance.

The *Rosarium Philosophorum* says: "Who therefore knows salt and its solution, he knows the hidden secret of the wise men of old. Therefore turn thy mind upon the salt, for in it (mind) alone (*in ipsa sola,* referring to *mens*) is concealed all science and the noblest and most hidden secret of all the ancient philosophers." [7]

We would have to assume a twofold typographical error in this passage if the secret were really related to the salt. Besides, "mind" and "salt" are close cousins (*cum grano salis!*).[8] The anonymous writer of the *Rosarium* says in another place that the work must be performed "with the true imagination, and not with the fantastic," and again that the stone will be found "when the search lies heavily upon the searcher." This remark can hardly be understood in any other way than as positing certain psychic factors as absolute requisites for the discovery of the wonderful stone. Thus both remarks make it seem possible that the author is actually of the opinion that the essential secret of the art is concealed in the human spirit; that, as we would put it today, it is in the unconscious.

The following alchemistic pronouncement agrees fairly well with the idea that the work is of a psychological nature:

"Thou seekest hard and findest not. Perhaps thou wilt find if thou doest not seek."

Such a precept would hardly be to the purpose for the synthesis of a chemical substance.

Not much effort is needed for the beginning of the work; it suffices that the student apply oneself to it with "a free and empty mind," as a text declares. But observance must be paid the important rule that "the mind (*mens*) is in accord with the work, which necessarily surpasses any other." In order to acquire the "golden understanding" (*aurea apprehensio*), he must, says another text, open wide the eyes of the spirit and of the soul, and contemplate and recognize things with the help of the inner light that God has kindled from the beginning in nature and in our hearts.

Now, since the artist's psyche is closely connected with the work, not only as a means, but also as a cause and point of departure, we can understand why such a strong emphasis was laid, even in the earliest treatises, upon the spiritual and mental constitution and attitude of the laboratory worker. Thus Alfidius says: "Know that thou canst not possess this science if thou doest not cleanse thy mind through God, by which is meant that thou purgest thine heart from all corruption." According to the ancient *Aurora Consurgens,* the treasure house of Hermetic wisdom is built upon fourteen cardinal virtues as a foundation; namely, health, humility, holiness, chastity, power, victory, faith, hope, love (*caritas*), kindness (*benignitas*), patience, moderation, mental discipline or culture, and obedience.

The pseudo Thomas of this same treatise mentions a citation that reads, "Cleanse the terrible darknesses of our spirit," and as a parallel to it cites the early alchemist Senior in a passage where he speaks about *nigredo* and *dealbatio*. In this way the "darknesses of our spirit" and the *nigredo,* the "blackness," unmistakably fall together into one; that is, the author feels or experiences the opening stage of the alchemistic process as coincident or even identical with his own psychological condition.

Another early authority is Geber. In the *Liber Perfecti Magisterii* he demands the following as psychological and characterological prerequisites for the *artifex* (artist). He must have a most subtle mind and possess sufficient knowledge of the metals and minerals. But he may not have a coarse and hard mind, nor may he be greedy and avaricious, undecided and vacillating; furthermore, he may not be in a hurry nor may he be conceited; on the contrary, he must be firmly resolved, tenacious, patient, mild, long-suffering, and moderate.

The author of the *Rosarium* says that he who wishes to be initiated in this art and wisdom must be not arrogant but pious, upright, of a deep understanding, affable, of a jovial mien and happy disposition. "My son," he continues, "above all I exhort thee to fear God, who knows thy nature and in whom there is help for every lonely one, whoever he be."

The introduction to the art that Morienus imparted to Khalid ben Yezid [9] is especially instructive: "For this thing that thou hast so long sought for, cannot be acquired or accomplished through force or passion. It is only acquired through patience and humility and through a determined and most perfect love. For God entrusts this divine and pure science to his believers and servants, to those, namely, to whom he resolved to entrust it from the primal state of things. [Here follow a few remarks about transmitting the art to pupils.] Nor were they [the elect] able to withhold anything of what God had entrusted to them in miraculous wise, nor could they themselves, any longer, direct their spirits except upon the goal that God had set for them. For God supports those of his servants whom he has purposely chosen so that they may search for this divine science, which is concealed from men, and may keep it to themselves. This is namely the science that draws its master [he who practises it] away from the misery of this world and leads to the knowledge of good things to be.

"When Morienus was asked by the king [Khalid] why he lived in mountains and deserts rather than in hermitages, he answered: I do not doubt that in hermitages and brotherhoods I would find greater peace, and find painful toil in the deserts and mountains, but no one reaps who does not sow . . . Most narrow is the entrance to peace, and no one can go to it except through suffering of the soul."

As to the last sentence, one must not forget that Morienus is not speaking for general edification, but with a particular regard to the divine art and its work. Michael Majer expresses himself in a similar way when he says: "In chemistry there is a certain noble substance (*lapis*) at whose beginning misery rules with vinegar, but at whose end gladness holds sway with joy; and I have assumed that it will happen so to me, namely, that I will first suffer difficulty, sadness and disgust, but finally will witness all the more pleasant and easy things."

The same author also testifies that "chemistry excites the *artifex* to meditation on the good things of heaven, and that he who is initiated of God in these mysteries casts aside all such insignificant cares as food and clothing, and so appears to himself as if he were born anew."

The difficulty and grief that stand at the beginning of the work are again made to coincide with the *nigredo*, like the "terrible darknesses of the spirit" of which the *Aurora Consurgens* speaks; and these, again, are no doubt the same as the *afflictio animæ*, the suffering of the soul, to which Morienus points. The expression with which he characterizes the attitude of the adept, *amor perfectissimus*, voices an extraordinary surrender to the work. If this *seria meditatio* (serious concentration) upon the work is not mere bragging —a supposition for which, indeed, we have no grounds— then we must surely conceive of these ancient adepts as pursuing their labours with unusual concentration, even with religious fervour.

Such devotion and self-sacrifice is, of course, especially fitted to project values and meanings into the object of the research, and to fill it with forms and figures that have their primary source in the unconscious of the investigator.

This interpretation is favoured by the curious and significant way in which the alchemists use the expressions *meditatio* and *imaginatio*. Ruland's *Lexicon Alchemiæ*, which dates from 1612, defines *meditatio* as follows: "The word *meditatio* is used when one has an inner dialogue with someone who is invisible, as also with God, when he is invoked, or with oneself, or with one's good angel."

This "inner dialogue" is a well-known matter to us psychologists, for it is an essential part of the coming to terms with the unconscious.[10] Ruland's definition proves beyond all doubt that, when the alchemists speak of *meditari*, they in no way mean a mere cogitation, but rather an inner dialogue, and therefore a living relation to the answering voice of the "other" in us, that is, the unconscious. And so when the Hermetic dictum, "And as all things come from the One through meditation of the One," employs the notion of meditation, it must, no doubt, be understood in this alchemistic sense of a creative dialogue by means of which things pass from an unconscious and potential state into a manifest one. Thus we read in a treatise of Philalethes: "Wonderful above all is it that our stone, howsoever it is already perfect and able to impart a perfect tincture, of its own free choice does humble itself again and will contemplate a new volatility apart from all manipulation." What is meant by a meditated volatility we learn a few lines below, where it says: "Of its own accord it will liquefy . . . and by God's command become endowed with spirit, which will fly upward and take the stone with it." [11] Again, therefore, to meditate means that, this time through a dialogue with God, additional spirit is contributed to the stone—which is to say, it is still further spiritualized, volatilized, or sublimated.

So, also, the above-mentioned *meditatio cælestium bonorum* must be understood in the sense of a living dialectic relation to certain dominants of the unconscious. We find this pointedly corroborated in a treatise by an anonymous

French alchemist who belonged to the seventeenth and eighteenth centuries. He says verbatim: "How often did I see them (the *sacerdotes Ægyptiorum*) overcome by joy at my understanding, how they most affectionately kissed me, for the true grasp of the ambiguities of a paradoxical doctrine was easily opened to me. How often did they let their pleasure in my beautiful discoveries concerning the figures of the intricate wisdom of old move them to show mine eyes and fingers the Hermetic vessel, the salamander, the full moon, and the rising sun."

Although this is no confession, but a picture of the golden age of alchemy, still it shows how the alchemist represented to himself the psychological nature of his work. The relation to the invisible powers of the psyche constituted the actual secret of the magistery. To give expression to this secret, the ancient masters readily resorted to the allegorical legend. One of the oldest monuments of this genre, and one which exerted a strong influence upon the later literature, is the *Visio Arislei*, which in its whole make-up is closely related to the series of visions known to us from the psychology of the unconscious.

I have mentioned before that, like the *meditatio*, so also the concept of *imaginatio* is of particular significance in the alchemistic work. We have already become acquainted with that remarkable passage in the *Rosarium* from which we learned that the work must be done with the right imagination, and we were likewise taught by another citation how, through contemplation, the tree of philosophy is made to grow. And now Ruland's dictionary helps us further to understand what *imaginatio* represents for the alchemist. For Ruland says, "Imagination is the star in man, the celestial or supercelestial body." This surprising definition throws a very particular light upon the fantasy processes connected with the *opus*: we must by no means conceive of them as the immaterial phantoms that we readily take fantasy pictures to be, but rather as something corporeal, as forming a "subtle body" of a semi-spiritual nature.

Such a concretization must necessarily predominate in an age when there was as yet no empirical psychology, for everything unconscious, inasmuch as it was activated, was projected upon corporeal things—that is, confronted the human being from without. It was in a sense a spiritual-physical hybrid, a concretization of the kind that one meets with very frequently in the study of the primitive mind. The *imaginatio,* or the act of imagining, is thus a physical activity that may be intercalated in the cycle of corporeal transformations—that brings these about and is brought about by them. In this way the alchemist related himself not only to the unconscious, but also directly to matter, in which he could hope to induce transformations through the power of imagination.

The peculiar expression *astrum* (star) is an alchemistic term that approximately means quintessence. *Imaginatio* is thus a concentrated extract of the forces of life, corporeal as well as psychic. The alchemist's requirement that the artist must have a sound physical constitution is understandable in this light, for he works with and through his own quintessence, and so inevitably conditions his own experiments. Just because of the intermixture of the physical and the psychic, a doubt remains as to whether the final transformations in the alchemistic process are to be sought for more in the material, or more in the spiritual, realm. But actually this question is wrongly put: no either-or existed for that age, but an intermediate realm between matter and mind, a psychic realm of subtle bodies to which a mental as well as a material manifestation was suitable. This is the only view of the question that helps us to grasp alchemistic ways of thought; on any other, they appear absurd.

Obviously, the intermediary realm of subtle bodies

ceases to exist as soon as one seeks to investigate matter in and for itself, apart from all projections; and it remains non-existent as long as one believes oneself in possession of final knowledge about matter and the soul. But in an age when physics touches upon a realm "where no one has trod, or may tread," and when psychology must recognize that there are forms of psychic existence apart from the acquisitions of the personal consciousness—in other words, when it likewise touches upon an impenetrable darkness—then the intermediary realm may come to life again, and the physical and psychic be once again blended into one, and inseparable. We have today come very near to this turning.

These, and similar, reflections are unavoidable if we wish in some measure to understand the peculiar conceptual language of alchemy. To speak of the "error of alchemy" has become today not only somewhat outdated, but a sign of intellectual poverty. There are very modern problems in alchemy, but they fall within another realm than that of chemistry.

The concept of *imaginatio* is perhaps the most important key to the understanding of the alchemistic *opus*. The anonymous author of the treatise *De Sulphure* speaks of the imaginative faculty of the soul in that passage where he meant to do just what the ancients had failed to do, that is, give a clear indication of the secret of the art. The soul, he says, stands in the place of God (*sui locum tenens seu vice Rex est*), and inhabits the life spirit in the pure blood. It rules the consciousness (*mens*), and this rules the body. The soul functions (*operatur*) in the body, but has the greater part of its function (*operatio*) outside of the body. (We may add by way of explanation: in projection.) This peculiarity is divine. For divine wisdom is only in part enclosed within the body of the world; for the greater part it is outside, and imagines far higher things than the body of the world can grasp (*concipere*); and these are outside of nature—God's own secrets. The soul is an example of this; it, too, imagines many things of the utmost profundity (*profundissima*) outside the body, as God does. To be sure, what the soul imagines happens only in the mind; but what God imagines happens in reality.

"The soul, however, has the absolute and independent power (*absolutam et separatam potestatem*) to do things that differ (*alia facere*) from those the body can grasp. But it has, when it wishes, the greatest power over the body (*potestatem in corpus*), for otherwise our philosophy would be in vain. . . . Thou canst grasp far greater matters, since we have truly opened the doors for thee."

This argument by the anonymous philosopher gives us some valuable insights into the manner of thought of the alchemists. The soul, in this text, is obviously an *anima corporalis* that inhabits the blood. It would, therefore, correspond to the unconscious, if this is taken as the psychic event that mediates between consciousness and the physiological functioning of the body. In the scheme of the chakras,[12] this anima would be located below the diaphragm. But, on the other hand, it is also God's lieutenant or viceroy, and the analogue of the *Deus Creator*.

There are people who have never been able to understand the unconscious except as the subconscious, and who always feel the need of putting a superconscious by its side—or, if possible, above it. Such concessions to spiritual weakness do not trouble our philosophers; they taught that every elementary form of existence contains its inner contradiction, a doctrine by which they have long ago anticipated the problem of opposites as Analytical Psychology conceives it. Our author has something to say about the element, air, that is important in this connection, and particularly so in connection with the subject of this essay. "The air," he tells us, "is a pure, uncorrupted element, in its kind the most worthy, uncommonly light and invisible, but heavy,

visible, and firm within. Enclosed in it (*inclusus*) is the spirit
of the Highest, which, before the Creation, hovered over
the waters according to the testimony of Holy Writ: 'And
he flew upon the wings of the wind.' In this element all
things are integrated (*integræ*) through the imagination of
the fire."

To understand such a pronouncement, we must obviously dismiss all modern conceptions of the constitution of
a gas, and take it as a purely psychological statement. So
understood, it deals with the projection of pairs of opposites
such as light-heavy, visible-invisible, etc. Now, the identity
of the opposites is the characteristic of every psychic event
that is unconscious. So the anima *corporalis* is at the same
time *spiritualis,* and the firm and heavy kernel of air is at the
same time the *spiritus creator* that hovers over the waters.
And as in the creative spirit "the images of all creation" are
contained, so also are all things imagined or "pictured" in
the air through the power of fire: this is so, on the one hand,
because fire surrounds the throne of God, and because out of
it are created—or "imagined"—the angels and all other living beings in descending rank and qualities through infusion
of the fiery anima in the life-air; [13] and it is so, also, because
fire destroys all that is composite, and restores its images to
the air again in the smoke.

Now, the soul, our author says, is only in part confined
to the body, as God, also, is only in part enclosed in the body
of the world. If we strip this statement of its metaphysics, it
declares that the psyche is only in part identical with our
conscious being, while for the rest it is in the state of projection, and in this state imagines or pictures those larger things
that the body cannot grasp—which is to say, cannot bring
to actuality. This "larger" (*majora*) corresponds to the
"higher" (*altiora*) of the all-creative imagination of God;
but this "higher," because it is imagined by God, becomes at
once substantial, instead of lingering in a state of potential

reality, like the contents of the unconscious. That the alchemistic *opus* is such an activity of the psyche *extra corpus*
comes out clearly from the remark that the soul has the
greatest power over the body, and that, if this were not so,
the royal art or philosophy would amount to nothing. "You
are able," says the author, "to grasp (*concipere*) the larger
things"; therefore, your body can actualize them—of course,
with the help of the art and with God's permission (*Deo
concedente*), this being a fixed formula of alchemy.

The *imaginatio,* as the alchemists understood it, is in
truth a key that opens the door to the secret of the *opus.*
We now know that it is a question of picturing and actualizing those "larger" things that the anima, on God's behalf,
presents creatively and *extra naturam;* or—putting it in
modern language—actualizing those contents of the unconscious [14] that are beyond nature—that is, not given in our
empirical world, and therefore constituting an *a priori* of
archetypal nature. The place, or the medium, of the actual-
ization is neither matter nor spirit, but the intermediate
realm of subtle actuality for which the symbol is the only
adequate expression. The symbol is neither abstract nor concrete, neither rational nor irrational, neither real nor unreal.
It is always both—it is *non vulgi,* the aristocratic affair of
one who is set apart, *cujuslibet sequestrati,* chosen and predestined by God from the very beginning.

The title-page vignette of the *Tripus Aureus* of 1677
clearly portrays the double face of alchemy already adumbrated in this chapter. The picture (Plate VI) is divided
into two parts: on the right is a laboratory where a man
clothed only in trunks is busy at the fire; on the left is a
library in which a bishop, a philosopher, and a man of the
world, probably a doctor, confer together. But in the centre,
upon the furnace, rises the tripod with the flask in which
appears the winged dragon. The dragon symbolizes the experience, the vision of the alchemist who works in the labora-

PLATE VI

See page 226]

PLATE VII

See page 227]

PLATE VIII

[*See page 242*

tory and "theorizes." [15] The dragon as such is a *monstrum*—
a symbol combining the earth-principle of the serpent and
the air-principle of the bird. But Mercury is the divine,
winged Hermes, the ancient god of revelation and the foremost psychopomp, appearing in ponderable matter. The
heavy metal quicksilver, the *argentum vivum,* was the wonderful substance that perfectly expressed the nature of the
στίλβων, that which glistens and animates from within.
When the alchemist speaks of *Mercurius,* he explicitly means
quicksilver, but implicitly the divine and all-creating spirit
concealed in matter. The dragon is probably the oldest pictured symbol known to us in alchemistic texts. It appears as
the ουροβορός, the tail eater, in the *Codex Marcianus* (Plate
VII) belonging to the tenth or eleventh century, accompanied by the legend: ἐν τὸ πᾶν: the One, the All.

The alchemists declare again and again that the *opus*
emerges from one thing and leads back again to the One; it
is thus in a certain sense a circle like a dragon that bites itself
in the tail. For this reason the work is often called *circulare,*
circular, or else the *rota,* the wheel. Mercury stands at the
beginning and at the end of the work. He is the *materia
prima,* the *caput corvi,* the *nigredo;* as the dragon he devours
himself, and as the dragon he dies and is resurrected in the
form of the *lapis.* He is the play of colour of the peacock's
tail, *cauda pavonis,* and the separation of the four elements.
He is the hermaphrodite of incipient being who divides into
two in the classic dualism of brother-sister, and unites in the
conjunctio, to appear again at the end in the radiant form of
the *lumen novum,* the stone. He is metal and yet fluid, matter and yet spirit, cold but fiery, poison but also the healing
draught—a symbol that unites the opposites.[16]

All these conceptions were the common property of
alchemy from the beginning. Zosimus, who belonged to the
third century, cites in his writing *About Virtue and Interpretation* one of the oldest authorities in alchemy, Ostanes,

an author whose place is on the very frontier of the historical period, and who was known even to Pliny. The relation of Ostanes to one of the first alchemistic authors, Democritus, falls within the first century before Christ. This Ostanes is supposed to have said the following: "Go to the streams of the Nile and there thou wilt find a stone that has a spirit (πνεῦμα). Take this, divide it, and reach with thy hand into its inner parts and draw out its heart; for its soul (ψυχή) is in its heart." An interpolating commentator remarks to this: "Thou wilt there, he says, find this stone that has a spirit, which refers to the expulsion of the quicksilver (ἐξυδραργύρωσις)."

When Nietzsche uses, in his *Zarathustra,* the emphatic metaphor, "For me an image slumbers in the stone," he is no doubt saying the same thing, but in the reverse order. In the time of Zosimus the world of matter was filled by the projection into it of a psychic mystery, which appeared as the mystery of matter from then on until the decline of alchemy in the eighteenth century. But Nietzsche's ecstatic intuition wished to snatch the secret of the superman from the very stone in which, until then, it had slumbered. It was in the shape of this image that he wished to create the superman whom we may well call, in the language of the classical world, the divine man.

The alchemists went the other way about: they sought the wonderful stone that harboured a pneumatic essence in order to win from it the substance that penetrates all bodies (because, indeed, this substance is the "spirit" that has penetrated the stone) and changes the common matter into noble by tinting it another colour. This "spirit-substance" is like quicksilver that lurks unseen within the ore, and that must first be expelled if one wishes to recover it in pure form. But if one holds this penetrating mercury, then one can "project" it upon other substances and bring them from an imperfect to the perfect state. The imperfect state is like the state of sleep; bodies lie in it like "the sleepers chained in Hades," and they are awaked as from death to a new and more beautiful life by the divine tincture extracted from the spirit-filled stone. It is quite clear that we observe here a tendency to locate the mystery of psychic transformation in matter, and to use it at the same time as a theoretical guide for effecting chemical transformations.

Nietzsche has carefully seen to it that no one could take the Superman for the spiritual and moral ideal. The alchemist similarly emphasizes the point that the tincture, or divine water, not only performs beneficent works of healing and ennoblement, but acts as a fatal poison that penetrates other bodies as deeply as it penetrates its own (which is to say, as the πνεῦμα its stone).

Zosimus is a Gnostic who is influenced by Hermes. In his advice to Theosebeia he recommends the "Krater" as a means of transformation: she should hasten to the Poimandres in order to be baptized in the Krater.

This Krater refers to the divine vessel of which Hermes speaks to Thoth in the treatise named ὁ κρατήρ. After the creation of the world, God sent this vessel down to earth as a kind of baptismal font, having previously filled it with νοῦς (πνεῦμα). Herewith God gave to human beings who wished to free themselves from their natural (imperfect, dormant) state of ἄνοια (we should say: insufficient consciousness) an opportunity to baptize themselves in νοῦς and thus to share in the higher state of ἔννοια (enlightenment, higher consciousness). The νοῦς is, therefore, a kind of βαφεῖον, dyestuff, or tincture, that ennobles ignoble substances. Its rôle corresponds exactly to that of the tincturing stone extract, which can also be a πνεῦμα, and which, in the form of Mercury, possesses the Hermetic double significance of redeeming psychopomp [17] and quicksilver.

It is, therefore, sufficiently clear that Zosimus possessed a kind of mystic or Gnostic philosophy whose basic ideas he projected upon matter. When we speak of psychological projection we must, as I have already pointed out, always remember the fact that projection is a pre-conscious process that works only as long as it has not yet become conscious. Zosimus is convinced, like all other alchemists, not only that his philosophy can be applied to matter, but that processes take place in matter that correspond in meaning to his philosophical assumptions. For that reason we must suppose that he experienced, with regard to matter itself, an identity of the events in his own psyche with the behaviour of matter. Since his experience of this identity is pre-conscious, Zosimus is no more able than the others to make any pronouncement concerning it. He simply comes up against it, and it serves as a bridge, binding psychic and material events into one, so that "what is within is also without."

An unconscious happening that is not grasped by consciousness nevertheless portrays itself somehow and somewhere—for instance, in dreams, visions, and fantasies. The idea of the pneuma as the Son of God descending into matter and later freeing himself from it, in order to bring healing and salvation to all souls, bears the traits of an unconscious mental content projected into matter. Such a content is an autonomous complex leading an independent existence, divorced from consciousness, in the psychic non-ego, and projecting itself whenever it is constellated in any way—which is to say, whenever it is attracted by analogies to external things.

The psychic autonomy of the pneuma, or νοῦς,[18] is attested in the Neo-Pythagorean literature; according to the view there expressed, the soul was devoured by matter and only the understanding, the νοῦς, was left. But the νοῦς is outside of man—he is his demon. One could hardly formulate his autonomy more aptly. This νοῦς is, no doubt, identical with the God Anthropos: he appears beside the Demiurge, but is an opponent of the planetary spheres. He rends the circle of the spheres and stoops to earth and water (that is, he is about to project himself into the elements). His shadow falls upon the earth, but his image is reflected in the water. This image inflames the love of the elements, and he himself is so charmed with the mirrored reflection of divine beauty that he would gladly take up his abode within it. But he has scarcely descended when Physis, or physical nature, embraces him with passionate love. From this embrace arise the seven first hermaphroditic beings.[19] The number seven clearly refers to the planets, and thus to the metals.

It is in such visionary images (the Anthropos descries his own mirrored image) that an unconscious happening— here the projection of an autonomous content—expresses itself. So these mythical pictures resemble dreams, which inform us not only of the fact that a projection has taken place, but also about what has been projected. In the epoch with which we are dealing it was the divine demon $\nu o \hat{\upsilon} s$, the God-man, the pneuma, etc., that were projected. In so far as the viewpoint of Analytical Psychology is realistic and bases itself upon the assumption that psychic contents are existencies, the above-named symbols stand for an unconscious component of the personality to which one might attribute a higher form of consciousness as well as a superiority to common humanity.

As an empirical fact, such figures always express superior insights or qualities that are not yet conscious, and that also raise the question of whether or not they may be ascribed to the personal psyche. The problem of ascribing them to a given source may appear a captious one to the layman, but in practical work is of great importance. Indeed, an incorrect ascription may cause dangerous inflations, which seem of no importance to the layman only because he does not know what misfortunes they cause to human beings and their affairs.

As a matter of fact, we are dealing here with a content

that up to the present has rarely been ascribed to the human personality. The one great exception is Christ. As υἱὸς τοῦ ἀνθρώπου, the Son of Man, and also as θεοῦ υἱός, the Son of God, he realizes the God-man; while as incarnation of the Logos through his pneumatic procreation, he is also a manifestation of the divine νοῦς. Thus the Christian projection involves the unknown in man, or the unknown man, who thus becomes the bearer of "the terrible and astounding secret."

Pagan projection, on the contrary, goes beyond man and concerns the unknown in the material world, the unknown substance, which in some way, like the chosen man, is filled with God. And as, in Christianity, the Godhead conceals itself in the man of low degree, so in the "philosophy" it hides itself in the unseemly stone. While in the Christian projection the *descensus spiritus sancti* stops at the living body of the Chosen One, who is at once true man and true God, in alchemy the descent goes on down into the darkness of lifeless matter, whose lower parts, according to the Neo-Pythagorean view, are ruled by Evil. Evil and matter together form the dyad (duality). This is of feminine nature, an *anima mundi*, the female Physis, who, after the embrace of the One, the Monad, longs for the good and the perfect. The gnosis of Justin presents her as Edem, virgin above and serpent below. Revengefully she strives against the πνεῦμα because, in the guise of the second form of God, the Demiurge, it had faithlessly abandoned her. But she is "the divine soul (ψυχή) imprisoned in the elements" who is to be liberated.

Now, since all these mythical pictures present a drama of the human psyche on the yonder side of consciousness, we see that man is the one who is to be redeemed, as well as the redeemer. The first formulation is the Christian one, the second the alchemistic. In the first case man ascribes to himself the need of salvation and leaves the work of salvation (the actual ἆθλον or opus) to the autonomous divine figure; in the last case man takes upon himself the duty of carrying out the work of redemption, and ascribes to matter in general the state of suffering and the need for redemption.

In both cases redemption is a work. In Christianity it is the life and death of the God-man, which, as a unique sacrifice, bring about the reconciliation of man, who craves redemption and is lost in materiality, with God. The mythical operation of the self-sacrifice of the God-man extends, in the usual acceptance, to all men, although it is effective only for those who submit through faith or are selected by divine grace; but furthermore, in the Pauline acceptance, it operates as an apocatastasis for extrahuman creation in general, which, in its imperfect state, awaits redemption like the merely natural man. By a certain "synchronism" of events, man, as the bearer of a soul submerged in the world (in the flesh), is potentially put into contact with God at the moment when He, as Mary's son, is incarnated in her, the *virgo terra* and the representative of matter in the highest form; and man is potentially redeemed at the moment when the eternal Son of God returns to the Father after suffering the crucifixion.

The ideology of this mystery is anticipated in the myth cycles of Osiris, Orpheus, Dionysus, and Hercules, as also in the Messianic conception in Hebrew prophecy.[20] Such anticipations can be found even in the primitive hero myths where the overcoming of death plays an important rôle.[21]

The projections upon Attis and Mithras, more or less contemporary to the alchemistic projection, are also worth mentioning. The Christian projection differs from all these manifestations of the mystery of redemption and transformation by reason of the historic and personal figure of the Rabbi Jesus. The mythical happening incarnated itself in him and so entered the realm of world history as a unique historical and mystic event.

In the God-hero the Godhead itself labours because of its imperfect and suffering creation; it takes upon itself the state of suffering, and by this sacrificial act accomplishes the *opus magnum,* the ἄθλον of healing and of the conquest of death. The human being can actually do nothing decisive in this matter; he looks to his Redeemer full of faith and confidence, and tries in his way, by a fitting moral attitude, at least to put no obstacles in the way of the Saviour's work of redemption.

We would have to be satisfied with this bare fact were it not for the existence of the church. But the institution of the church means nothing less than a constantly active continuation of the life of Christ and its sacrificial function. Christ's sacrifice, the accomplishment of salvation, constantly repeats itself in the *officium divinum,* or, as the Benedictines would say, in the *opus divinum,* while still remaining the unique sacrifice that was performed by Christ himself as a temporal fact. Outside the time order it is constantly performed anew. This *opus supernaturale* is presented in the sacrificial Mass. To a certain extent the priest presents the mystic act in the ritual, but the really active force is Christ who sacrifices himself constantly and everywhere. His sacrificial death had its place in the temporal order, and yet is an extratemporal event, as the holy Ambrosius formulates it: *umbra in lege, imago in evangelio, veritas in cælestibus.*

According to the view of Thomas Aquinas, the sacrificial Mass is not a true *immolatio* (sacrifice) of the body of Christ, but a representative picture of the sacrificial death. This interpretation would be sufficient and consistent if there were no transformation of the offered elements, the bread and wine. But this offering is supposed to be a *sacrificium,* literally a making sacred. The etymology of the German word for sacrifice, Opfer, seems to be obscure, for it is a question whether it comes from *offere,* to offer, or from *operari,* to effect, to be active. In the classical usage, *operari deo* meant to serve the god or to offer him a sacrifice. But if an Opfer is an *opus,* then it is far more than an *oblatio,* the offering of so modest a gift as bread and wine. It must be an effectual act that lends a causal significance to the ritualistic words of the priest. The words of consecration (*qui pridie quam pateretur,* etc.) are, therefore, to be taken not as merely representing the transformation, but as its true *causa efficiens.* That is why the Jesuit Lessius (died 1623) called the words of consecration the "sword" with which the sacrificial lamb is slaughtered.

The so-called theory of mactation (slaughtering for sacrificial purposes) occupies quite an important place in the literature of the Mass, although it has not always been tolerated in its more objectionable outgrowths. Surely the clearest of all is the Greek rite as it is described by Archbishop Nicholas Cabasilas of Thessalonica, who died about 1363. In the first (preparatory) part of the Mass, the bread and wine do not lie upon the main altar, but upon the πρόθεσις, a kind of sideboard. There the priest cuts a piece from the body of the bread, and the appropriate text is: "As a lamb he was led to the shambles." Then he lays it upon the table, and the text runs: "The lamb of God is sacrificed." Then a sign of the cross is imprinted in the bread, and a small lance is stabbed into its side, to the text: "But one of the soldiers with a spear pierced his side and forthwith came there out blood and water." With these words water and wine are mixed in the chalice. Then comes the oblation in a solemn procession, the priest carrying the offering (Cabasilas says) "as kings, when they bring a gift to God, bear it themselves and do not let it be born by others." (The δῶρον, the gift, represents the giver, which means that Christ as sacrificer is also the sacrificed.)

So the priest repeats the traditional event, and in so far

as Christ, in the sacramental state, possesses a *vita corpora actualis,* a true bodily life, one could say that a physical slaying (*mortificatio*) of his body takes place. This happens through the effect of the words of consecration spoken by the priest. By the destruction of the offering, and by the *oblatio occisi ad cultum Dei* (the offering of the slain to the service of God), the transformation, the transubstantiation comes about. The transformation is a transmutation of the elements, which, from a natural, tainted, imperfect, and material state, change into a subtle body. The bread, which must consist of wheat, signifies the body, and the wine, standing for blood, the soul. A piece of the host is mixed with the wine after the transformation, and in this way the *conjunctio* of the soul with the body—the living body of Christ, which is to say, the unity of the church—is restored.

The holy Ambrose named the altered bread *medicina.* It is the φάρμακον ἀθανασίας, the drug of immortality, which displays its characteristic effect upon the believer in the act of communion—the effect, namely, of uniting the body with the soul. But this takes place in the form of a healing of the soul (*et sanabitur anima mea*) and a reformation of the body (*et mirabilius reformasti*). The text of the Mass shows in what way this is intended: "Grant unto us through the mystery of this water and this wine to partake of the divinity of him who held himself worthy to partake of our humanity, Jesus Christ," etc.

Perhaps you will allow me to introduce a personal remark. It was a real discovery for me, a Protestant, to read the words of the offertory for the first time: *Deus, qui humanæ substantiæ dignitatem mirabiliter condidisti* (O Lord, thou who didst miraculously create the dignity of human substance) and *qui humanitatis nostræ fieri dignatus est particeps* (who held himself worthy to partake of our humanity). What respect for the worth of human nature! *Deus et homo!* There is here no reminder of that worthless sinner in whose disparagement Protestantism has so often taken pleasure, and to which it returns all too gladly and easily. But even more seems to be hidden in this somewhat transcendental valuation of man. For if God is *dignatus* to partake of human nature, then man also might think himself worthy of partaking of divine nature. In a certain sense the priest does so in performing the mystery of the offering, when he presents himself as the victim in the place of Christ; and the congregation does likewise when it eats the consecrated body, and so partakes of the divine substance.

Since the priest has a causative part in the transformation, he releases the creature within the bread and wine from its elemental imperfection. He therefore not only stands in the place of the redeemer, but is himself a redeemer. And at this point the whole problem of redemption is reversed. It is not man who is in need of redemption, but matter, in which the divine soul is imprisoned in a sleeping and confined condition. Matter, which contains the divine mystery, is everywhere, and also in the human body. It is easily had, and is found everywhere—even in the most horrible filth.

In this respect, the *opus magnum* is no longer a ritualistic *officium*, but rather the work of redemption that God himself performed for mankind through Christ, as an example, and that is recognized as his own individual work by the philosopher who has received the *donum spiritus sancti*, the divine art. The alchemists emphasize this point: "He who works through the spirit of another and through a paid hand will behold results that are far from the truth; and contrariwise, he who gives his services to another as a journeyman in the laboratory will never be admitted to the mysteries of the Queen." One could cite here the words of Cabasilas: "As kings, when they bring a gift to God, bear it themselves, and do not let it be borne by others."

As a matter of fact, the alchemists are decided solitaries; each says his own word in his own way. They rarely have

pupils, and there seems to have been very little direct tradition; nor have any secret societies or the like been shown to
exist. Each worked in his laboratory for himself, and suffered
from his loneliness. On the other hand, they did not combat
one another: their writings are remarkably free from
polemic, and the way in which they quote one another
demonstrates an astonishing agreement in principles, even
when we are frequently unable to recognize in what it is
that they actually agree. There is not a trace of the disputa-
tiousness and hairsplitting that so often mar theology and
philosophy. The reason for this is probably to be found in
the circumstance that true alchemy was never a business or
a career, but a real *opus* that a man carried on in silent, self-
sacrificing labour. The impression is given that each has
tried for himself to give expression to his particular experience and to adduce for this purpose those dicta of the masters
that seemed to have a similar content.

From the very earliest times they all agree that their
art is sacred and divine, and likewise that their work can be
accomplished only with the help of God. This science of
theirs is given only to the few and no man understands it
unless God or a master has opened his mind. Furthermore, he
may not impart the acquired discernment to others unless
they are worthy of such knowledge. Since all the essential
matters are expressed in metaphors, he can communicate
them only to the intelligent, who possess the gift of understanding. The foolish allow themselves to be deluded by
literal interpretations and recipes, and so fall into error. As
to the study of the treatises, the alchemist is warned that he
must not be satisfied with one book; he must possess many
books, for "one book opens another." Moreover, he must
read carefully, from paragraph to paragraph; then he will
make discoveries. The terms are admittedly quite undepend-
able. Occasionally a dream tells which is the sought-for
substance. The *materia lapidis* can be found by divine in-

spiration. The practice of the art is a hard road, and the longest road. The art has no enemies except the ignorant.

It goes without saying that there are good and bad authors in alchemistic literature, as in all others. There exist also spectacular works as well as crazy and deceitful ones. Such inferior writings are easily detected by their abundant recipes, their careless and unrefined composition, their obtrusive mystification, their terrible dullness, and their shameless insistence upon the manufacture of gold. Good books are recognized by the industry, the care, and the obvious mental integrity of the author.

The basis of the work, the *materia prima,* is one of the most famous secrets of alchemy. This secrecy is not surprising, since the *materia prima* represents matter, which is unknown and carries the projection of the autonomous psychic content. It was, of course, impossible to specify such a substance, because the projection derives from the individual, and is different for each individual. For this reason it is not correct to say that the alchemists have never stated what the *materia prima* is; on the contrary, they have given only too many hints, and so have unceasingly contradicted themselves. For one it was quicksilver; for others it was ore, iron, gold, lead, salt, sulphur, vinegar, water, air, fire, earth, blood, water of life, *lapis,* poison, spirit, cloud, sky, dew, shadow, sea, mother, moon, dragon, Venus, chaos, or microcosm. Ruland's *Lexicon* gives not less than fifty synonyms, and this list might be considerably increased.

The *materia prima* always has the quality of ubiquity; it can be found always and everywhere—which is to say, that the projection can always and everywhere come about. Sir George Ripley, the English alchemist (1415?-1490), says: "The philosophers tell the enquirer that birds and fishes bring us the *lapis;* [22] every man possesses it, it is in every place, in thee, in me, in every thing, in time and in space." It offers itself in lowly form (*vili figura*). From it arises our eternal water (*aqua permanens*). According to Ripley, the *materia prima* is water; it is the material principle of all substances, even of mercury. It is the Aristotelian hyle, or that which receives form or determination, and which emanated from chaos as a dark sphere [23] (*sphæricum opus*) through the creative act of God. Chaos is a "confused mass" out of which the stone arises. The hylic water contains a hidden, elemental fire. In the treatise *De Sulphure*, hell-fire (*ignis Gehennalis*) is attributed to the earth element as its inner contradiction. Hortulanus also has the stone arise from a *massa confusa* containing all the elements in itself.

As the world arose from a confused chaos, so also the stone comes into being. The idea of the rotating sphere of water reminds us of Neo-Pythagorean conceptions: according to Archytas, the world soul is a circle or a sphere and, according to Philolaus, it draws the world around with it in its rotation. The original idea is, no doubt, to be found in Anaxagoras, where the νοῦς gives rise to a whirlpool in chaos. The cosmogony of Empedocles is also of importance; here the union of the dissimilar (through the influence of the φιλία) gives rise to the σφαῖρος, the spherical. Its designation as εὐδαιμονέστατος θεός, most holy God, throws a particular light upon the "round" and perfect nature of the *lapis*, which arises from, and also constitutes, the initial sphere. This is why the *materia prima* is often called *lapis*.

The first state is the hidden one, but by the art and the grace of God it can be changed into a second state, which is manifest. And so the idea of *materia prima* occasionally blends into the idea of the initial stage of the process, the *nigredo*, blackness. It is then the black earth in which the gold, or the *lapis*, is sowed or scattered like the wheat grain. It is the black, magically fruitful soil which Adam took with him from Paradise; it is also called antimony, and is described as "black, blacker than black" (*nigrum nigrius nigro*).

As the grain of fire lies concealed in the hyle, so the king's son lies in the dark depths of the sea as though dead, but yet lives, and calls from the deeps: "Whosoever will free me from the waters and bring me to a dry state, him I will favour with ever-enduring (*perpetuis*) riches." Although many hear this call, no one will let himself be moved by pity and take it upon himself to seek the king. "Who," they say, "will dive into the sea? Who, when he himself is in danger of his life, will spring to another's side? Few indeed listen to his complaint, but the majority suppose that the voice they hear is the uproar and clamour of Scylla and Charybdis. Therefore they remain inactive, sitting at home, and are concerned neither for the kingly treasure nor for salvation."

The relation of the king's son to the *rex marinus* in the *Visio Arislei* is transparent. Arisleus (Archelaus),[24] the pupil of Anaxagoras, no doubt owes his influence to the fact that, in contradiction with his teacher, his cosmogonic *voûs* is intermixed with matter, namely, air. Naturally this idea has a particular value for alchemy. He tells in his vision of his adventure with the *rex marinus* in whose kingdom nothing prospers and nothing is propagated, and where there are no philosophers. Only the similar is intermixed, and as a result there is no procreation. The king must take the advice of philosophers and pair off his two children, Thabritius[25] and Beya, whom he has brought forth from his brain.

That the king is inanimate (*exanimis*), or that his realm is unfruitful, means that the hidden state is a latent or potential condition. The darkness and the depths of the sea pointedly signify the unconscious projection of a psychic content. Inasmuch as such a content belongs to the totality[26] of the personality, and is only apparently severed from the whole by the projection, something like an attraction always arises between consciousness and the projected content. This generally shows itself in the form of a fascination. The alchemistic allegory expresses this fact by the king's

cry for aid out of the depths of the dissociated and unconscious state. According to the alchemistic view, consciousness
should give heed to this cry; someone should render a service
to the king, *operari regi*, for this would be not only wisdom,
but salvation as well.[27] But this brings with it the necessity
of a descent into the dark world of the unconscious, the
ritualistic act of a κατάβασις εἰς ἄντρον, the adventure of
the night sea journey whose aim and end is the restoration
of life, the resurrection, and the conquest of death.[28] Arisleus
and his companions risk the venture, which ends with the
catastrophe of the death of Thabritius. This death is a pun-
ishment for the incestuous *conjunctio oppositorum*. The
brother-sister pair is an allegory of the idea of opposites in
general.

There are all kinds of opposites: dry-wet, hot-
cold, male-female, sun-moon, gold-silver, mercury-sulphur,
round-square, water-fire, ponderable-volatile, physical-
spiritual,[29] etc. The king's son is always a rejuvenated form
of the father king. The youth is frequently represented with
a sword, and stands for the spirit, while the father is the
body. In a variant text of the *Visio,* the death of the son
comes about by his disappearing, during the act of coitus,
into the body of Beya. There are other parallel representations: the father devours him—the sun is drowned in mercury or is swallowed by a lion (Plates VIII and IX).
Thabritius is the masculine, spiritual principle of light and
Logos, which, like the Gnostic νοῦς, sinks into the embrace
of physical nature. The death is, therefore, the completed
descent of the spirit into matter. The alchemists frequently
represented the sinfulness of this occurrence, but they never
grasped it; and this is why they rationalized or minimized
the incest, in itself so repellent.

Since the incest resulted from the advice of the philosophers, the death of the king's son was naturally a dubious
and dangerous matter. On descending into the unconscious,

See page 242]

PLATE IX

PLATE X

[See page 246

the conscious personality finds itself in a dangerous situation, for it seems as though it were extinguishing itself. It is the situation of the primitive hero who is devoured by the dragon. Since it is a question of the diminution or extinction of the conscious personality, and such an *abaissement du niveau mental* constitutes that "peril of the soul" of which primitive man stood in the greatest fear (namely, the fear of ghosts),[30] the intentional or wanton provocation of this state is a sacrilege or a breach of the taboo that is followed by the severest punishments.

Accordingly, the king imprisons Arisleus and his companions in a house of triple glass together with the corpse of the king's son. So the heroes are bound in the nether world, at the bottom of the sea, where they must undergo all kinds of terrors, and suffer for eighty days in an intense heat. By request of Arisleus, Beya was imprisoned with them. (The variant text of the *Visio* interprets the prison as the womb of Beya.) Clearly, they have been overpowered by the unconscious, and helplessly abandoned. This means that they have freely bound themselves over to death so as to engender fruitful life in a region of the psyche that has lain in dark unconsciousness and the shadow of death.

To be sure, the brother-sister pair suggests the possibility of life; but this unconscious contradiction must be activated by the intervention of consciousness, if it is not to remain latent. This, however, is a dangerous undertaking. We can understand the anxious plea contained in the *Aurora Consurgens: horridas nostræ mentis purga tenebras, accende lumen sensibus.* We can also understand Michael Majer, who supposed that only a few were willing to plunge into the sea. Arisleus was in danger of succumbing to the fate of Theseus and Pirithous, who, in their descent to the underworld, grew fast to its rocks—which is to say that consciousness, advancing into the unknown regions of the psyche, is overpowered by the archaic forces of the unconscious. The embrace of Nous and Physis is a cosmic allegory of such an occurrence. The reason for the descent, as the hero myth presents it, is that "the precious object hard to attain" (treasure, virgin, life potion, conquest of death, etc.) is to be found in the regions of danger (watery abyss, cave, forest, island, castle, etc.).

The fear of the descent to Hades is at bottom the timidity and the resistance experienced by every natural person when it comes to delving too deeply in himself. If he experienced the sense of resistance alone, it would not be such a serious matter. But the psychic substratum, that dark realm of the unknown,[31] actually exercises a fascinating attraction [32] that threatens to become the more overpowering the further he advances into it. And here arises the psychological danger of a dissolution of the conscious personality into its functional components—that is, into single functions of consciousness, complexes, hereditary units, etc.[33] Such a disintegration sometimes amounts to actual schizophrenia—and is just what happens to Gabricus (in the variant text of the *Rosarium Philosophorum*): he is disintegrated into atoms in the body of Beya.

The fate of Gabricus is a parallel to the *conjunctio* of Nous and Physis.[34] But the latter is a cosmogonic happening, while the former is a catastrophe brought about by the intervention of the philosopher. As long as consciousness does not come upon the scene, the contradictions of the unconscious remain latent. They are activated by consciousness. The *regius filius*, the spirit, the Logos or Nous, is then devoured by physical nature—that is, the body and its representative organs attain sovereignty over consciousness. The hero myth [35] presents this condition as the engulfment in the belly of the whale or dragon. So great a heat prevails there that the hero loses his hair; he is born again as bald as a babe at the breast.[36] This heat is the *ignis Gehennalis* of

Hell, to which Christ also descended, there to perform a part of his *opera* by conquering death.[37]

The philosopher makes the journey to Hell as a "redeemer." The "hidden fire" is the inner contradiction of the cold moisture of the sea. The *visio* clearly presents this fire as the warmth of incubation, which symbolizes the state of "brooding over" the self in the *meditatio*. In the Indian yoga we come upon the similar conception of *tapas*,[38] self-incubation. (The practice of *tapas* aims, like the *visio*, at transformation and resurrection.)

The "precious object hard to attain," whose presence was suspected in the dark *materia prima*, was symbolized by the alchemists in various ways. Christophorus of Paris, for instance, says that chaos (as *materia prima*) is the work of all-wise nature. Our understanding (*intellectus*), aided by the "heavenly and glowing spirit" (*spiritus*), must transform this natural work of art—that is, chaos—into the quintessence, which is of celestial nature, and into the life-giving essence (*vegetabilis*) of Heaven. The precious substance is potentially contained in chaos in the form of a *massa confusa* of the united elements, and man must diligently apply his understanding to it (*incumbere debet!*) so that he can change our Heaven "into actuality" (*ad actum*).

Johannes Grasseus mentions an opinion according to which the *materia prima* is the lead of the philosophers, also called the lead of the air (this being an allusion to the inner contradiction). This lead contains the radiant white dove called the "salt of the metals." The dove is the chaste, wise, and wealthy Queen of Sheba, covered with the white veil, who wished to give herself to King Solomon alone.

According to the view of Basilius Valentinus, the earth (as *materia prima*) is not a dead body, but is inhabited by the spirit, which is the life and soul of the earth. All created things, even the minerals, receive their powers from the spirit of the earth. The spirit is life, it is nourished by the stars, and gives nourishment to all living things, which it shelters in its womb. As the mother gestates the unborn child, so the earth, through the spirit it receives from on high, gestates the minerals in its womb. This invisible spirit, resembling a mirror image in the fact that it cannot be handled, is the root of the substance necessary to, or arising in, the process (*radix nostrorum corporum*).

A similar idea can be found in Michael Majer.[39] The sun has spun the gold in the earth by many millions of rotations around it. The sun has gradually imprinted in the earth its image, which is the gold. The sun is the image of God, and the heart [40] is the image of the sun in man. Gold is the sun's image in the earth, and is also called *deus terrenus;* God can be recognized in the gold. This image of God appearing in gold is no doubt the *anima aurea*, which, instilled into ordinary quicksilver, changes it into gold.

Ripley holds the view that one must draw the fire out of chaos and make it visible. This fire is the Holy Ghost which unites Father and Son. The Holy Ghost is often represented as a winged old man,[41] this being Mercury in the form of the god of revelation, who coincides with Hermes Trismegistus and forms an alchemistic trinity together with the king and the king's son (Plate X). God has created this fire in the earth, as he did the purging hell-fire. God himself glows in this fire with divine love.

It is not impossible that Christian symbolism was influenced by such ideas. I have been struck by the fact that, in representations of the unicorn, the hunters inflict upon the animal, when it already reposes in Mary's lap, such serious spear wounds that we may well ask whether the unicorn later recovered (Plate XI). The Jesuit Caussinus, who published a learned work about symbolism in 1623, reports that Basilius supposed the unicorn to stand for the Son of God. The same author holds that Ambrose seconded this view by maintaining that the procreation of Christ was as mysterious

PLATE XI

See page 246]

as that of the unicorn. Albertus alone is credited with the statement regarding the Virgin (the begetting through the Holy Ghost), that the *monoceros* (unicorn), a most violent animal, loved her (the *beata virgo*) and was captured by her as by a bait and a lure.

It is worthy of note that some alchemistic treatises ascribed to Albertus are regarded as forgeries. But it is certain that he knew the alchemy of his day and copiously cited Hermes. The *Tabula Smaragdina* contains the basic ideas: the *conjunctio* of Sol and Luna, the Son's penetration into the earth and his immense strength (*totius fortitudinis fortitudo fortis*). Caussinus mentions the strength of God, which equals that of the rhinoceros (like Behemoth in Job 40:10), and refers to Exodus 15:2, "the Lord is my strength," adding that "the earlier God of revenge, who sent down thunder and lightning and brought disorder upon the world, came to rest in the lap, in the very womb, of the virgin, taken captive by love." The unicorn will tolerate no other in its cave; and the Son of God, like the unicorn, built his sanctuary upon earth, that is, in the womb of the *beata virgo*. We should note the fact that the earth and the virgin are taken as one and the same (in astrology, also, the virgin is an earth symbol). We find this identity explicitly stated in the writings of Tertullian and Augustine. It is a tradition of ancient times that the horn of the unicorn has the property of freeing water from all harmful substances—of consecrating it, in a measure. In a similar way, says Caussinus, man is cleansed from the soilure of sin by baptism.

It is not inconceivable that the alchemistic views of Albertus fathered the idea of the *conjunctio* of virgin and unicorn, as also of the resulting transformation of God from an unfavourable and chaotic form into a perfect one—this transformation corresponding to the change of the sometimes poisonous *materia prima* into the alexipharmic, the counterpoison, the *medicina universalis* of the *lapis*. If this is so, we observe how a piece of Hermetic philosophy has gained entrance to Christian symbolism. This could happen all the more easily because the relationship of the virgin to God the Father and God the Son, who are yet one, is thoroughly obscure.

In the genealogical tree of Michael Majer, Gabritius in the form of Osiris is married to his mother, Isis. The incest takes place because there is no other possible choice; there exists only this one couple, the latent pair of opposites contained in the *materia prima*.

These examples show that a spirit lurked in the *materia prima* as it did in the stone of the Nile mentioned by Ostanes. This spirit was at length interpreted as the Holy Ghost in harmony with the old tradition of the Nous devoured by the darkness while in the embrace of Physis. The theme symbolizes the projection of a highly fascinating, unconscious content, which, like all such contents, displays the "divine," or "sacred," quality of the numen.

Alchemy sets itself the task of gaining and bringing to sight the "precious object hard to attain" in the form of physical gold, or of the panacea, or of the potently transformative tincture—in so far, that is, as the art busied itself in the laboratory. But inasmuch as the enterprise was never devoted purely to practical things and to chemistry, but also gave expression in and through itself to the unconscious contents, it was at the same time a psychic exercise that can best be compared to the so-called active imagination of which I have elsewhere given an example.[42] I have shown a process that is actively grasped by the imagination and that may, also, express itself in the dream life. Such a process reaches from the unconscious up into consciousness, and both its aspects have so close a relation to the world of alchemistic ideas that we are perhaps justified in assuming that alchemistic procedure deals with happenings that are the same as, or resemble, those in the processes of integration (or individuation) occurring both in the active imagination and in dreams.

A little while ago we abandoned Arisleus and his companions, together with Beya and the dead Thabritius, in the house of triple glass in which the *rex marinus* had imprisoned them. They suffered under an intense heat, like the three men in the fiery furnace into which King Nebuchadnezzar had thrown them. The king had a vision of a fourth companion, resembling a son of the gods, as told in Daniel 3:25. This vision is not without its bearing upon alchemy, inasmuch as the latter, in countless passages, repeats that the *lapis* is *trinus* and *unus* (threefold and one). It also consists of the four elements, fire representing, as we have seen, the spirit that is concealed in matter. This is the fourth who is missing and yet on hand, who always appears in the fiery distress of the furnace, and represents the divine presence, succour, the completion of the work.

Now, in their dire need Arisleus and his companions saw their master Pythagoras in dream, and they begged aid of him. But he sent them his disciple Harforetus, who is the "originator of nourishment." Therewith the work was completed, and Thabritius was alive again. We must obviously suppose that Harforetus has brought with him the miraculous food. That this is the case becomes apparent only through a discovery made by Ruska, who gave us access to the text of the *Codex Berolinensis*. There, in the introduction that is missing from the printed editions of the *Visio*, Pythagoras is made to say: "You write, and have already written down for posterity, how this most precious tree is planted and how he who eats of its fruits will nevermore go hungry." The *Visio* was composed for the purpose of leaving to posterity an example of the process. It speaks of the planting of trees, and the end of the legend is a demonstration of the marvellous, regenerating action of the fruits. While Arisleus was in dire straits, and while Thabritius lay in the sleep of death, the tree has apparently grown and borne fruit. The part played by Arisleus in the glass house is completely passive. The decisive action is taken by the master who sends his messenger, apparently with the food of life.

The alchemist maintained that a man could receive the secret knowledge only by divine inspiration or out of the mouth of a master, and also that no one could complete the work except with the help of God. In this case the legendary master, the divine Pythagoras, has taken the place of God and has completed the work of regeneration. This divine intervention, as we may well call it, takes place in dream, when Arisleus sees the master and beseeches him for aid. We are reminded of the offertory of the Mass by the union of the opposites—spirit and body—portrayed by Gabricius and Beya, by the slaying and the roasting in the oven. We likewise find an analogue to the entreaty of the helper in the *memento vivorum,* the petition for the living, and in the remembrance of the martyrs, which precede the transformation in the *ordo missæ.* This invocation is made *pro redemptione animarum suarum, pro spe salutis et incolumitatis suæ;* and the saints are held in remembrance in order that God, because of their merit and intercession, will allow *ut in omnibus protectionis tuæ muniamur auxilio.* The petition ends with the epiclesis, which ushers in the transformation: *ut nobis corpus et sanguis fiat,* that the body and the blood will come into being for us—namely, the miraculous sustenance, the φάρμακον ζωῆς. In the *Visio,* it is the fruits of the immortal tree that bring salvation. The *fructus sacrificii missæ,* the fruits of the sacrificial Mass, of which the church speaks, are somewhat different, for the phrase refers to moral effects and the like, and not to the consecrated substances, which likewise arise *ex opere operato.*

But at this point there is a division of minds. The Christian accepts the fruits of the sacrificial Mass for himself personally, and for his life circumstances in the widest sense. The alchemist, on the other hand, receives the *fructus arboris immortalis* not only for himself, but first and foremost for the king or the king's son, for the perfecting of the quested substance. He does, indeed, take part in the *perfectio,* which brings him health, riches, enlightenment and salvation, but since he is not the one to be redeemed, but a redeemer, he is more concerned to perfect his substance than himself. He always presupposes the moral qualities, and takes them into consideration only in so far as they can promote or obstruct the *opus.* His aim is not to achieve moral perfection for himself, but to procure for the mysterious substance an eternal and perfect existence, to create the *incombustibile* or *incorruptibile.* He lays a much higher emphasis upon the effect *ex opere operantis* than the church, because he takes the place of the Christ who offers himself in the sacrificial Mass. One should in no way suppose that religious megalomania makes him attribute to himself the rôle of redeemer. He has as little of this—and, all things considered, perhaps not so much— as the officiating priest, who at any rate immolates the Christ in a representative and causal capacity.

The alchemist always stresses his own humility, and frequently begins his treatise with an invocation of God. He does not dream of identifying himself with Christ; far otherwise, the alchemy of the later periods sets the quested substance, the *lapis,* in parallel to Christ. It is not a question of actual identification, but of the hermeneutic *sicut* (like, or as), which indicates the analogy. Nevertheless, analogy, for mediæval man, was not so much a mental tool as a secret correspondence—this being a survival of primitive thinking that had remained very much alive.

An instructive example is the rite of hallowing the fire on the Saturday before Easter. The fire is like Christ (*imago Christi*). The stone from which the spark is struck is the "cornerstone," a second *imago,* and the spark that springs from the stone is again an *imago Christi*. The analogy to the extraction of the pneuma from the stone, in the dictum of Ostanes cited by Zosimus, obtrudes itself. We are already familiar with the ideas of pneuma as fire, Christ as fire, and the earth's countersubstance, contained within it, as fire. But the stone from which the spark leaps is also the analogue to the rocky tomb, or the stone before it. Christ lay in it as one asleep or in the fetters of death, during the three days of the journey to Hell, when he had descended to the *ignis Gehennalis*. He arises thence as the new fire. An uncanonical word of the Master's goes: "Who is near unto me is near unto the fire, and who is far from me is far from the kingdom."

Accordingly, the church had to make a very important decision when it established the doctrine that the soul of Christ accomplished the *descensus ad inferos* according to its substance as well as according to its power. For, in the very nature of the case, the soul is fire from the central fire of the world.

It is rather surprising that alchemy did not stumble sooner upon the relation of the *lapis* to Christ, since the most important decision in the question of substance was taken as early as 1140, at the synod of Sens. We must, however, bear in mind that the alchemistic ideas of the early Latins were still very primitive, and that the *lapis* conception did not reach its most important developments until the fourteenth and fifteenth centuries. In his well-documented book: *The Secret Tradition in Alchemy, Its Developments and Records* (London: Kegan Paul, 1926), Arthur Edward Waite has expressed the opinion that the man who first identified the stone with Christ was Heinrich Khunrath, the author of *Amphitheatrum*, which appeared in 1609. Yet in the contemporary work of Jacob Boehme, who made extensive use of alchemistic terms, the *lapis* was already a metaphorical expression for Christ. Waite's opinion is undoubtedly mistaken, for we have much earlier attestations of the relation of the *lapis* to Christ. The oldest that I know of so far is contained in the *Codicillus* (Chapter ix) of Raymond Lully, who is supposed to have lived between 1235 and 1315. Even if many of the treatises ascribed to him were written by Spanish and Provençal disciples, this does not change the approximate date of the main body of writings to which the *Codicillus* belonged. In any case, I do not know that anyone has adduced convincing grounds for placing this treatise later than the fourteenth century. It contains the passage: "And as Jesus Christ, of the house of David, took upon himself human nature in order to free and to redeem mankind who were in the bonds of sin because of Adam's disobedience, so also, in our art, the thing that is unjustly defiled by the one will be absolved, cleansed and delivered from that foulness by another that is contrary to it."

We could cite as a still older source the *Tractatus Aureus* ascribed to Hermes, a book supposed by the Middle Ages itself to be of Arabian origin, if it contained any verbal reference to Christ. My reason for quoting it, in spite of this deficiency, lies in the fact that it describes matters that correspond in a curious way to the mysterious events of Eastertide, although presenting them in quite a different language.

The text deserves close attention from the psychological point of view. In abbreviated form, the passage reads: "Our most valuable stone, which was thrown upon the dung-heap, has become altogether mean . . . But when we marry the crowned king to the red daughter, then, in a weak fire, she is gotten with a son, and he lives through our fire . . . Then he is transformed, and his tincture remains as red as flesh. Our son of royal birth takes his tincture from the fire, whereupon death and darkness and the waters take to flight. The dragon fears the sunlight, and our dead son will live. The king comes out of the fire, and takes joy in the wedding. The hidden treasures are disclosed. The son, already come to

life, has become a warrior in the fire and surpasses the tincture, because he is himself the treasure and himself bears the
philosophical *materia*. Gather together, ye sons of wisdom,
and rejoice, for death's dominion has found an end, and the
son reigns, he wears the red garment and is clothed in the
purple."

We are hardly assuming too much if we take this text
as something like a variation upon the theme of the mythical
God-man and his conquest of death, and so as an analogue
of the Christian drama. Since the age and derivation of this
writing are still unknown, we cannot decide offhand how
much it owes to Christian influence, if, indeed, it owes anything. Very early texts, like that of Comarius, cannot be
suspected of showing the influence of Christianity. (Intro-
ductions and the like of a Christian nature have been added
to the manuscripts by Byzantine, monastic copyists.) And
yet it is just the text of Comarius that bears all the traits of
a regeneration mystery. After all, the ideas of rebirth, renewal, the overcoming of death, etc., were in no way the
exclusive products of Christian thought, but flourished many
centuries before our time reckoning began. Nor should we
take it for granted that Christianity had completely absorbed
or exterminated pagan culture. As Ruska has shown in the
cases of the *Tabula Smaragdina* and the *Turba*, there was the
possibility of a more or less direct and continuous tradition
within both Christianity and Islam, though the latter was
even more hostile to pagan culture than the former.

The oldest source that deals specifically with the relation of the stone to Christ seems, as far as I have been able
to determine, to be the *Margarita Pretiosa* of Petrus Bonus
of Ferrara, composed in 1330. Here is an epitome of the
discussion: The art is for one part natural, for the other
divine or supernatural. At the end of the sublimation there
germinates, through the mediation of the spirit, a radiant
white soul (*anima candida*), and with the spirit itself it flies

to heaven. And this is clearly and manifestly the stone. So far, the procedure is indeed somewhat marvellous, but still within the framework of nature. But as regards the fixation or the permanence of the soul and the spirit at the end of the sublimation, this comes about through the addition of the mysterious stone, which cannot be grasped by the senses, but only through the intellect, through inspiration or divine revelation, or through the teaching of one who knows.

Alexander says that there are two categories: perception through the eye and understanding through the heart.[43] The secret stone is a gift of God. It is the stone without which alchemy could not exist. It is the heart and the tincture of gold, regarding which Hermes said: "It is necessary that at the end of the world heaven and earth be bound together, this being the philosophical word." Pythagoras, also, said in the *Turba*: "This the god Apollo has concealed, so that the world may not be laid waste." Thus alchemy stands above nature, and is divine.

The whole difficulty of the art is contained in this stone. The intellect cannot grasp it, but must believe in it as it does in the divine miracles and the fundamentals of the Christian creed. Therefore, God alone is operative, while nature is passive in the process. From their knowledge of the art the ancient philosophers knew about the coming end of the world and about the resurrection of the dead. Then the soul will be united with its original body for all eternity. The body will become wholly transfigured (*glorificatum*), imperishable and almost unbelievably subtilized, and it will penetrate all solids. Its nature will be spiritual as well as corporeal. When the stone is disintegrated to powder like a man in his grave, God restores to it soul and spirit, and takes away all imperfection; then the substance (*illa res*) is strengthened and improved, as after the resurrection man becomes stronger and younger than he was before.

The ancient philosophers discerned the Day of Judgement in this art—that is, in the germination and birth of this stone—because there occurs in it the union of the soul to be transfigured (*beatificandæ*) with its original body, unto glory everlasting. So, also, the ancients knew that a virgin must conceive and give birth, because in their art the stone conceives and gets itself with child, and gives birth to itself. Such a thing can happen only through the grace of God. Therefore, Alphidius says of the stone that its mother is a virgin and its father has never known woman. They knew also that God becomes man on the Judgement Day of this art (*in novissima die huius artis*), when the work is completed (*in qua est operis complementum*), and that the begetter and the begotten, the old man and the boy, father and son, all become one.

Now, Bonus goes on, since no creature except man can unite with God, because of dissimilarity, God must become one with man. And this happened in the case of Jesus Christ and his virgin mother. For this reason Balgus says in the *Turba:* "O what miracles of nature, that have changed the soul of the old man into the body of the youth, and the father into the son."

Plato (*scribens in alchimicis*) has written to the same effect in a gospel which was completed long after by John the Evangelist. Plato has written the introductory words from "In the beginning was the Word" to "There was a man sent from God." God has given the philosopher this wonderful example so that he might be able to accomplish supernatural works. Morienus says that God entrusted the magistery to those of his philosophers or prophets for whose souls he had prepared a dwelling in his paradise.

This old text by Bonus, which is more than 270 years earlier than Khunrath, clearly shows that the relation between the mystery of Christ and the mystery of the stone was so obvious, even at the beginning of the fourteenth century, that the philosophical work seemed like a parallel and imitation—perhaps even like a continuation—of the divine work of redemption.

The next source, chronologically, is a Zurich manuscript of the fifteenth century found in the *Codex Rheno-vacensis,* in the monastery at Rheinau. This manuscript is unfortunately mutilated and begins with the fourth parable, as we discover by comparing it with a complete, but much later, manuscript at Paris. My attention was called to it by the fact that the printer (*typographus*) of the *Artis Aurif-eræ, quam chemiam vocant* has published only the second part of the *Aurora Consurgens* (1572). He prefixed to it a short notice to the reader in which he said that he had intentionally omitted the whole treatise of the parables or allegories, because the author, following the ancient manner of the obscurantists (*antiquo more tenebrionum*), had treated almost the whole of Sacred Writ, particularly Solomon, the Psalter, and the Canticles, in such a way as to make it appear that the Holy Scriptures had been written solely to do honour to alchemy. He had even profaned the most holy mystery of the incarnation and of the death of Christ by turning it into the mystery of the *lapis,* not, to be sure, with evil intent, as he (the printer, Conrad Waldkirch) freely admitted, but after the manner of that epoch of darkness (*seculum illud tenebrarum*). Waldkirch is referring here to the period before the Reformation, whose outlook upon man and matter, and whose experience of the divine presence in the mysterious *materia,* had disappeared from the field of vision of Protestants of his own day.

Because the first three parables, and a certain part of the fourth, are missing, I cannot cite from the *Aurora* as fully as I would choose. The sixth parable says: "It is written in the *Turba:* the earth suffers everything, because it is the foundation. Since it is the foundation of heaven, seeing that at the separation of the elements it appeared in a dry state, it is a way without hindrance in the Red Sea. When this great and wide sea [44] shattered the rock,[45] and the metallic waters flowed therefrom, then the rivers that delight the City of God vanished in aridity. When this mortal shall have put on immortality . . . then shall be brought to pass the word that is written . . . : Death is swallowed up in victory. O death, where is thy victory? For as all men die in Adam, so they will be brought to life again in Christ! [46] But Christ is the second Adam who, consisting of simple and pure essence, subsists for all eternity, as Senior says: 'He is the wine that never dies, since he persists through continual increase.' [47] . . . The second Adam speaks to his sons: [48] 'Come, ye blessed of my Father, inherit the kingdom prepared for you from the foundation of the operation [49] and eat my bread and drink the wine that I have mixed, for everything is prepared for you.' "

We actually get the impression that the anonymous author of this treatise has put the Holy Scriptures into the service of alchemy; while certain treatises of the Protestant *Musæum Hermeticum Reformatum,* which is two centuries later, rather give us the feeling that alchemy was to be estranged from its own nature and brought over to the Protestant Church. We can certainly understand that two such basically different spiritual movements as the church and alchemy represented no small conflict for mediæval man, although I know of nothing in the literature that betrays a consciousness of this conflict, or any animosity towards the church.

In any case, the author of the *Aurora* was in no way aware of the seriousness of the heresy he was committing. He had such a ready acquaintance with the Vulgate that we might almost suspect him of being in holy orders, and he was certainly an educated man with the liveliest interest in religion. We also have the testimony of the humanist Patrizzi for the fact that Hermetic philosophy was not felt to be contradictory to ecclesiastical Christianity. On the contrary, it was regarded as a support of Christian belief. Patrizzi, for instance, in the introduction to his book, petitioned Pope Gregory XIV to allow Hermes to take the place of Aristotle.

The text of the *Aurora* is of historical significance in so far as it is at least one hundred years earlier than Khunrath (1598) and Boehme (1610). Curiously enough, Boehme's first writing also bears the title: *Aurora, or the Dawn in its Ascent*. Could Boehme have known the *Aurora Consurgens,* or at least its title? It would not be impossible.

The next source, chronologically, for the identity of the *lapis* with Christ, is an interesting document from the end of the fifteenth or the beginning of the sixteenth century. It was addressed to Ladislaus, the king of Hungary and Bohemia. The author is named Nicholas Melchior, and calls himself a Hungarian. He has represented the alchemistic process as a form of the Mass. I will call attention only to a few essential points. After the reading of the Gospel, in the part of the Mass usually occupied by the creed, Melchior has put an Ave—not an Ave Maria, but an "Ave, præclara" —"of which I desire," he says, "that it be called the testament of the art, seeing that the whole chemical art is figuratively concealed in it, and blessed is he who understands this sequence." He goes on: "Salutations, O beautiful lamp of Heaven, thou beaming light [50] of the world, here thou unitest thyself with the moon, there doth arise (*fit*) the bond of Mars [51] (*copula martialis*) and the conjunction of Mercury.[52] From these three, above all, there is born in the river bed, through the magistery of the art, the strong giant whom a thousand times a thousand seek, after these three have dissolved themselves, not into rain water . . . but into mercurial water, into this our blessed resin,[53] which is dissolved by itself and which bears the name of Sperm of the Philosophers. Now he [54] hastens to ally himself, to betroth himself, to the virgin bride, and to fecundate her in the bath in a moderate fire. But the virgin does not become pregnant at once unless she is kissed in repeated embraces. Then she conceives in her body, and thus arises the luck-bringing embryo, all this corresponding to the order of nature. Then there appears at the bottom of the vessel the mighty Ethiopian, burned, calcined, bleached, wholly dead and lifeless.[55] He begs to be buried, to be sprinkled with his own humidity and slowly calcined,[56] until he arises in gleaming form from the strong fire . . . Behold a wonderful reconstruction or renewal of the Ethiopian! Because of the bath of rebirth he gives himself a new name, called by philosophers natural sulphur and their son, who is the stone of the philosophers. See, it is one thing, one root, one essence, to which nothing external is added, but from which much that is superfluous is taken away through the magistery of the art . . . It is the treasure of treasures, the supreme philosophical potion, the heavenly secret of the ancients. Blessed he who finds the like of it. He who has seen this thing, writes and speaks openly, and I know that he bears true witness. God be praised to all eternity."

The liturgy, properly speaking, ends here. There now follows a sort of recapitulation of the main parts. Melchior refers the offertory to the stone that the builders rejected and that became the cornerstone. "This was made by God and is wonderful in our eyes." After this comes the secret, which leads over to the oblation. The offering is the *opus:* "*nostrum artificium benedictæ artis alchemiæ*, which shall always be dedicated to the glorious name of God and to the salutary reformation of the Church, through our Lord Jesus Christ. Amen."

The transformation is missing; it has obviously been anticipated in the "Ave, præclara." The salutation "Ave," called the "Angelic Salutation," is associated in the ritual with Mary. But since we must, no doubt, complete the sense

LE
TABLEAV
DES RICHES
INVENTIONS
Couuertes du voile des feintes
Amoureuses, qui sont re-
presentees dans le

SONGE DE POLIPHILE
Desvoilees des ombres du Songe,
& subtilement exposees

PAR BEROALDE

A. PARIS.
Chez MATTHIEV GVILLEMOT, au Palais,
en la gallerie des prisonniers.
Auec priuilege du Roy.

PLATE XII

PLATE XIII

[*See page 265*

by adding *medicina* to *præclara,* we find here the intimation of a connection between the *aqua vitæ,* the *medicina catholica,* the quested substance in general, and the feminine principle. This possibility is given support by a passage from Senior Zadith, the Son of Hamuel, who is to be counted among the Arabic writers, and therefore precedes the thirteenth century. It goes: "The full moon is the water of the philosopher and the root of science . . . the perfect and round stone and the sea . . ."

The last to follow is the postcommunion: "Honour our king who comes out of the fire,[57] the one filled with divine light and crowned with the diadem, to all eternity." In conclusion there is a closing prayer for the reinforcement of Christian faith and the extermination of the Turks.

In spite of its bad taste and its absurdities, this text is highly illuminating in connection with our subject. Melchior has obviously recognized the analogy between the two *opera,* and has quite naïvely put the individual *opus,* in all its insufficiency, in the place of the time-honoured words of the holy service. One need not regard this too critically, if one is not a Catholic. Melchior is supposed to have lived in the time of the Reformation. Not so long afterward, over a wide extent of Europe, the Mass was replaced by the far from sacrosanct words of preachers. They announced the word of God, to be sure, but quite in their own way. Melchior did something similar. If we grant him the right to a personal confession of faith, he becomes acceptable. We can clearly discern from the text quoted above that he felt the alchemistic process to be the equivalent of the process of transubstantiation in the Mass, and that for that very reason he felt the need of representing his experience [58] in the form of the Mass. It is certainly strange that he did not make the alchemistic transmutation replace the transformation, but instead gave it a place near the creed, so that the liturgy ends before the consecration.

In the second version of the recapitulation, the transformation is again missing, and Melchior's rendering of the Mass jumps from the secret of the offertory directly to the post-communion. Since we can be fairly sure that the author was a Catholic, or at least had been one, this peculiarity could be ascribed to a kind of religious awe for the most solemn and moving part of the Mass, the transformation. And we could take this as an indirect, but sufficient, sign of a conflict in Melchior's conscience between the action upon him of the externally effective rite, and his own inner, individual experience. Although Christ is nowhere mentioned as the *lapis* or *medicina,* their identity emerges with convincing force from Melchior's text.

Additional evidence, which really should have been known to Waite, is furnished by a countryman of his, Sir George Ripley, canon of Bridlington. In the *Cantilena Riplæi* we read the following legend: There was once a noble king (the *caput corporum*) who had no descendants. He lamented his sterility: there must have arisen in him a *defectus originalis,* although he was "nurtured under the wings of the sun," and was without any natural faults of the body. In his own words he says: "But unfortunately I fear and know for a certainty that unless I can immediately partake of the aid of the species I cannot procreate. But I have heard with great astonishment that I shall be born anew through the tree of Christ." He says he now wishes to return again into the mother's womb, and to dissolve himself in the *materia prima.* It was the mother who prompted him to this undertaking, and she at once concealed him under her garment until such time as she had again made him incarnate through and in herself. She now became pregnant. During her pregnancy she ate peacock's meat and drank the blood of the green lion. At length she gave birth to the child; it resembled the moon and then changed into the radiance of the sun. The son once more became king. The text says: "God gave unto you the glorious, gleaming weapons of the four elements"—and the redeemed virgin (*virgo redimita*) was in their midst. There flowed from her a glorious balsam; she shone with a gleaming countenance, and was adorned with the precious stone. But in her lap lay the green lion, and blood flowed from his side. She was crowned with a diadem and raised to the empyrean as a constellation. The king became a triumphant victor among the highest, a great healer of all the sick, a redeemer (*reformator*) from all sins.

So far we have followed the *Cantilena:* in another place Ripley says: "Christ spoke: When I shall have been elevated, I will draw everything unto me. From that time forward when both parts, which are crucified and deprived of life, are betrothed to one another, man and wife shall be buried together, and afterwards animated again, by the spirit of life. They must then be raised up to heaven, so that body and soul may be transfigured there and may be enthroned upon the clouds; then they will draw all bodies unto their own worth."

If we realize that the author was no layman, but a learned canon, we can hardly suppose that he was unconscious of the parallel to the most fundamental dogmatic conceptions. Nowhere, to be sure, is it directly said that the *lapis* is Christ, but it is easy to recognize the sacred figures in the parts played by the king and the mother-virgin. Ripley, of course, has intentionally chosen these parallels without being conscious of any blasphemy. But the typesetter Conrad Waldkirch, of Basel, would have brought fire and brimstone raining down upon him had he done the like. Ripley happened to live in an epoch when God still inhabited nature with his mysteries, and when the secret of redemption still came to pass at every level of existence, because unconscious happening could still live in undisturbed, paradisaic participation with matter, and could still be experienced in matter.

As regards the particulars, the sick king, who was born without imperfection, is the man who suffers from a state of spiritual unfruitfulness. This unfruitfulness is, of course, due to the projection of the unconscious, which cannot further "develop" or "redeem" itself until it is integrated to consciousness. The peculiar idea that the king was nurtured "under the wings of the sun" is probably to be referred to the famous passage in Malachi (4:2) that helped to give a rational basis to the early worship of Christ as Helios or Sol—a tendency that Augustine, in his day, had still to combat. The passage runs: "But unto you that fear my name shall the Sun of righteousness arise with healing in his wings; and ye shall go forth, and grow up as calves of the stall."

This passage, of course, has always been understood as a Messianic prophecy, and it goes without saying that Ripley knew this. In the wings of the sun [59] we discover a very ancient image, but one which was very close to the Hebrew Malachi: it is the Egyptian sun symbol. The one who is nourished by this sun is the Son of God, the king.

The sick king who cannot procreate is connected with the *Visio Arislei;* there, to be sure, he figures as both the king and the king's son. He is in distress, and Pythagoras proffers aid by intervening in a dream. Here he demands to partake of the "species." We must understand by it a $\phi \acute{\alpha} \rho \mu \alpha \kappa o \nu \ \zeta \omega \hat{\eta} s$. The tree through which he is to be reborn is the cross of Christ, on the one hand, and, on the other, the immortal tree with the wondrous fruits, like that in the vision of Arisleus. The rebirth is accomplished according to the ritual of adoption followed by the classical world. The nourishment of the mother during her pregnancy is flesh and blood. The peacock is an early Christian symbol of the redeemer, but it is doubtful whether Ripley had knowledge of this fact. The peacock, however, is also closely related to the phœnix, a symbol of Christ which was surely known to Ripley. (Compare the figures on the Ripley scroll.) The blood flows from the green lion, who lies in the virgin's lap and bleeds from the wound in his side.[60] We are, therefore, dealing with the symbolism of communion, and with the wound in the side of the Christ prostrate in the lap of the Pietà. The green lion is an intermediate figure among the changing forms of Mercury.

As a giver of new birth, the mother is identical with the tree. In the *Pandora* of 1582, the tree is represented as a naked virgin (Pandora) wearing a crown. The *arbor philosophica* is a favourite symbol, and represents the philosophical process. When Ripley speaks of the tree of Christ, he is identifying the wondrous tree with the cross of Christ.[61]

At the end of the process, an apotheosis of the mother-virgin takes place. The *Pandora* presents the apotheosis in the form of an assumption of Mary, the so-called *assumptio Beatæ Mariæ Virginis*. After her death, her body was united again by a divine miracle with her soul, and both together were received into Heaven. This is the binding view of the church, although it has not yet been explicitly established as a dogma. In the picture (Plate XIII) she is labelled "*terra, corpus:* body, the joy of maidenhood"; the dove descends upon her, and God the Father touches her upon the right with his hand, in benison. She is crowned. The figure of God with the world sphere is labelled "*anima*—soul, Jesse —*pater, filius et mater.*" *Mater* refers to the queen of Heaven throning beside him, the king; in her the earth substance is absorbed in the godhead in transfigured form as the resurrection body.[62] Upon her left is a bearded figure of equal rank with God the Father, labelled "*sapientia*—wisdom." At the bottom of the picture is represented the freeing of the *rebis* from the *materia prima*. The whole is balanced, in the style of a mandala, by the animals that symbolize the

Evangelists. The inscription at the lower edge reads: "*Figura speculi Sanctæ Trinitatis.* Form of the mirror of the Holy Trinity." This picture (Plate XIV) is derived from one contained in an earlier work describing itself as a book about the holy threefoldness and the mystery of the transmutation of metals.[63]

Ripley gives to his king the traits of a triumphant victor, of a healer of all the sick, and of a redeemer from all sins. The *Rosarium* (1550) contains, at the end, the picture of Christ arising from the grave (Plate XV), with the inscription:

> After my many pains and heavy martyry,
> I have risen transfigured, of all blemish free.

From this source material we can now clearly discern what, in the last analysis, alchemy was seeking. It wished to produce a *corpus subtile,* the transfigured resurrection body. In this tendency it finds common ground with Chinese alchemy as we have come to know it from *The Secret of the Golden Flower.*[64] Chinese alchemy treats of the "diamond body," which is to say, of immortality attained through the transformation of the body. The diamond is a suitable symbol because of its transparency, its fire, and its hardness. So Orthelius tells us that the philosophers had found no better curative than the one which, because of its hardness, transparency, and ruby color, they called the noble and blessed Stone of the Philosophers.

This same Orthelius has also written in detail about the "theology" of the *lapis.* But he is probably later than Boehme, and I mention him only for the reason that he occupies himself with the question of the spirit found in matter. According to Orthelius, there are two treasures: the one is the written word and the other the word become fact (*verbum factum*). In the *verbum scriptum,* Christ is still "in swaddling clothes in his cradle" (*in cunis suis involutus*);

PLATE XIV

See page 266]

PLATE XV

[*See* page 266

while in the *verbum dictum et factum* the word is embodied
in God's creatures, and there, figuratively speaking, we can
touch it with our hands. It is from this source that we must
raise our treasure, for the word is nothing else than the
fire, the life and the spirit—the spirit which the Holy Trinity has spread abroad from the dawn of Creation, which
brooded (*incubavit*) over the primal waters, which was
breathed into (*inspiratus*) all things, and embodied in them,
through the word of God. As it was written: the spirit of
God fills the circumference of the earth. Some few had
expressed the opinion that this world-spirit (*spiritus mundi*)
was the third person of the Godhead, but they had not
taken into consideration the word "elohim," which, as a
plural form, covered all the persons of the Trinity. The
world-spirit arose from the Trinity, and was created by
it. The spirit became corporeal and is the chief constituent
of the Saviour (*salvatoris*) or Philosophical Stone, the real
means (*medium*) through which body and soul are kept
united during the course of life. The *spiritus mundi*, which
lay upon the primal waters, impregnated them and incu-
bated a seed within them, as the hen incubates her eggs. This
spirit is the *virtus* that inhabits the inner parts of the earth
and particularly the metals, and it is the task of the art to
separate the *Archæus*, the *spiritus mundi*, from matter, and
to produce a quintessence whose action can be compared
with Christ's action upon mankind.

As we have seen, the Gnostic vision of the *nous* en-
tangling itself in physical nature flashes out again from these
late-comers to alchemy. But the philosopher who, in earlier
days, descended like a Hercules into the darkness of the
Acheron to fulfill a divine *opus* has now become a laboratory worker given to speculation. Having lost sight of the
high aim of Hermetic mysticism, he labours to find a health
potion promising a renewal of strength—one that "holds

body and soul together," as his grandfather was probably wont to remark about a good wine. This change of direction in alchemy is due to the powerful influence of Paracelsus, who was the ancestor of modern medicine. Even Orthelius is inclined to natural science, and leaves all mystical experience to the church.

Alchemy was divided by Paracelsus and Boehme into natural science, on the one hand, and Protestant, Christian mysticism, on the other. The stone of alchemy became again what it was: *vilis vilissimus,* cheap among the cheapest, *in via ejectus,* thrown out upon the street, like the jewel in Spitteler's *Prometheus and Epimetheus.* Morienus might well repeat today what he had said before: "Take that which is trodden underfoot upon the dung-heap; if you do not, when you wish to climb the stairs, you will fall down upon your head." By which he means that if a man will not accept what he has cast aside, it will force itself upon him the moment he wishes to climb higher.

What the ancients meant by the *lapis* has never become quite clear. This question can be satisfactorily answered only when we know what content of the unconscious it was they projected. Today, the psychology of the unconscious alone is in a position to solve this riddle. As long as a content is in the projected state, it is inaccessible, and this is why all the efforts devoted in that bygone age to the alchemistic secret have betrayed so little to us. So much the greater, however, is the accumulation of symbolic material, and hence the reward to the researcher, for this symbolism has a more or less direct relation to what we know in psychology as the process of individuation.[65] By this I do not mean to say that we have in any way come closer to the secret of this process, but we see it in a new light, through the medium of symbols, clearly enough to make an attempt to save the honour of ancient alchemy.

In dealing with alchemistic philosophy, we must always bear in mind that it played an important rôle in the Middle Ages and gave rise to an extensive literature that had a far-reaching influence upon the spiritual life of the time. The parallel of the *lapis* to Christ is probably the clearest demonstration of the extent to which alchemy itself claimed to exert such an influence. When, in my discussion, I have touched upon subjects that seem to have nothing to do with alchemy, this may be explained—or excused—by these considerations.

As soon as we attempt to discuss alchemistic thought in its psychological aspects, we must give due importance to concatenations that seem very remote from the historical material taken at its surface value. By trying to understand the historical manifestations from within—which is to say, from the standpoint of the psyche—we start from a central point where many lines converge, however far apart their external sources may lie. We are confronted with the underlying human psyche, and this, unlike consciousness, has hardly changed at all in the course of many centuries; to the psyche, a truth of two thousand years ago is still the truth of today—it is still living and still effective. We come upon the fundamental psychic facts that remain unchanged for thousands of years and will remain unchanged for thousands of years to come. From this point of view, modern times and the present appear as episodes in a drama that began in dark prehistory, and that runs through the centuries towards a distant future. This drama is an *aurora consurgens:* humanity's coming to consciousness.

The alchemistic process of the classical period (from antiquity to the end of the sixteenth century) was a chemical research into which there entered an admixture of unconscious psychic material by the way of projection. For this reason the alchemistic texts frequently emphasize the psychological prerequisites for the work. The contents that come into consideration are those that suit themselves to projection upon the unknown chemical substance. Because of the impersonal nature of matter, it was the collective archetypes that were projected; and first and foremost, as the collective spiritual life of those centuries dictated, it was the image of the spirit imprisoned in the darkness of the world.

This image represents a state of relative unconsciousness that causes suffering and calls for redemption; and since matter acts as the mirror in which it is recognized, the image is treated in material terms. Psychologically considered, an unconscious content always embraces the paired opposites, being and non-being. So we find that the uniting of the opposites played a decisive rôle in the alchemistic process. To the outcome of the process we must grant the significance of a reconciling symbol, and such a symbol nearly always has about it the awesomeness of the numen.[66] This being so, we could almost expect the projection of the redeemer-image, which is to say, the correspondence of the *lapis* to Christ, and likewise the parallelism between the redeeming work, or *officium divinum,* and the chemical magistery. We must, however, note an important difference; for the Christian *opus* is an *operari,* to the honour of the redeeming God, on the part of the man who needs redemption, while the alchemistic *opus* is the labour of man the redeemer in the cause of the divine world-soul that sleeps in matter and awaits redemption. The Christian earns for himself, *ex opere operato,* the fruits of grace. The alchemist, on the other hand, achieves, *ex opere operantis* (in the literal sense), a "life remedy" (φάρμακον ζωῆς), which seems to him either an ill-concealed substitute for the means of grace of the church, or a completion of, and a parallel to, the divine work of redemption that is active in man. In the church formula of the *opus operatum* and the *opus operantis,* we find an expression for the two opposed points of view. In the last analysis they are irreconcilable.

We come in the end to the pair of opposites: collectivity and individual, or society and personality. This is a modern problem; for it seems as if the building up of collective life and the unprecedented massing together of men, so characteristic of our time, were needed to make the individual aware of the fact that he was being strangled in the meshes of the organized mob. The collectivism of the mediæval church seldom exerted sufficient pressure on the individual to turn his relation to society into a universal problem. So this question, also, remained undeveloped, at the level of projection; and the task of infusing into it at least a germ of consciousness, albeit under the mask of a neurotic individualism, was left to our own day.

Alchemy attained a final summit, and the historic turning point, in Goethe's *Faust,* which from beginning to end is saturated with alchemistic forms of thought. The change that makes its appearance in Faust is most clearly expressed in the scene of Paris and Helen. To the mediæval alchemist this scene would have meant the mysterious *conjunctio* of Sol and Luna in the retort; but the modern man who figures as Faust recognizes the projection, and, putting himself in the place of Paris, or Sol, possesses himself of Helen, or Luna, his female counterpart.

Here we unquestionably discover the true reason for the fact that, in Goethe's drama, all the "births" or rejuvenation figures—such as the Boy Charioteer, the Homunculus and Euphorion—go up in flames and disappear; and that the final rejuvenation takes place only after death, being thus projected into the future (as a symbol of the unconscious). Is it really an accident that the figure in which Faust attains his own completion bears a name that we have already met with: that of one of the outstanding alchemists of the early period, "Marianus"—or Morienus, as it is more commonly spelled?

By identifying himself with Paris, Faust transfers the alchemistic *conjunctio* from the projected state to the psychological sphere of personal experience, and thus to consciousness. This decisive step means nothing less than the unravelling of the alchemistic riddle, and the redemption of a previously unconscious part of the personality. But every increase in consciousness carries with it the danger of inflation, and the latter shows itself unmistakably in Faust's superhuman powers. His death was necessary in the circumstances of his day and age, but it was hardly a satisfactory answer. Birth and transformation, which follow the *conjunctio,* took place in the life after death—that is to say, in the unconscious.

Here was an unsolved problem which Nietzsche took up again in *Zarathustra:* the transformation into the superman. But Nietzsche came dangerously near to making it a worldly problem, and inevitably imbued his writing with Antichristian resentment. His superman is an aggravated form of the individual consciousness that must necessarily collide with the collective power of Christianity and lead to the catastrophic destruction of the individual. We know beyond peradventure, from the symptoms of his disease, that Nietzsche himself suffered this fate *tam ethice quam physice.* And what did the age to come have to offer in place of the individualism of Nietzsche's superman? It offered a collectivism, an aggregation of masses of people, that dwarfed anything of the sort that had gone before—and it offered this collective organization *tam ethice quam physice.* The unembellished balance sheet of our time shows us, on the one hand, the stifling of the personality and, on the other, a Christianity that is impotent and carries a perhaps fatal wound.

Faust's sin was his identification with that which is to

be transformed—and that which has been transformed. Nietzsche overshot the mark by identifying with the superman, Zarathustra, the component of the personality that is just coming to consciousness. But may we call Zarathustra a component of the personality? Is he not rather superhumanity—something which man is not, though he has his share in it? But then we must ask whether the God is really dead, of whom Nietzsche said that he has not been heard of for a long time. For it may be that he has come back again in the disguise of the "superhuman."

Faust again, in his blind reaching after the superman, brought about the murder of Philemon and Baucis. But who are these two humble old people? When the world had been bereft of gods, and would no longer offer a hospitable retreat to the divine strangers, Jupiter and Mercury, it was Philemon and Baucis who received the superhuman guests. And when Baucis was about to sacrifice for them her last goose, the transformation took place: the gods made themselves manifest, the humble cottage was changed into a temple, and the old couple became immortal servitors at the shrine.

The ancient alchemists, in a sense, stood nearer than Faust to the central truth of the psyche when they strove to redeem the fiery spirit from the chemical elements, and treated the *mysterium* as if it lay in the dark and silent bosom of nature. It was still outside themselves. To be sure, the development of consciousness, with its thrust upward, had to put an end to this projection, and to restore to the psyche what from the very beginning was of a psychic nature. But, from the Age of Enlightenment onward, and in the epoch of scientific rationalism, what was the psyche? It had become synonymous with consciousness. The psyche was "what I know." There was no psyche outside the ego. Inevitably, then, the ego identified itself with contents restored to the psyche by the withdrawal of the projection.

Gone were the times when the psyche was still for the most part "outside the body"—and still "imagined those greater things" that the body could not grasp. The contents of the former projection must now appear as personal possessions, as delusive fantasy pictures belonging to the ego-consciousness. The fire was chilled into air, and the air became the wind of Zarathustra and caused an inflation of consciousness that can apparently be checked only by the most terrible catastrophes to civilization—nothing less than the deluge with which the gods visited inhospitable humanity.

An inflated consciousness is always egocentric—never aware of anything but its own presence. It is incapable of learning from the past; incapable of grasping what is happening in the present, and of drawing correct conclusions for the future. It is hypnotized by itself, and therefore cannot be argued with. It is doomed to call upon itself catastrophes that strike it dead. Paradoxically enough, inflation means that consciousness has become unconscious. This is the case whenever consciousness takes upon itself the credit and responsibility for contents of the unconscious, and, loses that ability to differentiate which is indispensable to its existence.

When the fate of Europe carried it into a four years' war of stupendous horror—a war that no one wanted—hardly anyone asked who had caused the war and its continuation. No one realized that European man was possessed by something that robbed him of free choice. This state of unconscious possession will, no doubt, continue unchecked until at last European man becomes "afraid of his God-almightiness." But this is a change that can begin only with individuals, since masses—as we know only too well—are blind beasts.

It seems to me of some importance that individuals, or people individually, are beginning to understand that there exist contents that do not belong to the ego-personality, but are rather to be ascribed to a psychic non-ego. We must always come to this recognition if we wish to avoid a threatening inflation. To help us, we always have the useful and edifying pattern held up to us by the poets and philosophers —patterns or archetypes that one may well call remedies both for men and for times. What the archetypes show is, of course, nothing that can be held up to the masses, but always something hidden that we may set before ourselves in the private silence. But hardly anyone wants to know anything about this, for it is so much more convenient to proclaim the panacea for the ten thousand others; it is not necessary, then, to apply it to himself. And as we know, all suffering has an end when enough of us are exposed to it. No doubts can exist in the herd, and the greater multitude always has the better truth—but also the greater catastrophes.

What we may learn from the archetypes is this: the psyche harbours contents, and is exposed to influences, the assimilation of which may be attended by serious dangers. The ancient alchemists ascribed their secret to matter itself; and neither Faust nor Zarathustra is an encouraging example, should we be tempted to embody such a secret in the personal ego. Our part, then, surely, is to repudiate the arrogant claim of consciousness to be the whole of the psyche, and to grant the psyche a definite actuality, even if we cannot fully grasp it with our present means of understanding. I do not call the man who admits his lack of knowledge an obscurantist; I think it is much rather the man whose consciousness has not developed so far that he is aware of his lack of knowledge. I hold the view that the alchemist's hope of producing from matter the philosophical gold, or the panacea, or the wondrous stone, was only in part an illusion, an effect of projection; for the rest it corresponded to certain psychic facts that are of great importance in the study of the unconscious. As is shown by his texts and the symbolism they contain, the alchemist projected what I call the process of individuation upon the processes of chemical transformation. If I use "individuation" as a scientific term, this does not mean that we are dealing with a matter of which our knowledge is complete and sufficient.[67] It merely indicates an obscure field of research that calls for further study; it refers to the unconscious centralizing processes that form the personality.

We are dealing here with life processes endowed with the awesomeness of the numen, which, because of this very quality, have always been the most significant agents in the formation of symbols. These processes are mysterious to the extent in which they throw up problems that the human understanding will long, and perhaps vainly, strive to solve. We may well wonder whether, in the last analysis, the human intelligence is the suitable instrument for this task. It was not for nothing that alchemy called itself an *art*; it was right in the feeling that it was dealing with creative processes that can be fully grasped only in experience, although the intellect may designate them. Let us not forget that it was alchemy that coined the admonition:

Rumpite libros, ne corda vestra rumpantur.[68]

FOOTNOTES TO CHAPTER FIVE

1. The author's footnotes to the German edition (*Eranos-Jahrbuch*, 1936. Zurich: Rhein-Verlag) provide the reader with complete source references to the alchemistic texts, as well as with full quotation in the original tongues of the passages cited. The present English edition has preserved only those of the author's marginal comments that amplify his interpretation of the texts or deal with his psychology in general. [Translator's note.]

2. The *Rosarium Philosophorum*, as *secunda pars Alchemiæ*, is such a *theoria* in the proper sense of vision, contemplation (for example, the contemplating of scenes on the stage, etc.).

3. *Eranos-Jahrbuch*, 1935. Zurich: Rhein-Verlag.

4. *Problems of Mysticism and Its Symbolism*. New York: Moffat, Yard and Company, 1917.

5. Even in the twentieth century Gustav Meyrink, author of *The Golem*, still believed in the alchemistic methods. There is a remarkable account of his own experi-

ments in the introduction to *Thomas von Aquino, Abhandlung über den Stein der Weisen,* pp. 25 ff. Leipzig: Barth-Verlag, 1925.

6. There is a relation between this and the stipulation that the laboratory worker should be free from corporeal blemishes, should not be crippled in any way, etc.

7. *Pone ergo mentem tuam super salem, nec cogites de aliis. Nam in ipsa sola occultatur scientia & arcanum præcipuum, & secretissimum omnium antiquorum Philosophorum.* Several editions of the *Rosarium* have *ipsa sola.*

8. Compare the *sal sapientiæ,* which, according to ancient rite, was handed to the person presenting himself for baptism.

9. Morienus (Morienes or Marianus) was supposed to have been the teacher of the Omayyad prince Khalid ben Yezid (635-704).

10. I refer the reader to my treatment of the subject in *The Relation of the Ego to the Unconscious* in *Two Essays on Analytical Psychology.* London: Ballière, Tindall and Cox, 1928.

11. Compare to this the Mohammedan legend of the stone in the Mosque of Omar (Jerusalem). When Mohammed ascended to Heaven it wanted to fly with him.

12. Arthur Avalon, The Serpent Power, 1919. Madras: Ganesh & Company, 1924.

13. In a similar way, it is held, Christ is "imagined" in us.

14. Ripley says that all "our secrets" have arisen from an "image" (imago).

15. We can form some idea of such visions after the pattern of the one which Benvenuto Cellini describes in his autobiography: "One day when I was about five years old, my father was sitting in a ground-floor room of ours in which washing had been going on, and where a large fire of oak logs had been left; . . . his viola on his arm, [he] was playing and singing by himself near the fire—for it was very cold. Looking into the fire he chanced to see in the middle of the most ardent flames a little creature like a lizard disporting itself in the midst of the intensest heat. Suddenly aware of what it was, he called my sister and me and pointed it out to us children. Then he gave me a sound box on the ears, which made me cry bitterly, on which he soothed me with kind words, saying: 'My dear little fellow, I did not hurt you for any harm you had done, but only that you might remember that the lizard in the fire there is a salamander, which never has been seen for a certainty by anyone before.' Then he kissed me and gave me some farthings." *The Memoirs of Benvenuto Cellini,* translated by Anne Macdonell, Everyman's Library.

16. See my discussion of the reconciling symbol in *Psychological Types.* New York: Harcourt, Brace and Company, 1923.

17. Here, no doubt, we enter the realm of Neo-Pythagorean ideas. That the soul-pneuma has a penetrating quality that enabled it to permeate all bodies was, according to Zeller, taught by Ænedesimus. He also conceived the primal stuff as ἀήρ, air, corresponding to the πνεῦμα of the Stoics. The pneumatic (wind) nature of Hermes is indicated by his possession of wings. Alexander Polyhistor taught that Hermes guided the souls to the highest; the impure are bound by the Erinyes in the underworld in unbreakable chains (the imperfect who are "bound in Hades").

18. In the synchretistic Greek writings, the ideas of the νοῦς and the πνεῦμα are used interchangeably. The older meaning of πνεῦμα is wind; it is a phenomenon of the air, and from this comes the equivalence of ἀήρ and πνεῦμα (Zeller). Anaximenes held the primal matter to be ἀήρ; to Archelaus, the pupil of Anaxagoras, God was both ἀήρ and νοῦς. To Anaxagoras, the creator of the world was νοῦς; it gave rise to a whirlpool in chaos, and thus caused the separation of æther and air.

19. According to the Neo-Pythagorean view, even the godhead is of a hermaphroditic nature (Zeller).

20. The main points of comparison are the following: Osiris as God incarnated in man; his relation to wheat (holy wafer), his dismemberment and resurrection. As to Orpheus, his taming of the passionate instincts; the fisherman, the good shepherd, the teacher of wisdom, the fate of being rent asunder. As to Dionysus, his relation to wine, ecstatic revelations, the fish symbolism, his dismemberment and resurrection. As to Heracles, his subjection to Eurystheus and Omphale, the heavy labour (chiefly the liberation of tormented humanity from evils), the construction of symmetrical spaces and of the cross-form (the cardinal points in labours 7 to 10, the vertical in labours 11 and 12—compare the Paulinian allusion in Ephesians 3:18), his self-cremation and divine *sublimatio*.

21. As, for instance, in the Polynesian myths centring around Maui.

22. See Grenfell and Hunt, *New Sayings of Jesus*. Oxford: 1904. "Jesus saith: (Ye ask? who are those) that draw us (to the kingdom, if) the kingdom is in heaven? . . . the fowls of the air, and all the beasts that are under the earth or upon the earth, and the fishes of the sea . . ."

23. In the Ripley Scroll the sphere of water is represented with dragon's wings. The motto reads: "He goes round as a ball." Brit. Museum, Ms. Additional 10 302.

24. The name Arisleus is a corruption of Archelaus, owing to Arabic transcription.

25. Also Gabricus, Gabricius, Cabricius, Cabritis, Kybric—Arabic: kibrit = sulphur. Beja, Veya, Beua—Arabic: al-baida = the white one.

26. The "whole" or the "self" embraces conscious and unconscious contents. See *The Relation of the Ego to the Unconscious* in *Two Essays on Analytical Psychology*.

27. The evidence leaves us no room for doubt that when the philosophers used the terms *divitiæ, salus,* and *bona futura,* these terms are to be taken not only in the spiritual sense, as salvation of the soul, but also as physical well-being in every respect. We must not forget that the alchemist had no intention of inflicting moral torture upon himself on the assumption that man is a sinful nothing who complies with God's work of salvation by adopting an unobjectionable, ethical conduct. He finds himself in the rôle of a "redeemer," whose *opus divinum* is rather a continuation of the divine work of redemption than a preventive measure taken against eventual damnation on the day of judgement.

28. See Jung, *Psychology of the Unconscious*. New York: Moffat, Yard & Company, 1916.

29. The idea that the *ens primum* contained the opposites was universally held. In China the pair of opposites is yang and yin, odd and even numbers, heaven and earth, etc. Compare the union of the opposites in the hermaphrodite (Hastings, Encyclopedia of Religion and Ethics, iv, 140). In Empedocles, νεικος and φιλία of the elements (Zeus = fire, Hera = air). In the second period of creation arise hybrids resembling the Nordic Ymir and Buri (Hermann). In Neo-Pythagorean thought Monas is masculine, Dyas feminine (Zeller). In Nicomachus the godhead is even and odd number, and therefore androgynous (Zeller). Hermes Trismegistus: The *nous* is hermaphroditic. Among the Ophites the *pneuma* was androgynous.

30. The fear of ghosts means, in psychology, the overpowering of consciousness by the autonomous contents of the unconscious. This is the equivalent of mental derangement.

31. For the quadratic enclosure as the domain of the psyche, see Chapter Four. According to Pythagoras, the soul is a square (Zeller).

32. Symbolized by a magically enchanting woman or by dissolute girls. Similar themes are treated in Chapter Four.

33. Compare to this the interesting idea of *autofécondation* in Léon Daudet's *L'Heredo*.

34. Another version of the devouring: Mars feeds the king's body to the famished wolf, the son of Saturn (lead). The wolf symbolizes the appetite of the *materia prima* for the king, who often takes the place of the son.

35. See *Psychology of the Unconscious.*

36. Compare the feeding with honey and milk of those presenting themselves for baptism in early Christian ritual.

37. "O death, where is thy sting? O grave, where is thy victory?" I Corinthians 15:55.

38. See *Psychology of the Unconscious.*

39. An analogous idea is to be found in Emerson's Essay: "History."

40. The heart and the blood as the seat of the soul.

41. In Indian thought we meet with the corresponding idea of the "swan."

42. In Chapter Three, "Archetypes of the Collective Unconscious."

43. These two categories correspond, in psychology, to conscious comprehension based upon sense data, and to the projection of unconscious contents. The latter is fitly designated by the "heart," for the heart region represents an earlier localization of consciousness, and, even at a more developed stage, still harbours the thoughts that are charged with emotion—that is, the contents that are strongly under the influence of the unconscious.

44. The "sea" of the philosophers. Hermes was called a *mare sapientiæ.*

45. From the "stone" from which the pneumatic spark flies there flows also the healing water. In later alchemistic literature this stone is often compared to Christ.

46. I have reduced the text to its essentials by omitting all subsidiary and merely ornamental matter.

47. The wine is here the *medicina catholica*, the panacea. Like the *lapis*, so also the miraculous healing draught increases or completes itself, generally by the help of the art.

48. The philosophers.

49. Instead of "the foundation of the world" (Matthew 25:34) we have here the beginning of the alchemistic *opus*.

50. The sun.

51. Perhaps a reference to Venus and Mars, caught in the net of Vulcan.

52. The conjunction of Mercury with what? Perhaps the conjunction of two Mercuries, the ♂ and the ♀. We seem to have before us the union of Sol with Luna, Mars, and Mercury.

53. The peculiar substance with which Mary the Prophetess, the sister of Moses, is supposed to have occupied herself.

54. Presumably Sol, perhaps in the form of "resin."

55. The *caput mortuum*, the head of Osiris in the state of *nigredo*.

56. Calcination probably corresponds to incineration, and the glowing of the ash approaches to vitrification. This operation is also connected with Mary.

57. Compare what was said above about Christ's relation to the fire: I should add

that Melchior recommends the reading of Luke 10 before the Credo. This chapter bears no apparent relation to Melchior's theme, but closes with these significant words: "But one thing is needful: for Mary hath chosen the good part, which shall not be taken away from her."

58. That the experience was of a subjective nature is shown by the author's incidental remark: *et scio quod verum est testimonium ejus.*

59. The Vulgate says: *sub pennis.* The feathers of the phœnix and of other birds have an important place in Ripley's writings and in alchemy in general.

60. The wounding of the lion means his sacrifice and mortification in the process. He is also pictured in a maimed condition, with his paws chopped off. Compare also the wounded unicorn lying in the lap of the Virgin.

61. It is still an open question for me whether Germanic influences are to be found in alchemy; think of the tree symbolism (Odin upon the tree!).

62. Compare the vision of Guillaume de Digulleville, in Chapter Four.

63. Codex Germanicus, number 598 in the state library of Münich.

64. Wilhelm and Jung, *The Secret of the Golden Flower.* New York: Harcourt, Brace and Company, 1931; London: George Routledge and Company, 1931.

65. See Chapter Four, where I have presented an "alchemistic" dream series. It shows us that the philosopher's stone is one of the many symbols of the Self.

66. See Chapter V of *Psychological Types.*

67. *Psychological Types,* "Definitions: Individuation."

68. "Rend the books, lest your hearts be rent asunder."

CHAPTER SIX

The Development of Personality

> Folk and serf and conqueror
> These concede in every age:
> *The sons of earth find greatest joy*
> *In personality alone.*

In somewhat free-handed fashion the last two verses of Goethe's stanza are often quoted:

> *Höchstes Glück der Erdenkinder*
> *Sei nur die Persönlichkeit.*[1]

This gives expression to the view that everyone's ultimate aim and strongest desire lie in developing the fullness of human existence that is called personality. "Education to personality" has become a pedagogical ideal that turns its back upon the standardized—the collective and normal—human being. It thus fittingly recognizes the historical fact that the great, liberating deeds of world history have come from leading personalities and never from the inert mass that is secondary at all times and needs the demagogue if it is to move at all. The pæan of the Italian nation is addressed to the personality of the Duce, and the dirges of other nations lament the absence of great leaders.[2]

The yearning for personality has become a real problem that occupies many minds today, whereas earlier there was only one man who foresaw this question—Friedrich Schiller—and his letters on æsthetic education have lain dormant like a Sleeping Beauty of literature while more than a century has passed.

We may confidently assert that the Holy Roman Empire of the German nation has taken no notice of Friedrich Schiller as an educator. On the contrary, the *furor teutonicus* has thrown itself upon pedagogy—the education of children—has practised child psychology, ferreted out the infantile elements in the adult, and thus made of childhood such an important condition of life and fate that beside it the creative meaning and possibilities of later, grown-up existence were completely overshadowed. Our own time has even been exuberantly lauded as the age of the child. This boundless extension and expansion of the kindergarten is equivalent to complete forgetfulness of the problems of education divined by the genius of Schiller.

No one will deny or even underestimate the importance of childhood years; the severe injuries, often lasting through life, caused by a nonsensical upbringing at home and in school are too obvious, and the need for reasonable pedagogic methods is too urgent. But if this evil is to be attacked at the root, one must in all seriousness propose the question of how it came about, and still comes about, that stupid and limited methods of education are employed. Obviously it is for the one and only reason that there exist stupid educators who are not human beings, but personified automatons of method. Whoever wishes to educate should himself be educated. But learning by heart and the mechanical application of methods, which is still practised today, is no education, either for the child or for the educator himself.

People are constantly saying that the child should be reared to personality. Of course, I admire this lofty educational ideal. But who rears children to personality? In the first and most important place we have the ordinary, incompetent parents who are often themselves, all their lives, partly or wholly children. Who would expect in the last analysis that all the ordinary parents should be "personalities," and who has ever thought of devising methods for instilling personality into the parents? So we naturally expect more of the pedagogue, of the trained professional upon whom psychology has been grafted for better or worse in the form of viewpoints of this or that denomination, usually diametrically opposed, as to how the child is presumably constituted and is to be handled. It is presupposed that the young people who have chosen pedagogy as their occupation in life are themselves brought up. No one, surely, will choose to assert that they are one and all personalities as well. By and large, they have themselves had the same defective upbringing as the children they are supposed to instruct, and as a rule are no more personalities than these.

In general, our approach to education suffers from a one-sided emphasis upon the child who is to be brought up, and from an equally one-sided lack of emphasis upon the deficient upbringing of the adult educator. Everyone who has finished his course of studies appears to himself to be fully brought up—which is to say, grown up. He must appear so to himself; he must have this solid conviction of his own competence in order to hold his ground in the struggle for existence. Doubt and feelings of uncertainty would cripple and hinder him, would undermine the necessary belief in his own authority and unfit him for the professional life. Moreover, he is expected to be able and confident, and not to have doubts of himself and his capability. The expert is simply condemned to unhesitating competence.

Everyone knows that these are not ideal conditions. But under the given circumstances we may say, with some reservations, that they are the best possible. We cannot conceive how they could be different. We simply cannot expect more from the average educator than from the average parent. If they are good in their profession, we have to content ourselves with that, just as with parents who bring up their children as well as they can.

It is best not to apply to children the high ideal of education to personality. For what is generally understood by personality—namely, a *definitely shaped, psychic abundance, capable of resistance and endowed with energy*—is an adult ideal. It is only in an age when the individual is still unconscious of the problem of his so-called adulthood, or —still worse—when he consciously evades it, that people could wish to foist this ideal upon childhood. In fact, I suspect our contemporary pedagogical and psychological enthusiasm for the child of a dishonourable intent: people speak of the child, but should mean the *child in the grownup. For in the adult there is hidden a child—an eternal child, something that is always becoming, is never completed,* and that calls for unceasing care, attention, and fostering. This is the part of human personality that wishes to develop and to complete itself.

But the human being of our time is as far from this completion as heaven is from earth. Darkly divining his own defect, he seizes upon the education of children and fervently devotes himself to child psychology on the favourite assumption that something must have gone wrong in his own upbringing and childhood development—something that can be weeded out in the next generation. This purpose is praiseworthy, to be sure, but it comes to shipwreck against the psychological fact that we cannot correct in a child a fault that we ourselves still commit. Children, of course, are not so stupid as we believe. They notice only too well what is genuine and what is not. Andersen's fairy tale about the king's new clothes contains an immortal truth.

How many parents have announced to me the laudable intention of sparing their children the experiences they had to go through in their own childhood! And when I asked, "But are you sure that you have yourself overcome these mistakes?" they were firmly persuaded that the damage had long ago been corrected in them. Actually, however, it was not. If as children they had been brought up too severely, then they spoiled their own children with a tolerance that bordered upon bad taste; if in childhood certain realms of life had been painfully concealed from them, these were then thrown open to their own children by methods of enlightenment that were just as painful. Thus they had simply fallen into the other extreme, the strongest of all evidence for the tragic survival of the old sin. This they had wholly failed to see.

If there is anything that we wish to change in the child, we should first examine it and see whether it is not something that could better be changed in ourselves. As an example, take our enthusiasm for pedagogy. Perhaps we misconstrue the pedagogical need, because it would remind us uncomfortably that we are ourselves still children in some ways and are in urgent want of bringing up.

In any case, this doubt seems to be thoroughly pertinent if we set out to educate mere children to the end of becoming personalities. Personality is a germ in the child that can develop only by slow stages in and through life. No personality is manifested without *definiteness, fullness,* and *maturity*. These three characteristics do not, and should not, fit the child, for they would rob it of its childhood. It would become an unnatural, precocious pseudo adult; yet modern education has already turned out such monsters, especially in those cases where the parents have set themselves with true fanaticism always and ever to do their "best" for the children and "to live only for them." This ideal, which is so often appealed to, most effectively prevents the parents from developing themselves, and enables them to force their own "best" upon the children. But this so-called best is actually what the parents have most badly neglected in themselves. In this way the children are goaded on to achievements that the parents have never compassed, and ambitions are loaded upon them that the parents have never fulfilled. Such methods and ideals engender educational monstrosities.

No one can educate to personality who does not himself have it. And not the child, but only the adult can attain personality as the mature fruit of an accomplishment of life that is directed to this end. The achievement of personality means nothing less than the best possible development of all that lies in a particular, single being. It is impossible to foresee what an infinite number of conditions must be fulfilled to bring this about. A whole human life span in all its biological, social, and spiritual aspects is needed. Personality is the highest realization of the inborn distinctiveness of the particular living being. Personality is an act of the greatest courage in the face of life, and means unconditional affirmation of all that constitutes the individual, the most successful adaptation to the universal conditions of human existence, with the greatest possible freedom of personal decision.

To educate someone to *this* seems to me to be no small matter. It is surely the heaviest task that the spiritual world of today has set itself. And, indeed, it is a dangerous task— dangerous to a degree that Schiller himself was far from suspecting, though his prophetic foresight made him the first who dared confront these problems. It is as dangerous as the bold and unconsiderate undertaking of nature to let women bear children. Would it not be a sacrilegious, Promethean, or even Luciferian enterprise if a superman should venture in his alchemistic retort to give rise to a homunculus, who would then grow into a golem? And yet he would only be doing what nature does every day. There is no human horror or abnormity that did not lie in the womb of a loving mother. As the sun shines upon the just and the unjust, and as women who bear and give suck protect the

children of God and of the devil with equal love, uncon-
cerned about the possible results, so we, too, are parts of
this singular nature and, like it, carry within us the unpredictable.

Personality develops itself in the course of life from
germs that are hard or impossible to discern, and it is only
our actions that reveal who we are. We are like the sun
that nourishes the life of the earth and brings forth every
kind of lovely, strange, and evil thing; we are like the
mothers who bear in their wombs unknown happiness and
suffering. At first we do not know what deeds or misdeeds,
what destiny, what good or evil we contain, and only the
autumn can show what the spring has engendered; only in
the evening will it be seen what the morning began.

Personality as a complete realization of the fullness
of our being is an unattainable ideal. But unattainability· is
no counterargument against an ideal, for ideals are only sign-
posts, never goals.

As the child must develop in order to be brought up,
so the personality must first unfold before it can be subjected to education. And here the danger already begins.
We are dealing with something unpredictable; we do not
know how and in what direction the budding personality
will develop, and we have learned enough of nature and
the reality of the world to be rightly somewhat distrustful.
We have been brought up in the Christian teaching of belief in the original evil of human nature. But even persons
who no longer hold to the Christian teaching are naturally
distrustful and anxious with regard to the possibilities that
lie in the underground chambers of their being. Even enlightened, materialistic psychologists like Freud give us a
very unpleasant picture of the things that slumber in the
background and in the depths of human nature. It is, therefore, something of a hazard to put in a good word for the
unfolding of personality. But the human spirit is full of the

strangest contradictions. We praise "sacred motherhood" and never think of holding it responsible for all such human monsters as criminals, the dangerously insane, epileptics, idiots, and cripples of every kind who yet are born. But we are beset by the most serious doubts when it comes to granting a free development to human personality. "But then anything would be possible," people say. Or they warm up the feeble objection of "individualism." Yet individualism has never been a natural development, but only an unnatural usurpation, an unadapted, impertinent pose that often proves its hollowness with collapse before the slightest obstacle. Here we are dealing with something else.

Now, no one develops his personality because someone told him it would be useful or advisable for him to do so. Nature has never yet allowed herself to be imposed upon by well-meaning advice. Only coercion working through causal connections moves nature, and human nature also. Nothing changes itself without need, and human personality least of all. It is immensely conservative, not to say inert. Only the sharpest need is able to rouse it. The development of personality obeys no wish, no command, and no insight, but only need; it wants the motivating coercion of inner or outer necessities. Any other development would be individualism. This is why the accusation of individualism is a cheap insult when it is raised against the natural development of personality.

The saying, "For many are called, but few are chosen," applies here as nowhere else; for the development of personality from its germinal state to full consciousness is at once a charism and a curse. Its first result is the conscious and unavoidable separation of the single being from the undifferentiated and unconscious herd. This means isolation, and there is no more comforting word for it. Neither family, nor society, nor position can save him from it, nor the most successful adaptation to actual surroundings, nor yet the most frictionless fitting in with them. The development of personality is a favour that must be paid for dearly. But people who talk the most about the development of personality are those who least consider the results, which are such as to frighten away all weaker spirits.

Yet the development of personality means more than the mere fear of bringing monsters into the world, or the fear of isolation. It also means fidelity to the law of one's being.

For the word "fidelity" I should prefer, in this connection, to use the Greek word of the New Testament, πίστις, which is mistakenly translated as "faith." It really means trust, trustful loyalty. Fidelity to the law of one's being is a trust in this law, a loyal perseverance and trustful hope; in short, such an attitude as a religious man should have to God. And now it becomes apparent that a dilemma heavily weighted with consequences emerges from behind our problem: personality can never develop itself unless the individual chooses his own way consciously and with conscious, moral decision. Not only the causal motive, the need, but a conscious, moral decision must lend its strength to the process of the development of personality. If the first, that is, need, is lacking, then the so-called development would be mere acrobatics of the will; if the latter is missing, that is, the conscious decision, then the development will come to rest in a stupefying, unconscious automatism. But a man can make a moral choice of his own way only when he holds it to be the best. If any other way were held to be better, then he would live and develop that other personality in place of his own. The other ways are the conventions of a moral, social, political, philosophic, or religious nature. The fact that the conventions always flourish in one form or another proves that the overwhelming majority of mankind chooses not its own way, but the conventions, and so does not develop itself, but a method and a collectivity at the cost of its own fullness.

Just as the psychic and social life of mankind at a primitive level is exclusively a group life with a high degree of unconsciousness in the individual, so the later historical process of development is also a collective matter and will, no doubt, remain so. This is why I believe in convention as a collective necessity. It is a makeshift and not an ideal, whether in respect to morals or religion, for subjection to it always means repudiation of wholeness and a flight from the final consequences of one's own being.

To undertake to develop personality is in fact an unpopular venture, an uncongenial deviation from the highway, an idiosyncrasy smacking of the recluse—or so it seems to those who stand outside. No wonder, then, that from the beginning only the few have hit upon this strange adventure. If they had all been fools, we could drop them from the field of vision of our interest as ἰδιῶται, as persons who have retired from spiritual activity. But, unfortunately, personalities are as a rule the legendary heroes of mankind, those who are wondered at, loved, and worshipped, the true sons of God whose "names do not perish in æons." They are the true blossoms and fruits of the tree of humanity, the seeds that continue to engender.

The reference to historical personalities sufficiently explains why growth into personality is an ideal, and why the accusation of individualism is an insult. The greatness of historical personalities has never consisted in their unconditional subjection *to* convention, but, on the contrary, in their liberating freedom *from* convention. They thrust themselves up like mountain peaks out of the mass that clung to its collective fears, convictions, laws and methods, and chose their own way. And to the ordinary human being it always seemed wonderful that someone should prefer to the beaten track, with its known destination, a small and steep path that leads into the unknown. This is why it was always believed that such a man, if not out of his mind, was yet inhabited by a demon or god; the miracle of a man acting otherwise than in the way humanity had always acted could be explained only as due to his being gifted with demonic power or divine spirit. For what, except a god, could counterbalance the dead weight of the whole of mankind and eternal habit? From the beginning, therefore, the heroes had demonic attributes. According to the Nordic conception they had serpents' eyes, and their birth or derivation was strange; certain ancient Greek heroes had serpent souls, others had a personal demon, were magicians or the chosen of God. All these attributes, and many more that could be cited, show that for the ordinary man the commanding personality is a *supernatural manifestation,* as we may call it, and one that can be explained only by the supervention of a demonic factor.

What, in the last analysis, induces a man to choose his own way and so to climb out of unconscious identity with the mass as out of a fog bank? It cannot be necessity, for necessity comes to many and they all save themselves in convention. It cannot be moral choice, for as a rule a man decides for convention. What is it, then, that inexorably tilts the beam in favour of the *extraordinary?*

It is what is called vocation: an irrational factor that fatefully forces a man to emancipate himself from the herd and its trodden paths. True personality always has vocation and believes in it, has fidelity to it as to God, in spite of the fact that, as the ordinary man would say, it is only a feeling of individual vocation. But this vocation acts like a law of God from which there is no escape. That many go to ruin upon their own ways means nothing to him who has vocation. He must obey his own law, as if it were a demon that whisperingly indicated to him new and strange ways. Who has vocation hears the voice of the inner man;

he is *called*. And so it is the legendary belief that he possesses a private demon who counsels him and whose mandates
he must execute. A familiar example of this kind is Faust,
and a historic case is the "daimon" of Socrates. Primitive
medicine men have their snake spirits, and Æsculapius, the
patron of doctors, is represented by the serpent of Epi-
daurus. Moreover, he had the Cabir Telesphoros as his private demon to read the recipes to him, as was supposed—
that is, to inspire him.

To *have vocation* means in the original sense *to be addressed by a voice*. We find the clearest examples of this in
the confessions of the Old Testament prophets. Nor is this
merely an ancient manner of speech, as is shown by the confessions of historic personalities such as Goethe and Napoleon, to mention two familiar examples, who made no secret of their feeling of vocation.

Now, vocation, or the feeling of vocation, is not per-
chance the prerogative of great personalities, but also belongs
to the small ones all the way down to the duodecimo format;
only, with the decrease of proportions, it becomes more
veiled and unconscious. It is as if the voice of the inner
demon moved further and further off and spoke more rarely
and indistinctly. The smaller the personality is, so much the
more unclear and unconscious it becomes, till it finally
merges into one with society, surrendering its own wholeness and dissolving instead into the wholeness of the group.
In the place of the inner voice appears the voice of the
social group and its conventions, and in the place of vocation, the collective necessities.

But it happens to not a few, even in this unconscious
social state, to be summoned by the individual voice, whereupon they are at once differentiated from the others and
feel themselves confronted by a problem that the others do
not know about. It is generally impossible for a man to
explain to his fellow beings what has happened, for under-

standing is cut off by a wall of the strongest prejudices. "I am just like everyone else"; there is "no such thing," or if there is, then, of course, it is "morbid" and moreover quite inexpedient; it is "a monstrous presumption to suppose that anything of that sort could have any significance"; indeed, it is "nothing but psychology."

This last objection is highly popular today. It arises from a singular undervaluation of psychic life, which people apparently regard as something personal, arbitrary, and therefore completely futile. And this, paradoxically enough, along with the present-day enthusiasm for psychology. After all, the unconscious is "nothing but fantasy"! He "merely thought" so and so, etc. People take themselves for magicians who conjure the psychic hither and yon and mould it to suit their moods. They deny what is uncomfortable, sublimate the unwished for, explain away anything that causes anxiety, correct faults, and suppose in the end that they have finally arranged everything beautifully. In the meanwhile they have forgotten the main point, which is that psychic life is only to the smallest extent identical with consciousness and its sleight-of-hand tricks, while for much the greater part it is unconscious fact that lies there hard and heavy as granite, immovable and inaccessible, yet ready, whenever unknown laws shall dictate, to plunge down upon us. The gigantic catastrophes that threaten *us* are not elemental happenings of a physical or biological kind, but are psychic events. We are threatened in a fearful way by wars and revolutions that are nothing else than psychic epidemics. At any moment a few million people may be seized by a madness, and then we have another world war or a devastating revolution. Instead of being exposed to wild beasts, tumbling rocks, and inundating waters, man is exposed today to the elemental forces of his own psyche. Psychic life is a world-power that exceeds by many times all the powers of the earth. The enlightenment, which stripped nature and human institutions of gods, overlooked the one god of fear who dwells in the psyche. Fear of God is in place, if anywhere, before the dominating power of psychic life.

But these are all mere abstractions. Everyone knows that the intellect—that handy man—can put it this way and in quite a different way too. It is wholly a different matter when this objective, psychic fact, hard as granite and heavy as lead, confronts the individual as an inner experience and says to him in an audible voice, "This is what will and must happen." Then he feels himself called, just as do the social groups when a war is on, or a revolution, or any other madness. Not for nothing is it just our own epoch that calls for the liberating personality, for the one who distinguishes himself from the inescapable power of collectivity, thus freeing himself at least in a psychic way, and who lights a hopeful watchfire announcing to others that at least *one* man has succeeded in escaping from the fateful identity with the group soul. The fact is that the group, because of its unconsciousness, has no freedom of choice, so that, within it, psychic life works itself out like an uncontrolled law of nature. There is set going a causally connected process that comes to rest only in catastrophe. The people always longs for a hero, a slayer of dragons, when it feels the danger of psychic forces; hence, the cry for personality.

But what has the single personality to do with the need of the many? First of all, he is a part of the people as a whole and as exposed to the force that moves the whole as are all the others. The only thing that distinguishes this person from all the others is his vocation. He has been called away from the all-powerful, all-oppressing psychic life that is his own and his people's affliction. If he listens to the voice, then he is different and isolated, for he has decided to follow the law that confronts him from within. His "own" law, everyone will cry. He alone knows better—has to know better:

it is *the* law, *the* vocation, as little his "own" as the lion that fells him, although it is undoubtedly this particular lion that kills him, and not any other lion. Only in this sense can he speak of "his" vocation, "his" law.

With the very decision to put his own way above all other ways he has already in large part fulfilled his liberating vocation. He has cancelled the validity of all other ways for himself. He has placed *his* law above all conventions, and so has shoved aside, as far as he is concerned, all those things that not only failed to prevent the great danger, but actually brought it on. For conventions are in themselves soulless mechanisms that can never do more than grasp the routine of life. Creative life is always on the yonder side of convention. This is how it comes about that, when the mere routine of life in the form of traditional conventions predominates, a destructive outbreak of the creative forces *must* follow. But such an outbreak is only catastrophic as a *mass phenomenon*, and never in the individual who consciously subordinates himself to these higher powers and places his abilities at their service. The mechanism of convention keeps people *unconscious*, and then, like wild game, they can follow their customary runways without the necessity of conscious choice. This unintentional effect of even the best conventions is unavoidable, and it is also a terrible danger. For when new conditions not provided for by the old conventions arise, then panic seizes the human being who has been held unconscious by routine, much as it seizes an animal, and with equally unpredictable results.

But personality does not allow itself to be seized by the panic of those who are just awaking, for it already has terror behind it. It is equal to the changing conditions brought by time, and is unknowingly and unwillingly a *leader*.

Certainly, all human beings resemble one another, for otherwise they could not succumb to the same delusion; and the foundation of the psyche, upon which individual consciousness rests, is universally the same, beyond a doubt, for otherwise people could never reach a common understanding. In this sense, personality with its peculiar psychic make-up is itself not something absolutely unique and happening but once. The uniqueness holds only for the *individuality* of the personality, as it does for each and every individuality. To become a personality is not the absolute prerogative of the man of genius. He may even have genius without either having personality or being a personality. In so far as every individual has his own inborn law of life, it is theoretically possible for every man to follow this law before all others and so to become a personality—that is, to achieve completeness. But since life can only exist in the form of living units, which is to say, of individuals, the law of life in the last analysis always tends towards a *life that is individually lived*. Although, at bottom, one cannot conceive the objective-psychic in any other way than as an actuality that is universal and uniform, and although this means that all men share the same primary, psychic condition, still the objective-psychic must individuate itself as soon as it manifests itself, for there is no way in which it can express itself except through the single individual. The only exception to this is when it seizes upon the group; but in that case it leads by rules of nature to a catastrophe, and for the simple reason that it acts only through unconscious channels and is not assimilated by any consciousness so as to be assigned its place among all the other conditions of life.

Only the man who is able *consciously* to affirm the power of the vocation confronting him from within becomes a personality; he who succumbs to it falls a prey to the blind flux of happening and is destroyed. The greatness and the liberating effect of all genuine personality consists in this, that it subjects itself of free choice to its vocation and consciously translates into its own individual reality what would lead only to ruin if it were lived unconsciously by the group.

One of the most shining examples of the life and meaning of personality that history has preserved for us is the life of Christ. In Christianity, which—it may be mentioned in passing—was the only religion really persecuted by the Romans, there appeared a direct opponent of the Cæsarean madness of Rome, a trait that distinguished not only the emperor, but every Roman as well: *civis Romanus sum.* The opposition showed itself wherever the cult of Cæsar and Christianity clashed. But as we know from what the Evangelists intimate as to the psychic evolution of the personality of Christ, this opposition also played the decisive rôle in the soul of the founder of the Christian religion. The story of the temptation clearly shows us with what kind of psychic power Jesus had collided: it was the power-devil of the contemporary mind that led him into serious temptation in the wilderness. This devil was the objective-psychic that held all the people of the Roman imperium under its spell; this is why it promised to Jesus also all the kingdoms of earth, as if it desired to make a Cæsar of him.

Following the inner voice, his vocation and his calling, Jesus freely exposed himself to the attack of the imperialistic delusion that filled everyone, conqueror and conquered alike. In this way he recognized the nature of the objective-psychic, which had plunged the whole world into a state of suffering and had produced a yearning for salvation that found its expression even in the heathen poets. He did not suppress this psychic onslaught, but consciously let it act upon him; nor did he allow himself to be suppressed by it, but assimilated it. And so world-conquering Cæsarism was changed into a spiritual kingship, and the *imperium Romanum* became a universal and unworldly kingdom of God. While the Jewish people as a whole was expecting an imperialistic and politically active hero, Jesus fulfilled the Messianic vocation less for his nation than for the Roman world, and pointed out to humanity the old truth that, where force rules, there is no love, and where love rules, force does not count. The religion of love was the exact psychological counterpart to the Roman bedevilment with power.

The example of Christianity perhaps best illustrates the abstract discussions I have presented above. This apparently unique life has become a sacred symbol because it is the prototype of the only meaningful life, that is, of a life that strives for the individual realization of its own particular law, such realization being absolute and unconditional. In this sense one may exclaim with Tertullian: *anima naturaliter christiana!*

The deification of Jesus as well as of Buddha is not surprising, but strikingly shows the enormous valuation that humanity puts upon these heroes, and so upon the ideal of the development of personality. Though it seems at present as if the blind and destructive prevalence of senseless, collective force would thrust the ideal of personality into the background, yet this is only a passing revolt against the ascendancy of the past. When once tradition has been sufficiently lopped off by the revolutionary, unhistorical, and therefore uneducated inclinations of the new generation, then heroes will again be sought for and found. Even Bolshevism, which can hardly be surpassed in radicalism, has embalmed Lenin and made a saviour of Karl Marx. The ideal of personality is an indestructible need of the human soul, and it is the more fanatically defended the more unsuitable it is. Even the cult of Cæsar was a misconstrued cult of personality, and modern Protestantism, whose critical theology has brought the divinity of Christ to the vanishing point, has taken its last refuge in the personality of Jesus.

Yes, what is called personality is a great and mysterious question. All that can be said about it is curiously unsatisfactory and inadequate, and there is always the threatening danger that the discussion will lose itself in mere talk that is as redundant as it is hollow. The very concept of personality is so vague and badly defined in common usage that hardly two minds will take the word in the same sense. Though I here propose a particular conception of it, I do not imagine that I have thus said the last word. I should like to consider everything that I say here as a mere attempt to approach the problem of personality, without making any claim to solve it. Or rather, I should like to consider my attempt as a description of the psychological problem of personality.

All the usual little remedies and medicaments of psychology fall somewhat short in this connection, just as they do with the man of genius or the creative human being. Derivation from ancestral heredity and from the milieu does not quite succeed; inventing fictions about childhood, which is so popular today, ends—to put it mildly—in the inappropriate; the explanation from necessity—"he had no money, was ill," and so forth—remains caught in mere externalities. Something irrational, that cannot be rationalized, must always supervene, a *deus ex machina* or an *asylum ignorantiæ*—that well-known superscription standing for God. Here the problem seems to extend into an extrahuman realm, and this, from the beginning, has been covered by some one of the names of God.

As can be seen, I also have had to refer to the inner voice, the vocation, and to designate it as a powerful objective-psychic element in order to characterize the way in which it acts in the developing personality and appears subjectively in any given case. Mephistopheles, in *Faust*, is not personified merely because this gives a better dramatic or theatrical effect, as though Faust moralized himself and painted his own devil on the wall. The first words of the dedication: *Ihr naht Euch wieder, schwankende Gestalten* ("You draw near again, vacillating figures"), are more than

merely for æsthetic effect. Like the concretization of the
devil, it is an admission of the objectivity of the psychic
experience, a whispered confession that it happened in this
way *after all,* not because of subjective wishes, fears, or
judgements, but somehow quite of itself. Surely, only a
blockhead would think of ghosts, and yet something like
a primitive blockhead seems to lurk everywhere under the
surface of reasonable, daytime consciousness.

And so we have the eternal doubt whether what appears to be the objective-psychic is really objective or
whether it is imagination after all. But the question at once
arises: have I intentionally imagined such and such, or has
it been imagined in me? The problem is similar to that of
the neurotic who suffers from an imaginary carcinoma. He
knows, and he has been told a hundred times, that it is imagination, and he asks me in a browbeaten way, "Yes, but
how does it happen, then, that I imagine such a thing? Naturally I don't want to." The answer to this is that the idea
of the carcinoma has imagined itself in him without his
foreknowledge and without his permission. The basis of this
happening is that a psychic growth, a "proliferation," is
taking place in his unconscious without his being able to
make it conscious. Before this inner activity he has the sense
of fear. But as he is entirely persuaded that within, in his
own psyche, there cannot be anything of which he does not
know, he must refer this fear to a physical carcinoma of
which he knows that it does not exist. And if, in spite of
all, he should still be afraid of it, a hundred doctors will
confirm the view that his fear is entirely groundless. Neurosis is thus a protection against the objective, inner activity
of the psyche; or rather, it is an attempt, somewhat dearly
paid for, to escape from the inner voice and so from vocation. For this proliferation is the objective activity of the
psyche, independent of conscious caprice, that wishes to
speak to consciousness through the inner voice and so to

guide a person to the attainment of his full stature. Behind the neurotic perversion is concealed vocation, destiny, the development of personality, the complete realization of the life-will that is born with the individual. The man without *amor fati* is the neurotic; he wastes himself, and is unable to say with Nietzsche, "A man never raises himself higher than when he does not know whither his destiny will still lead him."

In so far as a man is untrue to his own law and does not rise to personality, he has failed of the meaning of his life. Fortunately, in her kindness and patience, Nature has never put the fatal question as to the meaning of their lives into the mouths of most people. And where no one asks, no one needs to answer.

The neurotic's fear of carcinoma is, therefore, right; it is not an imagination, but the consistent expression of a psychic fact that exists in the extraconscious realm, inaccessible to the will and the understanding. If he should go alone into the wilderness and listen in his isolation to the inner world, he might perhaps hear what the inner voice has to say. But as a rule the miseducated, civilized human being is quite incapable of perceiving the voice, which is not vouched for by the current doctrines. Primitives are qualified for this in a much higher degree; at least the medicine men are able, and are even professionally fitted, to talk with spirits, trees, and animals, which is to say that the objective-psychic, the psychic non-ego, confronts them in these forms.

Because neurosis is a disturbance of the development of personality, we physicians of the psyche are compelled by professional necessity to occupy ourselves with the problem of personality and the inner voice, however remote it may seem to be. In practical psychotherapy these psychic facts, otherwise so vague and so often degenerated into empty phrases, emerge from their obscurity and are brought nearer to sight and knowledge. It is extremely rare, however, that this happens spontaneously as in the case of the Old Testament prophets; as a rule, the psychic circumstances that have caused the disturbance must with effort be made conscious. Yet the contents that come to light strictly correspond to the "inner voice" and have the significance of a fateful vocation. When this is accepted by consciousness and integrated, it brings about the development of personality.

Just as great personality acts upon society to alleviate, liberate, transform, and heal, so the birth of personality has a restoring effect upon the individual. It is as if a stream that was losing itself in marshy tributaries suddenly discovered its proper bed, or as if a stone that lay upon a germinating seed were lifted away so that the sprout could begin its natural growth.

The inner voice is the voice of a fuller life, of a wider, more comprehensive consciousness. That is why, in mythology, the birth of the hero or the symbolic rebirth coincides with sunrise: the development of personality is synonymous with an increase of awareness. For the same reason most heroes are characterized by solar attributes, and the moment of the birth of their great personalities is called illumination.

The fear that the majority of natural human beings feels before the inner voice is not so childish as one might suppose. The contents that confront a limited consciousness are in no sense harmless, as is shown by the classic example of the life of Christ, or the equally significant experience of Mara in the legend of Buddha; as a rule, they spell the very danger that is specific to the individual concerned. What the inner voice brings close to us is generally something that is not good, but evil. This must be so, first of all, for the reason that we are generally not as unconscious of our virtues as of our vices, and then because we suffer less from the good than from the bad.

As I have explained above, the inner voice brings to consciousness whatever the whole—whether the nation to which we belong or the humanity of which we are a part —suffers from. But it presents this evil in individual form, so that at first we would suppose all this evil to be only a trait of individual character. The inner voice brings forward what is evil in a temptingly convincing way, so as to make us succumb to it. If we do not succumb to it in part, then nothing of this apparent evil goes into us, and then also no renewal and no healing can take place. (I call the evil of the inner voice "apparent," and this sounds too optimistic.) If the "I" completely succumbs to the inner voice, then its contents act as if they were so many devils, and a catastrophe follows. But if the "I" succumbs only in part, and if by self-assertion it can save itself from being completely swallowed, then it can assimilate the voice, and it is seen that the evil was only an evil semblance, while in reality it brought healing and illumination. The character of the inner voice is "Luciferian" in the most proper and unequivocal sense of the word, and that is why it places a man face to face with final moral decisions, without which he could never attain consciousness and become a personality. In a most unaccountable way the lowest and the highest, the best and the most atrocious, the truest and the falsest are mingled together in the inner voice, which thus opens up an abyss of confusion, deception, and despair.

It is, of course, ridiculous to accuse the voice of nature, the all-good and the all-destroying, of evil. If it appears to us pre-eminently bad, this is at bottom a matter of the old truth that the good is always an enemy of the better. We would be foolish if we did not cling to the traditional good as long as ever possible. But as Faust says:

When we attain the good the world presents us,
We call the better lie and sham!

Something good is unfortunately not eternally good, for otherwise there would be nothing better. If the better is to come, then the good must stand aside. This is why Meister Eckhart said, "God is not good, or else he could be better."

There are times in the history of the world (our own may be one of them) when something that is good must make way; what is destined to be better thus appears at first to be evil. This last sentence shows how dangerous it is even to touch upon these problems, for how easy it would be, according to this, for evil to smuggle itself in by simply explaining that it is the potentially better! The problems of the inner voice are full of hidden pits and snares. It is a most dangerous and slippery region, just as dangerous and devious as life itself when it rejects the aid of handrails. But whoever is unable to lose his life by the same token will never gain it. The birth of the hero and the heroic life are always threatened. Typical examples are the serpents of Hera that threaten the infant Heracles; Python, who wishes to destroy the light god Apollo at birth; and the slaying of the first-born in Bethlehem. The development of personality is a wager, and it is tragic that the demon of the inner voice should spell greatest danger and indispensable help at the same time. It is tragic, but logical. It is artlessly so.

May we, therefore, be thankful to humanity, to all the well-meaning shepherds of the flock, and to all the anxious fathers of the hosts of children, when they erect protective walls, set up efficacious pictures, and recommend passable roads that sinuously wind around the abysses?

When all is said and done, the hero, leader, and saviour is also the one who discovers a new way to greater certainty. Everything could be left as it was if this new way did not absolutely demand to be discovered, and did not visit humanity with all the plagues of Egypt until it is found. The undiscovered way in us is like something of the psyche that is alive. The classic Chinese philosophy calls it "Tao," and compares it to a watercourse that resistlessly moves towards its goal. To be in Tao means fulfilment, wholeness, a vocation performed, beginning and end and complete realization of the meaning of existence innate in things. Personality is Tao.

FOOTNOTES TO CHAPTER SIX

1. From Goethe's *West-Oestlicher Divan, Buch Suleika*. Although the verses in question are generally quoted as a pronouncement of the poet, he has put them in the mouth of Suleika and makes Hatem reply:

> May well be! So they suppose;
> But I am on another track:
> All the joys of earth I find
> United in Suleika's self.   [Translator's note]

2. This chapter was originally given as a lecture entitled *Die Stimme des Innern* at the Kulturbund, Vienna, in November, 1932. Since then Germany, too, has found its leader.

Collected Papers on Analytical Psychology. London: Baillière, Tindall and Cox, 1916; New York: Moffat, Yard and Company, 1917.

Contributions to Analytical Psychology. New York: Harcourt, Brace and Company, 1928.

Modern Man in Search of a Soul. New York: Harcourt, Brace and Company, 1933; London: Kegan Paul, Trench, Trubner & Co., Ltd., 1933.

Psychological Types. New York: Harcourt, Brace and Company, 1933; London: Kegan Paul, Trench, Trubner & Co., Ltd., 1923.

Psychology and Religion. New Haven: Yale University Press, 1938; London: H. Milford, Oxford University Press, 1938.

The Psychology of Dementia Præcox. New York: Nervous and Mental Disease Publishing Company, 1936.

Psychology of the Unconscious. New York: Moffat, Yard and Company, 1916; Dodd, Mead & Company, 1931.

Studies in Word-Association. London: W. Heinemann, Ltd., 1918.

The Theory of Psychoanalysis. New York: Nervous and Mental Disease Publishing Company, 1915.

Two Essays on Analytical Psychology. New York: Dodd, Mead & Company, 1928.

With Richard Wilhelm

The Secret of the Golden Flower. New York: Harcourt, Brace and Company, 1931; London: George Routledge and Company, 1931.

INDEX

A

Abtala Jurain, treatise of 1732, 213-215
Ace of clubs, 166; as a dream symbol, 117
Aesculapius, 174, 292
Agathodaimon, 192
Albertus Magnus, 247
Alchemistic images, traditional, 89
Alchemists, real nature of matter unknown to, 212; solitary character of, 237
Alchemy, 27; as exemplar of individual-ism, 28; Taoist, 50; basic concept of, 205; amplification method in, 207; es-sential points of, 208; psychic processes of, 210; heterogeneous currents in, 211; "projections" in, 212; psychic nature of, 216; *meditatio* in, 220; physical and psychic intermixed in, 222; conception of opposites in, 241; in relation to Christian doctrine, 250, 251; importance in Middle Ages, 269; science and mys-ticism in, 268; projection of psychic material in, 269; as aid to study of un-conscious, 275
Alfidus, 217
Ambrosius, 234, 236
America, attitude towards intellect in, 113
Amithaba, 128
Amplification, in dream interpretation, 207
Ancestral psychical conditions, 45
Ancestral spirits, in primitive rites, 146
Angelus Silesius, 59
Anima, 22, 114, 225; definition of, 19; in mythology and legend, 73; one aspect of the unconscious, 76; various projections of, 79; as chaotic life-urge, 80; as rep-resenting the inferior function, 156
Animal symbolism, 147
Animus, the, defined, 19
Anthropos, or God-man, 230, 231, 233
Antimony, 240
Ape, as dream symbol, 155, 175, 196
Apuleius, 82, 107
Archetypes, anima and animus natural, 23; in collective unconscious, 50; as con-tents of the same, 53; myth and fable as, 53, 54; dogmatic, in Catholic ritual, 60; of meaning, 82; the "old wise man", 87, 88; of transformation, 89; remedial, 275
Archytas, 240
Asiatic cults, imported by Romans, 61
Astrology, 55, 213
Atman, personal and superpersonal, in Upanishad, 133
Augustine, St., 53, 101, 247, 264
Avalokiteshvara, 128
Aztecs, 175

B

Ball, as dream symbol, 137, 158
Bardesanes, 67
Basilius Valentinus, 211, 245, 247
Benoit, Pierre, 78, 80, 221
Bernhardus Trevisanus, 206
Bernoulli, Prof., 89, 197, 208
Beya, in *Visio Arislei,* 241-244
Bhagavad-Gita, 140
Black Mass, 92, 155
Blue flower, as dream symbol, 165
Bodhisattva, 145
Boehme, Jacob, 59, 206, 252, 268
Bolshevism, 298
Brahma on world-mountain Meru, 134
Buddha, 128, 145
Buddhism, 24

C

Cabasilas, 237
Cabiri, 182, 190; creative dwarf gods in *Faust,* 160, 162
Caesarism, effect of Christianity on, 297
Carbon, 198
Carus, C. G., 5, 52
Caussinus, Jesuit, 246, 247
Cave, as dream symbol, 158
Central Australia, natives of, 146
Centre, as dream symbol, 168, 169; as totality of psychic being, 191; properties of the unknowable, 197